Business or Hobby?

Are you running a Business, or is it an expensive Hobby?

Planning for Profits

I've learned the hard way that asking clients about their Business Plans can be a touchy subject. For many, the question feels like an insult—especially when I point out that running a business without a plan often looks more like managing a hobby. Unsurprisingly, some clients were upset when I shared this perspective.

However, after explaining that a solid Business Plan, one that's consistently referenced and revised, often eliminates the need for my intervention. Over time, most clients recognized the connection between having a clear plan and their struggles, and their frustration gave way to understanding.

Helping clients grasp the difference between a profitable business and an expensive hobby isn't always easy—particularly for new entrepreneurs who may be deeply passionate but lack structure. Yet, this distinction is critical. It's the foundation for achieving long-term success, sustainability, and, ultimately, financial freedom.

Story about Paul's Restaurant

The aroma of sizzling steaks mingled with the comforting scent of freshly baked bread as Holly and Sean stepped into their favorite restaurant. It was a place that felt like home, where the warm glow of the lights matched the familiar smile of the owner, Paul, who greeted them as they entered. They instinctively made their way to their usual table, Holly already pulling out her phone to capture a few snapshots of the cozy ambiance. Meanwhile, Sean was preoccupied with scrolling through his schedule, trying to juggle the demands of his next grocery store shift.

Their server, Emily, appeared almost instantly. Her cheerful demeanor matched the vibrancy of the bustling dining room. With a smile, she took their orders and whisked away toward the kitchen. Holly and Sean couldn't help but admire the seamless energy around them. Servers darted between tables with practiced ease, busboys swiftly cleared plates and refilled drinks, and even the cooks lent a rhythm to the scene, creating a kind of culinary choreography. At the center of it all was Paul, orchestrating the symphony with the precision of a maestro.

As they waited for their meal, their conversation shifted to their own lives and jobs. Holly, a retail cashier with a knack for social media and photography, gushed about her love for capturing fleeting moments—though she rarely shared the photos she so carefully curated. Sean, a grocery store manager by day and a customer service agent by night, spoke of his constant hustle, though his juggling act often left him overwhelmed and unsure of how to move forward.

When their food arrived, it was as if art had been plated. Perfectly cooked and beautifully presented, the meal was everything they had come to expect from Paul's restaurant. Holly and Sean couldn't help but compliment him on his incredible team and the flawless operation he had built. Paul, ever humble, credited his success to meticulous planning and an unwavering commitment to his vision. His employees weren't just staff; they were part of a shared dream, executing his well-crafted strategy with precision and pride.

As Holly and Sean enjoyed their meal, they couldn't help but reflect on the contrasts between themselves and Paul. Holly lived in the moment, snapping countless photos without ever taking the next step to share them or create something more meaningful. Sean, with his scattered approach, felt like he was perpetually running in circles, yearning for progress but unsure how to achieve it. And then there was Paul—methodical, driven, and always a step ahead, his plans unfolding like clockwork.

When they finished their meal and settled the bill, they said their goodbyes to Paul, who remained the epitome of composure amidst the chaos of a busy evening. As they stepped outside into the cool night air, they felt inspired, albeit in different ways. Paul's restaurant was more than a place to eat—it was a testament to the power of clarity, vision, and relentless effort. Holly and Sean couldn't wait to return, not just for the delicious food and impeccable service but for the spark of motivation they always seemed to find within its walls.

Why is Paul's Restaurant performing so well?

How could Holly apply planning to her Photography hobby and Social Media Interests?

How could Sean use planning as a manager at a grocery store or his side gig of Customer Service?

Chapter 1: Business or Hobby?

Key indicators help you assess whether you're running a business that generates profit or just indulging in a costly hobby.

1. Revenue vs. Expenses

- **Profitable Business**: A profitable business generates consistent revenue that exceeds its operating expenses. It has a clear path to profitability and sustainable cash flow.
    - Example: If your revenue consistently covers your costs with money left over, you're likely running a business or a high-potential hobby.
- **Expensive Hobby**: In a hobby, revenue may be sporadic, inconsistent, or insufficient to cover operating costs. Even if you're generating sales, you might find yourself spending more on supplies, tools, or other resources than you earn.
    - Example: If you're spending more on materials, marketing, or personal enjoyment than you're earning, it could be a hobby rather than a business.

2. Clear Business Plan

- **Profitable Business**: A business has a clear, repeatable, and scalable model that includes defined products or services, a target market, a pricing strategy, and operational processes. There's a plan for customer acquisition and retention.
    - Example: You have a structured plan to attract and retain customers, and you can measure the success of each marketing or sales tactic.
- **Expensive Hobby**: A hobby often lacks a structured, repeatable model. The focus is on passion or personal interest, not profit. There might not be a clear strategy for scaling or expanding the business.
    - Example: You may have a great product but are unsure about how to effectively market it or attract a broad customer base.

3. Profit Margins

- **Profitable Business**: A profitable business has strong profit margins—meaning it can sell products or services for more than the cost of production, labor, and overhead, leaving enough to reinvest or pay owners.
    - Example: If you're able to cover overhead costs (such as rent, salaries, and marketing) while earning enough to grow or pay yourself, you have a profitable business.
- **Expensive Hobby**: In a hobby, the focus might be more on quality or passion rather than profitability, which can lead to high expenses that eat into your potential margins. You might not be pricing your products correctly or may not be able to control costs.
    - Example: If the products or services are sold at break-even or below cost due to emotional or personal attachment, it could indicate a hobby.

4. How Time and Effort are Invested in operation

- **Profitable Business**: A profitable business requires time, effort, and resources to run. It grows through strategic planning and continuous effort to optimize processes, improve efficiency, and meet customer demands. The owner is focused on long-term profitability.
    - Example: The business owner actively seeks ways to improve profitability, whether by increasing sales, reducing costs, or expanding operations.
- **Expensive Hobby**: While a hobby may involve significant time and effort, the primary motivation is personal enjoyment, not financial success. There might be no interest in improving the business structure or systems.
    - Example: If you spend a lot of time on activities that don't lead to revenue generation or business growth (like perfecting a product you aren't selling), it may be a hobby.

5. Return on Investment (ROI)

- **Profitable Business**: A business generates a positive return on investment (ROI). The financial return justifies the initial investment, time, and resources.
    - Example: You earn more than what you invested (money, time, and energy) in terms of revenue or profits, and the business is capable of reinvesting in growth.
- **Expensive Hobby**: An expensive hobby may have no clear ROI. Even if you enjoy the activity, it's costing more than it's bringing in financially.
    - Example: If you spend $10,000 on materials, equipment, and marketing but only bring in $5,000 in sales, you're operating at a loss, signaling a hobby rather than a profitable business.

6. Growth and Scaling Potential

- **Profitable Business**: A business has the potential for growth and scaling. You have strategies for expanding operations, increasing sales, or extending your product/service line.
    - Example: You can identify key metrics to measure growth, and there are plans for expansion, whether geographically, online, or by increasing market share.
- **Expensive Hobby**: Hobbies typically don't have scalability. The focus is on maintaining personal satisfaction or craftsmanship rather than growing a marketable, profitable enterprise.
    - Example: There might be no clear plan or interest in scaling your activities or broadening your audience beyond the immediate circle.

7. Customer Demand

- **Profitable Business**: A profitable business operates based on customer demand. It's market-driven and offers products or services that customers need or want, with plans to maintain or increase demand.
  - Example: You track customer feedback, monitor sales patterns, and have a marketing plan to ensure customers return or refer others.
- **Expensive Hobby**: A hobby might not be driven by market demand. You may create products based on personal interests rather than customer needs.
  - Example: You enjoy creating something for yourself or a small group of people, but there is no broad demand or effort to reach a larger audience.

8. Financial Sustainability

- **Profitable Business**: A business can sustain itself financially over time. It has adequate cash flow to cover costs and pay for growth. It can also survive economic downturns or shifts in customer behavior.
  - Example: The business has financial systems in place that allow it to weather changes in the market or economy without losing profitability.
- **Expensive Hobby**: A hobby might require outside funding (personal savings, loans, etc.) to cover its ongoing costs without a clear plan for self-sufficiency or profitability.
  - Example: You might continue to put your own money into the business without a clear return on that investment.

Conclusion on Business of Hobby:

- **A Profitable Business**: Generates consistent revenue, covers its expenses, and has a clear path to growth and sustainability. It is driven by market demand, profitability, and scaling potential.
- **An Expensive Hobby**: Driven more by passion and personal enjoyment rather than profitability. Revenue may be inconsistent, and expenses often exceed income, with no clear path to growth or financial sustainability.

The difference between a business and a hobby lies in the **intent, structure,** and **financial outcomes**. A profitable business is **built to be sustainable, scalable**, and **driven by market demands**. In contrast, a hobby is typically personal, with **no clear strategy** for generating consistent income.

A Business Plan is what separates the two—it's the roadmap that transforms a passion project into a thriving enterprise. By carefully researching, thoughtfully drafting, fully implementing, and regularly updating a Business Plan, you create the foundation for success and ensure your venture is far from just a costly pastime. If you take the steps to research, draft, implement, and update your business plan, then I accomplished the GOAL of this book.

But what if you're **making profits from your hobby without a Business Plan?** In that case, it's time to decide: either **create a solid Business Plan to formalize your operation or consider selling the business**— even then, having a Business Plan can significantly increase its value. Alternatively, a plan **might enhance the joy you get from your hobby** if your goal is personal fulfillment rather than profit.

When I say, "No Hobbies," I'm not discouraging you from pursuing your interests or talents. Instead, I'm advocating for intentionality and planning. Enjoy your hobbies and businesses with purpose. Don't mistake an expensive hobby for a business simply because you didn't make time to plan. With focus and a clear strategy, you can find fulfillment and financial success in both.

Self-Assessment Quiz: Is Your Venture a Business or a Hobby?

This quiz will help you evaluate the current state of your venture and determine if you're running a business or indulging in a hobby. Answer each question honestly, and tally your points to see where your venture stands.

Section 1: Financial Sustainability

1. Do you generate consistent revenue from your venture?

    - A. Yes, I generate consistent revenue that covers my expenses and leaves a profit. *(3 points)*
    - B. Sometimes, but revenue is inconsistent. *(2 points)*
    - C. Rarely or never. *(1 point)*

2. Have you priced your products or services based on a clear understanding of costs and market demand?

    - A. Yes, my pricing ensures profitability and aligns with market standards. *(3 points)*
    - B. Somewhat, but I often estimate prices. *(2 points)*
    - C. No, I haven't fully calculated my costs or market position. *(1 point)*

3. Do you track your income and expenses regularly?

    - A. Yes, I use a detailed system to track finances. *(3 points)*
    - B. Occasionally, but not consistently. *(2 points)*
    - C. No, I don't track them at all. *(1 point)*

Section 2: Planning and Structure

4. Do you have a written business plan or strategy?

    - A. Yes, I have a comprehensive plan that I regularly update. *(3 points)*
    - B. I have a general idea but nothing formal. *(2 points)*
    - C. No, I don't have a plan. *(1 point)*

5. Do you set specific, measurable goals for your venture?

    - A. Yes, I set and review goals regularly. *(3 points)*
    - B. Sometimes, but I don't always follow through. *(2 points)*
    - C. No, I don't set goals for my venture. *(1 point)*

6. Do you have systems in place to manage operations (e.g., production, customer service, inventory)?

    - A. Yes, I have efficient systems for all aspects of my venture. *(3 points)*
    - B. Partially, but there's room for improvement. *(2 points)*
    - C. No, I manage everything on an ad hoc basis. *(1 point)*

Section 3: Market and Customers

7. Do you have a clear target market for your products or services?

    - A. Yes, I've researched and identified my ideal customers. *(3 points)*
    - B. I have a general idea but haven't done detailed research. *(2 points)*
    - C. No, I sell to whoever is interested. *(1 point)*

8. Do you actively market your products or services?

- A. Yes, I have a consistent marketing strategy. *(3 points)*
- B. Occasionally, but it's not consistent. *(2 points)*
- C. No, I rely on word-of-mouth or chance. *(1 point)*

9. Do you gather and act on customer feedback to improve your offerings?

    - A. Yes, I regularly collect feedback and make improvements. *(3 points)*
    - B. Sometimes, but not systematically. *(2 points)*
    - C. No, I don't actively seek feedback. *(1 point)*

Section 4: Time and Commitment

10. How much time do you dedicate to your venture each week?

    - A. 20+ hours, treating it like a full-time commitment. *(3 points)*
    - B. 10-20 hours, depending on my schedule. *(2 points)*
    - C. Less than 10 hours when I have free time. *(1 point)*

11. Do you prioritize your venture over other hobbies or personal interests?

    - A. Yes, it's my main focus. *(3 points)*
    - B. Sometimes, but I juggle it with other interests. *(2 points)*
    - C. No, it's just one of many activities I enjoy. *(1 point)*

12. Are you committed to growing your venture long-term?

    - A. Yes, I'm fully committed to its growth and success. *(3 points)*
    - B. Somewhat, but I'm unsure about its future. *(2 points)*
    - C. No, I treat it as a short-term interest. *(1 point)*

Scoring Guide

- **30-36 points**: **You're Running a Business!**
  Congratulations! Your venture is well-structured and has the foundation for profitability and growth. Keep refining your strategies to achieve even greater success.

- **20-29 points: You're on the Fence.**
  Your venture shows potential but lacks consistency or structure in certain areas. Focus on formalizing your business plan, tracking finances, and setting measurable goals to transition fully into a business.

- **12-19 points: It's a Hobby.**
  Your venture is likely driven by passion, but it isn't operating like a business yet. To turn it into a profitable enterprise, invest time in creating a plan, identifying your market, and committing to financial and operational goals.

Reflection Questions:

Assessing Your Venture:

- What is your current monthly revenue, and does it consistently exceed your expenses?

- List three reasons why you started your venture. Are they driven by passion, profit, or both?

- Do you have a clear understanding of your target market? Describe it in 2-3 sentences.

Defining Your Motivation:

- How much time do you dedicate to your venture weekly? Is it consistent with your goals for growth?

- What is your desired income from this venture in the next year? How does that align with your current operations?

Evaluating Growth Potential:

- List two areas where you believe your venture could scale (e.g., new products, markets, or customer segments).

- Are you reinvesting profits into growth? If not, why?

Case Study: Sarah's Gourmet Jam – From Hobby to Profitable Business

Background

Sarah loved making homemade jams from fresh, locally sourced fruits. What started as a weekend activity quickly gained attention from friends and family who couldn't get enough of her unique flavors like "Peach Lavender" and "Spiced Fig Delight." Encouraged by their feedback, Sarah decided to sell her jams at a local farmers' market.

While the initial reception was positive, Sarah struggled to scale her hobby into a profitable business. She often underestimated her costs, lacked a marketing plan, and struggled to differentiate her brand from other vendors.

Challenges

1. **Inconsistent Pricing**:
   - Sarah initially set prices based on what "felt fair," leading to minimal profit margins.

2. **Limited Reach**:
   - She relied solely on farmers' markets for sales, missing out on online opportunities.

3. **Operational Inefficiencies**:
   - Without a production plan, Sarah often ran out of inventory or had surplus jams that spoiled.

Strategies for Growth

1. **Crafting a Business Plan**:
   - **Mission Statement**: "To bring the joy of artisanal, gourmet jams to food enthusiasts while supporting local farmers."

- **Target Market**: Health-conscious individuals, foodies, and gift shoppers looking for unique, high-quality products.

- **Financial Goals**: Achieve $50,000 in revenue within the first year of formalizing the business.

2. **Pricing and Financial Analysis**:

    - Sarah calculated her costs, including ingredients, jars, labels, and labor. She discovered she needed to charge $8 per jar (instead of $5) to achieve a 40% profit margin.

    - Introduced a subscription model: Customers received a monthly delivery of seasonal jam flavors at a discounted rate.

3. **Expanding Sales Channels**:

    - Launched a website with an online store to reach customers nationwide.

    - Partnered with local gourmet stores and gift shops to stock her products.

    - Used social media to showcase recipes featuring her jams, creating engagement and driving traffic to her site.

4. **Streamlining Operations**:

    - Invested in small-scale commercial kitchen space, increasing production capacity.

    - Adopted a batch production schedule, reducing waste and ensuring consistent supply.

    - Created a simple inventory tracking system using spreadsheets.

5. **Building a Brand**:

    - Designed elegant, eco-friendly packaging with a rustic feel, appealing to her target audience.

    - Developed a tagline: "Homemade Happiness in Every Jar."

    - Attended food expos to network and gain exposure.

Results

1. **Revenue Growth**:
   - Within six months, Sarah's revenue increased by 75%, largely due to online sales and bulk orders from local stores.
   - The subscription service added predictable, recurring income.

2. **Brand Recognition**:
   - Sarah's jams were featured in a local food magazine, boosting her visibility.
   - Customer testimonials highlighted the unique flavors and high quality, creating word-of-mouth referrals.

3. **Operational Efficiency**:
   - With streamlined production, Sarah reduced spoilage by 30% and increased her output by 50%.

4. **Personal Transformation**:
   - Sarah gained confidence in running her business and hired a part-time assistant, freeing her time to focus on strategy and product development.

Lessons Learned

1. **Understand Your Costs**:
   - Pricing products correctly is essential to ensuring profitability.

2. **Diversify Sales Channels**:
   - Relying on a single outlet limits growth potential. Exploring online sales and partnerships opens new revenue streams.

3. **Invest in Branding**:
   - A memorable brand and strong packaging can differentiate you in a crowded market.

4. **Plan for Growth**:
   - Streamlined operations and clear financial goals lay the foundation for scaling.

This case study illustrates how Sarah transitioned from a hobbyist to a business owner by addressing her challenges and implementing practical strategies. Her journey highlights the importance of planning, branding, and adaptability in achieving success.

Chapter 2: Power of a Business Plan

A Business Plan: The Effort That Pays Off

No matter how you approach it, creating a business plan is a highly valuable investment of your time and energy. The benefits far outweigh the effort required to draft one, acting as a guiding framework for success.

Business Plan Components:

1. **Executive Summary**: Typically completed last.
2. **Business Description**: Outlines your mission, vision, and core values.
3. **Products and Services**: Details what you offer and how it stands out.
4. **Marketing and Sales Strategy**: Specifies how you will attract and retain customers.
5. **Operations Plan**: Covers logistics, processes, and team organization.
6. **Financial Plan**:
   - Includes projections and funding requests, if applicable.
   - Appendices for additional details and documentation.

These Six Steps Will Build and Grow Your Business or Hobby A business plan can bridge the gap between a hobby and a profitable venture. If you're hesitant to start, consider these questions to motivate action:

- What challenges could a lack of planning create?
- How would a business plan clarify your goals and improve decision-making?
- How can it attract potential investors or collaborators?

Reasons a Business Plan is Essential for Success

Why a Business Plan is Essential for Success

A business plan is far more than just a document; it serves as a comprehensive blueprint for transforming your vision into tangible results. Here's why creating one is a critical step toward achieving success:

Chapter 3: Planning for Profits

A well-designed business plan acts as a strategic roadmap, ensuring entrepreneurs and business owners maintain focus and alignment. It establishes a clear framework for:

- **Defining Goals**: Outlining both short- and long-term objectives, making it easier to track progress.

- **Guiding Decision-Making**: Offering a reference point for evaluating choices and ensuring actions align with overarching goals.

- **Prioritizing Efforts**: Helping allocate time, energy, and resources to what truly matters.

Without this structure, businesses risk losing focus, getting distracted by non-essential tasks, or spreading themselves too thin. This can result in missed opportunities, inefficiency, or failure to achieve meaningful outcomes.

Defining Goals: Outlining Short- and Long-Term Objectives

Setting clear, measurable goals is the cornerstone of a successful business plan. Well-defined goals provide a sense of purpose and direction, ensuring you know where you're headed and what steps are necessary to get there. These goals typically fall into two categories:

Short-Term Goals

Short-term goals are specific milestones designed to be achieved within a few months to a year. These are focused, actionable steps that drive immediate progress. Examples include:

- Securing a set number of clients.
- Launching a new product or service.
- Reaching a specific revenue target or increasing monthly sales by a certain percentage.

Long-Term Goals

Long-term goals are broader strategic objectives that span multiple years and contribute to the overall vision of the business. These goals often involve more significant growth or development, such as:

- Expanding into new markets or regions.
- Building a franchise or scaling operations.
- Achieving a targeted profit margin or market share.

Why Defined Goals Matter

Clearly defined goals are transformative. They:

- **Turn Ideas into Action**: Break down broad aspirations into concrete, actionable steps.
- **Drive Progress**: Establish benchmarks for measuring success and identifying areas for improvement.
- **Foster Accountability**: Provide a framework for tracking progress and ensuring that team members stay aligned with objectives.

By defining both short- and long-term goals, you create a roadmap that not only clarifies your business's direction but also motivates consistent effort and strategic growth.

Example: A Small Business

A small bakery's business plan might include:

- **Short-term goal**: Increase monthly sales by 20% within six months through online orders and delivery services.
- **Long-term goal**: Open a second location in a neighboring city within three years.

By outlining these objectives, the **business owner stays focused on specific, measurable targets** rather than being distracted by unrelated opportunities.

Benefits of Goal Definition:

- Creates measurable targets to track progress.
- Ensures alignment of all team members and stakeholders.
- Provides motivation and focus, especially when challenges arise.

Guides Decision-Making: Making Informed Choices

Strategic Framework for Decisions

A business plan establishes a clear framework for making decisions. With defined strategies, priorities, and benchmarks, you can evaluate opportunities or challenges against your plan and determine whether they align with your goals. This structured approach prevents reactive, impulsive choices that may derail your business.

- **Example: A New Opportunity**
  Imagine a small marketing agency receives an opportunity to branch into event planning. While enticing, their business plan may show that their core strength lies in social media services, and expanding into unrelated areas would divert time and resources. By consulting their plan, they make an informed decision to stay focused on their strengths.

Avoiding Pitfalls

A well-structured business plan is instrumental in identifying and sidestepping common pitfalls that can derail your progress. By offering clear strategies and a focused framework, it helps ensure that your efforts are aligned with your objectives. Common pitfalls that a business plan can help avoid include:

- **Overextending Resources**: Spreading yourself too thin by taking on too many projects or opportunities at once, which can lead to burnout or inefficiency.
- **Wasting Money**: Allocating resources to initiatives that don't align with the core mission of the business, resulting in reduced profitability.
- **Losing Focus**: Getting sidetracked by short-term gains or trends at the expense of long-term priorities and sustainable growth.

Data-Driven Decisions

A strong business plan includes critical data points—such as financial projections, market research, and competitor analysis—that guide informed decision-making. With these insights, you can evaluate opportunities and challenges with clarity and confidence. For instance:

- Decide whether to hire additional staff based on growth projections.
- Evaluate the ROI of investing in new technology or equipment.
- Assess whether to expand operations into new markets or focus on optimizing current ones.

Guiding Decisions

By grounding decisions in your business plan, you can:

- **Reduce Uncertainty**: Minimize guesswork by relying on data and analysis.

- **Align Choices with Goals**: Ensure that every decision supports your overall business objectives and vision.
- **Boost Confidence**: Approach challenges and opportunities with clarity, increasing your ability to make sound, strategic decisions.

With a business plan as your guide, you're equipped to navigate the complexities of entrepreneurship, stay focused on your mission, and make impactful choices that drive success.

Prioritizing Efforts: Focusing on What's Most Critical

Limited resources—such as time, money, and manpower—are a common challenge for businesses, particularly small ones. A business plan helps address this by ensuring these resources are allocated strategically to the most critical priorities that drive growth and success. Without such focus, businesses risk inefficiency and spreading their efforts too thin on low-impact tasks.

Example: A Start-Up Company

A new tech startup designs its business plan to prioritize:

- **Product Development**: Building a minimum viable product (MVP) to test the market.
- **Customer Acquisition**: Identifying and targeting early adopters.
- **Brand Awareness**: Establishing a strong market presence through targeted campaigns.

Instead of investing time in creating advanced features not yet in demand, the startup focuses on refining its MVP and gathering user feedback. This approach allows for efficient resource utilization and informed future developments.

Identifying Key Priorities

A business plan highlights the actions most essential to achieving your goals, such as:

1. **Product or Service Development**: Creating offerings that meet customer needs.
2. **Market Penetration and Customer Acquisition**: Expanding your reach and building a customer base.
3. **Revenue Generation and Cost Management**: Ensuring profitability and financial stability.
4. **Brand Positioning and Marketing**: Establishing and maintaining a competitive presence.

By concentrating on these high-impact areas, businesses can take deliberate, impactful steps that lead to measurable success.

Benefits of Prioritizing Efforts

- **Prevents Wasted Resources**: Reduces time and money spent on low-priority tasks.
- **Aligns the Team**: Ensures everyone works toward common goals that drive growth.
- **Increases Productivity**: Fosters efficiency by focusing on core activities that yield the greatest results.

Example: Bringing It All Together

Jane's Mobile Pet Grooming Business

- **Defining Goals**:
    - Short-term: Serve 50 clients per month within six months.
    - Long-term: Expand services to neighboring cities within two years.
- **Guiding Decisions**: Jane contemplates purchasing a second van for expansion. However, her business plan highlights that her short-term goals should prioritize marketing efforts to increase her current client base.
- **Prioritizing Efforts**: Jane focuses on launching digital marketing campaigns and forming partnerships with local pet stores rather than investing in secondary initiatives like new services.

By maintaining direction and clarity, Jane avoids distractions, allocates her resources effectively, and steadily grows her business.

A well-crafted business plan helps businesses like Jane's remain focused on what truly matters, driving intentional progress and sustainable growth.

Key Takeaways for Readers

1. **Define Goals for Clear Direction**:
    - Short- and long-term goals give you a roadmap to follow, helping you stay motivated and accountable.

2. **Use Your Plan to Guide Decisions**:

    ◦ With clear strategies and data-driven benchmarks, you can evaluate choices to ensure they align with your objectives.

3. **Prioritize What Matters Most**:

    ◦ Focus your time, energy, and resources on high-impact activities that directly contribute to your success.

Final Thought on Goal Setting

A business plan isn't just a document—it's a tool for clarity, decision-making, and focus. By defining your goals, guiding strategic choices, and prioritizing efforts, it empowers you to navigate challenges, seize opportunities, and keep your business on the path to success. Whether you're launching a start-up or scaling an existing venture, a well-developed plan ensures you're always moving in the right direction.

Reflection Questions

Executive Summary:

    ◦ Write a one-sentence mission statement for your business.

    ◦ What is the primary problem your business solves? Who does it solve it for?

Market Research:

    ◦ Who are your top three competitors, and what sets your business apart?

    ◦ Identify three characteristics of your ideal customer.

Chapter 4: Funding Your Venture

Facilitates Funding: A Role of a Business Plan in Securing Capital

Securing funding is often a pivotal step for businesses, whether they are in the startup phase or aiming to scale. A well-structured business plan serves as a compelling tool to attract investors, lenders, or financial institutions by presenting a clear, credible case for why the business is worth supporting. Here's how a business plan facilitates funding:

1. Essential for Investors and Lenders

Investors and financial institutions require assurance that their funds will be used effectively and yield a return. A detailed business plan provides this confidence by addressing key concerns and demonstrating your preparedness and viability as an entrepreneur.

The Requirement for a Structured Plan

Investors and lenders approach funding with caution. A business plan acts as evidence that:

- You have thoroughly analyzed your market, competition, and financial needs.
- You understand the operational aspects of running your business.
- You have identified potential risks and devised strategies to mitigate them.

What Investors Look For in a Business Plan

To secure funding, your business plan must address the following critical elements:

1. A Clear Value Proposition

- Define the unique problem your business solves and the benefits it provides.
- Explain why customers will choose your product or service over competitors.

Example: "Our app leverages AI to provide personalized fitness coaching, addressing the need for affordable, adaptive workout solutions not offered by traditional gyms or existing fitness apps."

2. Thorough Market Analysis

- Provide evidence of demand by identifying your target audience and their needs.
- Highlight the size, growth potential, and trends within your market.
- Detail your competitive landscape and how your business is positioned to succeed.

Example: "Our target market consists of urban millennials, a demographic with a 20% annual growth rate in health app adoption, presenting a $500 million market opportunity."

3. Realistic Financial Projections

- Outline clear timelines for profitability and expected financial returns.
- Include revenue forecasts, expense estimates, and break-even analysis.
- Highlight key financial metrics, such as gross margins and cash flow.

Example: "We project $2 million in revenue within three years, with profitability reached in year two due to low overhead costs and high scalability of our subscription model."

4. A Well-Structured Operational Strategy

- Detail how your business will execute its plan effectively and scale over time.
- Include logistics like production processes, supply chain management, and distribution.
- Highlight any partnerships, technology, or expertise that strengthen your business model.

Example: "Our strategic partnership with a leading fitness equipment manufacturer ensures efficient distribution and high-quality product integration."

2. Building Trust and Confidence

A business plan demonstrates your expertise and dedication to your venture. Key components that inspire confidence include:

- **Transparent Funding Requirements**: Clearly articulate how much funding you need, why it is required, and how it will be used.

- **Comprehensive Risk Mitigation**: Address potential challenges and provide strategies to minimize risks.

- **Tangible ROI**: Outline how investors will recoup their investment and the potential for long-term gains.

Case Study: A SaaS Startup Securing Funding

Scenario: A startup developing a subscription-based project management software seeks $500,000 in seed funding.

Key Business Plan Highlights:

1. **Value Proposition**: The software simplifies complex workflows for small businesses, offering intuitive AI-driven features at a competitive price.
2. **Market Analysis**: Research shows a $1 billion addressable market with an underserved segment of small businesses with under 50 employees.
3. **Financial Projections**: The plan predicts $1 million in revenue by the second year, with a 70% gross margin due to low software maintenance costs.
4. **Operational Strategy**: A phased rollout ensures scalability, starting with a beta launch in one region, followed by a national release.

Outcome: The well-structured plan secured funding from venture capitalists who appreciated the clear strategy, market research, and financial viability.

Key Tips for Creating a Fundable Business Plan

- **Focus on Clarity**: Use concise language and visuals (charts, graphs) to present complex data.
- **Highlight Financials**: Provide detailed but realistic projections and show how the funding will directly impact growth.
- **Tailor for the Audience**: Emphasize aspects most relevant to the funders, such as ROI for investors or risk mitigation for banks.
- **Demonstrate Passion and Dedication**: Convey your commitment and belief in the venture through a polished and professional presentation.

By addressing these elements, a business plan becomes a persuasive tool that not only attracts funding but also builds lasting relationships with stakeholders who share your vision for success.

Example:

A tech startup looking for seed funding submits a comprehensive business plan to venture capitalists. The plan outlines their innovative product, growth projections, and market demand. By addressing key concerns—such as scalability, competitive analysis, and financial forecasts—the startup gains investor confidence and secures funding.

For Lenders: Securing Loans

Traditional lenders, such as banks, require a business plan as part of the loan application process. They use it to assess the risk involved in lending money and ensure the business has a clear path to repayment. Key sections they analyze include:

- **Financial forecasts**: Cash flow projections, profit and loss statements, and break-even analysis.

- **Repayment strategy**: How and when the loan will be paid back.

- **Collateral and risk management**: What assets can be leveraged in case of default?

Example:

A small bakery owner seeking a $50,000 bank loan provides a business plan that includes detailed financial projections, a timeline for loan repayment, and a breakdown of how the funds will be used (e.g., purchasing equipment and raw materials). The plan reassures the bank that the bakery will generate sufficient income to repay the loan.

2. Demonstrates Credibility

A Mark of Professionalism

A detailed, well-structured business plan conveys that you have put serious thought into your venture. It highlights your commitment, preparation, and ability to manage resources effectively, which builds trust with potential backers. Investors and lenders are far more likely to fund businesses that present themselves professionally.

Why Credibility Matters:

- It reassures financiers that you understand your market, competitors, and potential challenges.
- It shows you are proactive and have contingency plans for risks.
- It reflects your ability to manage finances responsibly and achieve milestones.

Example:

An entrepreneur pitching their eco-friendly cleaning business to angel investors presents a data-driven business plan. It includes a breakdown of market research, cost structure, and growth strategies. By demonstrating expertise and preparation, the entrepreneur earns the trust of investors, who see the venture as a credible and promising opportunity.

3. Explains Financial Needs

Communicating Why Funding is Needed

Financiers want to know exactly why you are requesting funding, how much you need, and how you plan to use it. A business plan provides clarity on your financial needs and ensures that backers understand the purpose of their investment.

- **Key Components for Explaining Financial Needs:**
    - **Breakdown of costs**: Where the funding will go (e.g., inventory, staffing, marketing, equipment).
    - **Return on investment (ROI)**: What investors or lenders will gain in return.
    - **Timelines**: When you expect to use the funding and when they can anticipate results (e.g., profitability, market expansion).

Example:

A fashion retailer seeking $100,000 in funding outlines in their business plan:

- **$50,000** for inventory expansion to meet customer demand.
- **$20,000** for a digital marketing campaign to increase brand awareness.
- **$30,000** for store renovations to attract foot traffic.

By clearly explaining where the funds will go and the anticipated ROI, the retailer demonstrates responsible financial planning, increasing the likelihood of approval.

Why This Matters to Financiers

1. **Risk Reduction**: A clear explanation of financial needs reassures backers that their money will be used effectively to generate growth or repay loans.
2. **Measurable Progress**: Financial forecasts and funding breakdowns allow investors to track progress and hold business owners accountable for milestones.
3. **Profit Potential**: Investors want a clear picture of when and how their investment will yield returns, and lenders need confidence in the repayment strategy.

Key Sections in the Business Plan That Facilitate Funding

A business plan is a critical tool for securing funding, and specific sections play a pivotal role in convincing investors, lenders, or financial institutions of the venture's viability. Below are the key sections and their importance in facilitating funding:

1. Executive Summary

The executive summary is the first section funders read, making it one of the most critical. It should:

- Provide a clear and concise overview of your business.
- Highlight the purpose of the business and its unique value proposition.
- Summarize market opportunities, key financial goals, and projected outcomes.

Why It Matters: A compelling executive summary grabs attention and sets the tone for the rest of the plan, encouraging investors or lenders to explore further.

Example: "Our company provides eco-friendly packaging solutions, addressing the growing demand for sustainable alternatives in the $50 billion packaging industry. With a projected annual revenue of $5 million by year three, we seek $1 million in funding to scale production and expand market reach."

2. Market Analysis

This section demonstrates your understanding of the market dynamics, target audience, and competitive landscape. It should:

- Define your target market and its size, demographics, and preferences.
- Showcase industry trends, growth potential, and existing demand.
- Analyze competitors, identifying gaps or weaknesses you can exploit.

Why It Matters: Funders want assurance that there's a real market demand for your product or service and that you understand your competitive positioning.

Example: "Market research reveals a 20% annual growth rate in demand for eco-friendly packaging. While competitors focus on large-scale B2B clients, our niche targets small- and medium-sized businesses seeking customizable, sustainable solutions."

3. Financial Projections

This section outlines your business's financial health and potential, including:

- **Cash Flow Statements**: Show how money will flow in and out of the business.
- **Income Statements**: Project revenue, expenses, and profits over a specified period.
- **Break-Even Analysis**: Identify when the business will become profitable.

Why It Matters: Financial projections provide funders with the data needed to assess the profitability and sustainability of your business.

Example: "Our financial projections estimate $500,000 in revenue in year one, growing to $2 million by year three, with a 65% gross profit margin. Break-even is anticipated within 18 months."

4. Funding Requirements

This section clearly outlines:

- How much funding is needed?
- Why the funds are required (e.g., equipment, hiring, marketing).
- How the funds will be allocated and the expected impact.

Why It Matters: Funders want a transparent breakdown of how their money will be used and how it contributes to achieving business milestones.

Example: "We are seeking $1 million to cover:

- $400,000 for production equipment.
- $300,000 for marketing and sales efforts.
- $200,000 for expanding our team.
- $100,000 for operational overhead."

5. Risk Mitigation

This section identifies potential challenges and outlines strategies to manage or mitigate risks. Include:

- Internal risks (e.g., operational inefficiencies, staffing challenges).
- External risks (e.g., economic downturns, regulatory changes, competition).
- Contingency plans and solutions.

Why It Matters: Funders need reassurance that they've anticipated potential obstacles and have plans in place to navigate them effectively.

Example: "To mitigate supply chain disruptions, we have secured agreements with multiple suppliers. Additionally, our operational model includes maintaining a three-month inventory buffer to address unforeseen demand surges."

Why These Sections Are Crucial

These sections collectively demonstrate that your business:

1. Has a clear purpose and potential market opportunity.
2. It is financially viable and capable of generating returns.

3. Can effectively utilize funding to achieve growth milestones.
4. Anticipates risks and has strategies to manage them.

A well-prepared business plan, with these key sections thoroughly detailed, not only increases the likelihood of securing funding but also establishes credibility and confidence with potential backers.

Example: A Realistic Funding Pitch

A health-tech startup seeking $500,000 for a wearable fitness device provides a business plan that includes:

1. **The Problem**: Lack of accurate, affordable fitness trackers in the market.
2. **The Solution**: A new wearable device with advanced features at a competitive price.
3. **Financial Needs**:
    - $200,000 for product development and manufacturing.
    - $150,000 for marketing and customer acquisition.
    - $150,000 for building inventory and logistics.
4. **Revenue Forecast**: A timeline showing profitability within 18 months.
5. **Investor ROI**: A projected 3x return within 5 years.

This level of detail ensures the investors understand the opportunity, financial needs, and potential rewards, making the case for funding much stronger.

Key Takeaways for Readers

1. **Investors and Lenders Require a Plan**: A business plan is non-negotiable for securing funding. It shows your business is viable and worth the investment.
2. **Credibility Builds Trust**: A detailed, well-researched plan highlights your commitment, preparation, and expertise, earning the confidence of financiers.
3. **Clearly Outline Financial Needs**: Specify how much funding you need, why you need it, and how you will use it. Demonstrate the ROI or repayment strategy to reassure backers.

Final Thought on Funding

A business plan is not just a formality—it's the key to unlocking funding. By demonstrating your business's viability, financial potential, and strategic approach, you inspire confidence in investors and lenders. A clear, detailed plan positions your venture as a worthy investment, turning your vision into reality with the financial support you need to succeed.

Reflection

Financial Planning:

- What is your current profit margin? If you don't know, calculate it: (Revenue - Costs) ÷ Revenue × 100.

- List three expenses you can reduce or eliminate to improve profitability.

Chapter 5: Building Adaptability

Business Plan Reduces Risks

A well-structured business plan serves as a risk management tool, helping businesses identify, anticipate, and prepare for potential challenges before they arise. By forcing you to analyze all aspects of your venture—financials, operations, market trends, and competition—a business plan reduces uncertainty and enables proactive decision-making. Instead of reacting to problems as they occur, you can devise strategies in advance to mitigate risks, ensuring your business is better equipped to navigate hurdles and capitalize on opportunities.

1. Identifies Challenges: Addressing Risks Proactively

The Importance of Risk Identification

The process of planning requires a deep dive into the internal and external factors that could impact your business. This forces you to analyze potential risks—operational, financial, market-based, and competitive—and determine how they can be mitigated or managed. By identifying challenges early, you can devise strategies to address them, avoiding costly surprises down the road.

- **Key Areas to Assess for Risk Identification:**
    - **Operational Risks**: Supply chain disruptions, equipment failure, or staffing issues.

- **Financial Risks**: Cash flow problems, insufficient capital, or unexpected expenses.
- **Market Risks**: Changes in consumer preferences, increased competition, or economic downturns.
- **Regulatory Risks**: New laws, taxes, or compliance requirements that impact your operations.

Example:

A retail store owner creating a business plan identifies a potential supply chain risk due to reliance on a single overseas supplier. To mitigate this, they devise a contingency strategy that includes partnering with local suppliers to ensure inventory availability during disruptions.

Benefits of Identifying Challenges:

- Allows you to develop contingency plans to manage risks.
- Reduces the likelihood of costly disruptions.
- Ensures you're prepared for challenges before they escalate.

2. Prepares for Uncertainty: Forecasting Financials and Trends

Anticipating Hurdles Through Forecasting

Business plans typically include financial projections, market analysis, and growth forecasts, helping you anticipate future scenarios. By analyzing data and trends, you can identify potential challenges—like cash flow shortages or market saturation—and adjust your strategies in advance. Forecasting also enables you to build flexibility into your operations so you can pivot when circumstances change.

- **Key Tools for Forecasting:**
  - **Cash Flow Projections**: This helps you anticipate periods of low revenue and plan for them.
  - **Sales Forecasts**: Estimates demand for your product or service, allowing you to adjust production or marketing efforts.
  - **Market Trend Analysis**: Identifies shifts in consumer behavior, industry trends, and potential growth areas.

Example:

A small tech startup projects that cash flow will be tight during the first six months of operation. With this forecast, they secure additional funding upfront and reduce unnecessary expenses, ensuring the business can survive the lean period.

Benefits of Preparing for Uncertainty:

- Enables businesses to anticipate and prepare for cash flow shortfalls.
- Helps adjust strategies when market conditions shift.
- Builds resilience by planning for multiple scenarios.

3. Improves Decision-Making: Navigating Uncertainties with Data

The Role of Data in Reducing Risk

A business plan equips you with clear data—financial projections, operational insights, and market research—enabling informed decision-making. Instead of relying on guesswork, you can base your decisions on realistic forecasts, ensuring you allocate resources effectively and address risks proactively.

- **Example of Data-Driven Decision-Making:**
    - If your financial projections show that you're nearing your cash flow limit, you can decide to delay hiring or renegotiate supplier payment terms to conserve funds.
    - If market research reveals a growing demand for eco-friendly products, you might pivot your strategy to focus on sustainability initiatives.

Scenario Planning

A business plan allows you to create scenarios that account for best-case, worst-case, and moderate outcomes. This approach ensures you're ready to act regardless of what happens.

- **Example:**
  A restaurant owner plans for three scenarios:
    - **Best Case**: High customer turnout enables expansion within a year.
    - **Moderate Case**: Steady growth requires maintaining current operations.
    - **Worst Case**: Slower-than-expected growth leads to budget cuts and revised marketing efforts.

By planning for different outcomes, the restaurant owner can make proactive decisions instead of panicking when challenges arise.

Benefits of Improved Decision-Making:

- Helps allocate resources more effectively.
- Reduces reliance on intuition or guesswork.
- Provides clarity during uncertain or stressful situations.

Case Study: Small Manufacturer Navigating Challenges

Scenario: A small business specializing in custom furniture identifies several risks during the business planning process:

1. **Supply Chain Risk:** Rising costs of raw materials.
2. **Market Risk:** Competition from low-cost mass-market furniture retailers.
3. **Financial Risk:** Seasonal demand fluctuations that impact cash flow.

Strategies Identified in the Business Plan:

- **Diversify Suppliers:** Partner with multiple suppliers to reduce dependence on any single source.
- **Focus on a Niche Market:** Target high-value clients looking for customized, artisanal furniture to differentiate the business.
- **Manage Cash Flow:** Build a financial cushion by setting aside funds during peak seasons to cover slow periods.

Outcome:
The manufacturer successfully mitigates supply disruptions, positions itself as a premium brand, and maintains stable cash flow throughout the year, avoiding the risks identified during planning.

How to Use Planning to Reduce Risks

1. **Perform a SWOT Analysis**
   Conduct a SWOT analysis (Strengths, Weaknesses, Opportunities, Threats) to identify internal and external risks. Use this analysis to devise proactive strategies for overcoming challenges.

   - **Example:** A food truck identifies "weather-dependent sales" as a threat. The solution: invest in catering services to generate income regardless of weather.

2. **Create Financial Contingency Plans**
   Develop cash flow projections and contingency plans to manage unexpected expenses or revenue shortfalls.

   - **Example:** A retailer plans to cut discretionary spending and renegotiate rent if sales fall below a certain threshold.

3. **Monitor Market and Industry Trends**
   Stay informed about shifts in the market, emerging competitors, and industry challenges. Regularly update your business plan to account for these changes.

   - **Example:** A fitness studio adapts to the rise of virtual classes by offering online memberships to counter decreased in-person attendance.

4. **Test Assumptions Through Data**
   : Use market research and historical data to test your assumptions. Build realistic, data-driven forecasts to guide your decision-making.

   - **Example:** A startup uses survey data to confirm demand for their product before committing significant resources to production.

Key Takeaways for Readers

1. **Identify Risks Proactively:** A business plan forces you to address challenges and devise solutions before they become critical problems.
2. **Prepare for Uncertainty:** Forecasting financials and market trends allows you to anticipate hurdles and plan flexible strategies.
3. **Make Data-Driven Decisions:** Clear data and projections reduce uncertainty, enabling you to navigate challenges confidently and strategically.
4. **Build Resilience:** Scenario planning helps you prepare for a range of outcomes, ensuring you're ready to act, no matter what the future holds.

Final Thought on Risk

A business plan is a critical risk management tool that equips you to anticipate challenges, prepare for uncertainty, and make confident, informed decisions. By proactively identifying risks and creating contingency strategies, you transform uncertainty into opportunity, ensuring your business remains resilient and adaptable in an ever-changing market. Planning doesn't eliminate risks—it makes them manageable.

Enhances Communication

A well-crafted business plan is more than a tool for outlining goals and strategies; it also serves as a powerful communication resource. By documenting your mission, objectives, and operational strategies, the plan becomes a **shared point of reference** that aligns teams, clarifies your vision, and facilitates collaboration among all stakeholders. Whether you're communicating with employees, partners, advisors, or investors, a detailed business plan ensures everyone is on the same page and working toward the same objectives.

1. Aligns Teams: Unifying Stakeholders Around Goals

The Importance of Alignment

A clear and structured business plan ensures that all stakeholders—employees, partners, managers, and advisors—understand the company's mission, values, and objectives. By creating a common understanding, the plan aligns individuals and teams, ensuring that efforts are focused on shared priorities.

- **Why Team Alignment Matters:**
    - Ensures consistency in decision-making and execution.
    - Prevents misunderstandings and conflicting efforts.
    - Motivates employees by showing how their work contributes to the bigger picture.

Example: A Start-Up with Rapid Growth

A growing start-up hires new employees and brings on advisors to expand operations. Without a clear plan, confusion arises about priorities and responsibilities. By sharing the business plan, leadership ensures that:

1. **Employees** understand their roles and the specific goals they are working toward.
2. **Advisors** are aligned with the company's strategies and financial benchmarks.
3. **Partners** know their contributions to achieving the company's overall mission.

This alignment allows the start-up to scale efficiently, reducing wasted effort and fostering a sense of unity.

Benefits of Team Alignment:

- Everyone knows their role and responsibilities.
- Teams work in the same direction, reducing conflicts or duplication of efforts.
- It improves morale by connecting individual contributions to organizational success.

2. Clarifies Vision: Turning Ideas Into Actionable Plans

Bringing Ideas to Life

A business plan translates abstract ideas and ambitious goals into **clear, actionable strategies**. This clarity makes it easier to communicate your vision to others, whether they are employees, partners, investors, or stakeholders. It bridges the gap between what you envision and how that vision will be achieved.

- **Key Elements That Clarify Vision:**
    - **Mission Statement**: Outlines the core purpose and values of the business.
    - **Goals and Milestones**: Provides tangible objectives for short- and long-term success.

- **Operational Strategies**: Break down how the vision will be executed, step by step.

Example: A Social Enterprise Seeking Buy-In

An entrepreneur with a vision for an eco-friendly clothing line develops a business plan that includes:

- The mission: To produce a sustainable, ethical fashion that reduces environmental impact.
- Goals: Launch the first product line within 12 months and reach $100,000 in sales in the first year.
- Strategies: Build supplier partnerships, invest in digital marketing, and create a customer loyalty program.

By translating their vision into actionable steps, the entrepreneur effectively communicates their plan to investors, partners, and team members, building confidence in the venture.

Benefits of Clarifying Vision:

- Makes it easier to inspire and gain support from stakeholders.
- Translates big-picture ideas into a practical roadmap.
- Ensures that everyone understands the "why" and "how" of the business.

3. Facilitates Collaboration: Creating a Shared Understanding

Driving Effective Communication Across Teams

A business plan serves as a shared document that outlines goals, strategies, and timelines, making it an essential tool for fostering collaboration. It helps teams and stakeholders coordinate efforts, share responsibilities, and track progress. By providing a unified point of reference, the business plan removes ambiguity and ensures everyone knows what needs to be done and by when.

- **How a Business Plan Facilitates Collaboration:**
  - **Centralizes Information**: Teams can refer to the plan to understand objectives and priorities.
  - **Creates Accountability**: Assigns roles and deadlines, ensuring that everyone is responsible for their contributions.
  - **Encourages Cross-Functional Cooperation**: Aligns departments or partners to work collaboratively toward shared outcomes.

Example: A Product Launch with Cross-Team Collaboration

For a new product launch, a company uses its business plan to coordinate between departments:

- **Marketing**: Plans the promotional campaigns to generate buzz.
- **Sales**: Focuses on outreach to retailers and customers.
- **Operations**: Ensures the product is manufactured, packaged, and delivered on time.

The business plan outlines goals, timelines, and dependencies, ensuring that all teams work collaboratively toward a common launch date. By creating shared visibility and clarity, the business avoids miscommunication and delays.

Benefits of Facilitating Collaboration:

- Improves teamwork by providing clear roles and responsibilities.
- Reduces miscommunication and overlapping efforts.
- Enhances efficiency by keeping everyone on the same page.

Practical Tips for Enhancing Communication with a Business Plan

1. **Share the Plan with Stakeholders**

    - Regularly share the plan with employees, advisors, and partners to keep everyone informed and engaged.
    - Update stakeholders as strategies or goals evolve, ensuring alignment over time.

2. **Use Visual Aids to Communicate Complex Information**

    - Incorporate charts, timelines, and infographics to make key elements (like financial projections or milestones) easier to understand.
    - **Example:** A Gantt chart can illustrate project timelines for cross-team collaboration.

3. **Set Up Regular Check-Ins**

    - Schedule meetings to review progress, address concerns and ensure that teams are aligned with the business plan.
    - Use the business plan as a guide to track progress and adjust strategies as needed.

4. **Keep the Plan Accessible**

- Store the plan in a central location (e.g., cloud storage) so stakeholders can access it anytime.
- **Example:** Platforms like Google Drive or Asana allow teams to view and track updates to the business plan.

5. **Tailor Communication to the Audience**

    - For employees: Highlight how their work aligns with the business goals.
    - For investors: Focus on financial projections, ROI, and growth strategies.
    - For partners: Emphasize collaboration opportunities and shared objectives.

Case Study: Aligning Teams with a Business Plan

Scenario:
A mid-sized marketing agency struggling with miscommunication among teams developed a comprehensive business plan.

Steps Taken:

1. Clearly outlined the company's goals: Expand into two new markets within 18 months.
2. Assigned roles to each department:
    - **Sales**: Identify target clients in new markets.
    - **Operations**: Set processes to onboard new clients.
    - **Marketing**: Develop campaigns tailored to the new markets.
3. Created a shared timeline for milestones, ensuring accountability across teams.

Outcome:
The business plan provided a clear roadmap, aligning all departments and reducing confusion. Teams collaborated efficiently, and the company successfully entered two new markets on schedule.

Key Takeaways for Readers

1. **Align Your Team**: A business plan unifies all stakeholders by clearly defining the mission, goals, and roles, ensuring everyone moves in the same direction.
2. **Clarify Your Vision**: Translating ideas into actionable steps makes it easier to communicate with investors, employees, and partners, gaining their support and confidence.

3. **Facilitate Collaboration**: A shared plan improves teamwork, accountability, and coordination, allowing teams to work together seamlessly toward common goals.

4. **Improve Communication Practices**: Use visuals, regular updates, and audience-specific messaging to make your business plan an effective communication tool.

Final Thought on Communication

A business plan is not just a tool for planning—it's a communication powerhouse. It aligns teams, clarifies your vision, and fosters collaboration, ensuring that everyone, from employees to investors, understands your mission and contributes effectively. With a shared understanding of goals and strategies, your business can operate cohesively, tackle challenges efficiently, and achieve success with confidence.

Tracks Progress and Performance

A well-designed business plan serves as a dynamic tool for monitoring your business's progress and ensuring performance stays on track. By establishing clear, measurable milestones, the plan allows you to assess achievements over time, identify areas for improvement, and make necessary adjustments to meet evolving market conditions. Beyond just providing a roadmap, it fosters accountability by assigning responsibility for specific goals and ensuring that teams and individuals are aligned with your objectives.

1. Sets Milestones: Monitoring Achievements Over Time

The Role of Milestones in Measuring Progress

Milestones are essential tools for tracking a business's progress and ensuring alignment with overall goals. By breaking down larger objectives into smaller, actionable checkpoints, milestones provide clarity and focus while helping businesses monitor performance in real-time. They serve as benchmarks to measure success, identify challenges early, and make necessary adjustments to stay on track.

Key Characteristics of Effective Milestones

To be impactful, milestones must possess the following attributes:

1. **Specific**
    - Milestones should be clearly defined, leaving no room for ambiguity.
    - They address a particular task or goal and outline exactly what is to be accomplished.

- **Example**: "Launch a new marketing campaign targeting a 10% increase in website traffic."

2. **Measurable**
   - Use quantifiable metrics to gauge success.
   - Measurability ensures that progress can be tracked and evaluated against clear criteria.
   - **Example**: "Achieve $50,000 in sales within the first quarter."

3. **Time-Bound**
   - Link milestones to specific deadlines to instill urgency and maintain momentum.
   - Deadlines ensure accountability and help prioritize tasks.
   - **Example**: "Finalize prototype design by the end of Q2."

4. **Actionable**
   - Milestones must be achievable within the resources and constraints of the business.
   - This practicality ensures that the team can realistically reach the targets.
   - **Example**: "Hire three new sales representatives within the next 90 days."

Benefits of Using Milestones

- **Clear Benchmarks for Success**: Provide tangible points to measure achievements and progress.

- **Early Problem Detection**: Highlight areas that may need attention before they escalate.

- **Motivation and Focus**: Smaller, frequent wins help maintain momentum and team morale.

- **Accountability**: Ensure all stakeholders stay aligned and committed to achieving goals.

Example: A Retail Startup's Milestones

A retail startup sets the following milestones in its business plan:

1. **Month 1**: Secure vendor contracts and finalize inventory.
2. **Month 3**: Launch an e-commerce platform and achieve 100 sales.
3. **Month 6**: Expand product offerings by 20% based on customer feedback.
4. **Year 1**: Reach $250,000 in annual revenue and establish partnerships with two national retailers.

By dividing its larger goal into these smaller, time-bound steps, the startup ensures steady progress and creates opportunities to refine its strategy along the way.

Effective milestones are the building blocks of a successful business plan, ensuring that progress is measurable, actionable, and aligned with overarching objectives. They enable businesses to stay focused, make informed decisions, and achieve long-term success.

Benefits of Setting Milestones:

- Provides clarity on what success looks like at each stage.
- Breaks complex goals into manageable steps, reducing overwhelm.
- Creates momentum by celebrating small achievements along the way.

Facilitates Adjustments: Pivoting to Meet Market Demands

A business plan is not meant to be rigid; it is a dynamic, living document that evolves as circumstances change. Regular reviews of your business plan ensure that you remain adaptable and responsive to new challenges, market trends, and customer needs. This flexibility helps businesses stay competitive, refine strategies, and align resources with emerging opportunities.

The Need for Regular Reviews

Consistently revisiting and evaluating your business plan allows you to assess what's working, address what's not, and make necessary adjustments based on data and insights. This process ensures that your business remains aligned with its goals while staying relevant in a rapidly changing environment.

Why Regular Reviews Matter:

- **Respond to Shifting Trends**: Quickly adapt to industry or market developments, such as changes in consumer behavior or emerging technology.
- **Address Operational Issues**: Evaluate performance against milestones to identify bottlenecks or inefficiencies.
- **Maintain Relevance**: Ensure your strategies and goals reflect the latest business realities and external conditions.

How Regular Reviews Drive Adjustments

1. **Identify Gaps**

   - Regular reviews help pinpoint where you've fallen short of expectations. By analyzing unmet milestones, you can uncover root causes and take corrective actions.
   - **Example**: If your sales numbers are below projections, reviews may reveal issues such as ineffective marketing, pricing problems, or changes in consumer preferences.

2. **Adapt to Market Changes**

   - Market dynamics such as competitor activity, regulatory changes, or evolving customer demands can necessitate shifts in strategy.
   - **Example**: If a competitor introduces a new product feature that disrupts your market, reviews allow you to evaluate your offerings and determine how to differentiate further.

3. **Optimize Strategies**

   - Regular evaluations allow you to focus on high-impact activities while refining or eliminating underperforming initiatives.
   - **Example**: If a particular advertising channel shows a low return on investment, you can reallocate your budget to more effective platforms.

Benefits of Regular Reviews and Adjustments

- **Improves Efficiency**: Ensures resources are directed to activities that drive the most value.
- **Increases Agility**: Allows your business to pivot quickly in response to external changes.
- **Enhances Competitiveness**: Keeps your strategies and offerings aligned with current market demands.
- **Minimizes Risk**: Identifies potential problems early and implements solutions before they escalate.

Case Study: Pivoting to Meet Market Demands

Scenario: A brick-and-mortar bookstore notices declining sales due to the rising popularity of e-books and online retailers.

Review Findings:

- Gaps: Foot traffic has decreased, and in-store events aren't attracting enough customers.

- **Market Changes**: Competitors like Amazon dominate the online space, and consumers are increasingly seeking convenience.

Strategic Adjustments:

- Launch an online store to sell e-books and physical copies nationwide.
- Develop a subscription model offering discounts and early access to new releases.
- Shift resources toward online marketing, targeting book clubs and literary enthusiasts.

Outcome: By adapting to market demands and leveraging technology, the bookstore not only stabilized sales but also expanded its customer base beyond its physical location.

Practical Steps for Regular Reviews

1. **Set a Schedule**: Conduct monthly, quarterly, or annual reviews depending on your business needs.
2. **Use Data**: Analyze metrics such as sales performance, customer feedback, and financial reports to guide decisions.
3. **Involve Stakeholders**: Include team members and advisors to provide diverse perspectives.
4. **Document Changes**: Update your business plan to reflect adjustments and new strategies.

A business plan that is regularly reviewed and adjusted becomes a powerful tool for navigating change. By staying flexible and data-driven, businesses can effectively pivot to meet market demands, maintain relevance, and achieve long-term success.

Example: A Fitness App Business

A fitness app company sets a goal of acquiring 10,000 downloads within six months.

After the first quarter, they analyzed their progress and discovered they'd only achieved 3,000 downloads due to low ad engagement. Instead of sticking rigidly to the plan, they pivot:

- Adjust the marketing strategy by focusing on social media influencers and partnerships.
- Optimize ad copy and visuals to target fitness enthusiasts better.

- Revisit their goals and extend the milestone timeline slightly while monitoring the new strategy's performance.

The ability to analyze performance, identify roadblocks, and make swift adjustments ensures the business continues to move forward instead of stagnating.

Benefits of Facilitating Adjustments:

- Ensures the business remains agile and adaptable to change.
- Prevents small issues from snowballing into larger challenges.
- Helps optimize strategies and resources for maximum efficiency.

3. Encourages Accountability: Assigning Responsibility for Results

Accountability Drives Results

A business plan doesn't just outline goals—it assigns ownership for achieving those goals. By clearly defining who is responsible for each milestone or key task, it holds individuals, teams, and departments accountable for delivering results. Accountability fosters a sense of ownership, ensuring that everyone understands their role in contributing to the overall success of the business.

- **Key Tools for Accountability:**
    - **KPIs (Key Performance Indicators)**: Metrics to measure individual and team performance.
    - **Timelines**: Specific deadlines for achieving tasks or milestones.
    - **Performance Reviews**: Regular check-ins to assess progress and provide feedback.

Example: A Marketing Agency

A marketing agency includes the following in its business plan:

- **Goal**: Increase client leads by 25% in six months.
- **Milestones**:
    - Month 1: Launch social media campaigns (owned by the marketing team).
    - Month 3: Generate 100 high-quality leads (owned by the sales team).
    - Month 6: Assess the ROI of campaigns and report results (owned by the operations team).

By assigning responsibility for each milestone, the business ensures accountability at every level. Teams and individuals have clear roles, understand expectations, and are motivated to meet their targets.

Benefits of Encouraging Accountability:

- Improves team productivity and focus.
- Reduces ambiguity around roles and responsibilities.
- Builds a culture of ownership where everyone takes pride in achieving results.

Tracking Progress and Performance: Practical Tips

1. **Use KPIs to Measure Success**
   Establish clear Key Performance Indicators to monitor progress toward milestones. For example:

   - **Sales Targets**: Achieving specific revenue goals.
   - **Customer Metrics**: Acquisition rates, retention rates, or customer satisfaction scores.
   - **Operational Metrics**: Production timelines, delivery rates, or inventory turnover.

2. **Schedule Regular Progress Reviews**
   Set up periodic check-ins—monthly, quarterly, or bi-annually—to assess progress. Use these meetings to evaluate what's on track, address challenges, and adjust plans.

3. **Leverage Technology for Tracking**
   Use project management tools like **Trello**, **Asana**, or **Monday.com** to keep track of tasks, milestones, and team responsibilities. Financial tools like **QuickBooks** or **Excel** can help track budgets and forecasts.

4. **Celebrate Achievements**
   : Acknowledge when milestones are met to boost morale and reinforce a sense of accomplishment. Celebrating small wins creates motivation to keep progressing toward larger goals.

5. **Stay Flexible and Adaptable**
   Be open to revising your milestones or strategy based on performance data, market trends, or unforeseen challenges. Flexibility ensures continued progress.

Case Study: Tracking Progress in a New Restaurant

Scenario:
A new restaurant sets clear milestones in its business plan to track its progress:

1. **First 3 Months**: Attract 500 customers and receive at least 50 positive reviews online.
2. **6 Months**: Reach profitability by managing food costs and increasing customer loyalty.

3. **12 Months**: Introduce catering services and expand marketing efforts.

Actions Taken:

- Regular reviews of weekly customer traffic and feedback allowed the restaurant to identify slow days and adjust promotions.
- Financial analysis helped reduce waste and improve profit margins.
- The team was held accountable for their roles—front staff for customer service, marketing for outreach, and chefs for consistent food quality.

Outcome:
By tracking progress, the restaurant met its milestones, became profitable, and successfully launched a catering arm in year one.

Key Takeaways for Readers

1. **Set Measurable Milestones**: Break large goals into smaller, actionable checkpoints to monitor achievements over time.
2. **Track and Adjust Regularly**: Use progress reviews and performance data to identify challenges and adapt strategies as needed.
3. **Foster Accountability**: Assign clear roles and responsibilities to ensure everyone is committed to achieving their goals.
4. **Celebrate Progress**: Recognize small wins to maintain motivation and momentum.
5. **Stay Agile**: A business plan is a living document. Be open to adjusting goals to keep pace with changes in the market or business environment.

Final Thought on Tracking Performance

Tracking progress and performance is the key to turning a business plan into a tool for success. By setting clear milestones, regularly assessing progress, and fostering accountability, businesses can stay focused, adaptable, and motivated. Progress doesn't happen by accident—monitoring and measuring your journey ensures that every step you take moves you closer to your ultimate goals.

Chapter 6: Enhancing Market Understanding

Increases Market Understanding

A business plan is a powerful tool for deepening your understanding of the market. It forces you to conduct thorough research, evaluate competitors, and analyze your target audience, enabling you to make better strategic decisions. By exploring market dynamics, you gain valuable insights into customer behavior, industry trends, and competitive landscapes. This knowledge not only helps you position your business effectively but also uncovers opportunities to innovate and differentiate your offerings.

1. In-depth Research: Understanding Your Industry, Competitors, and Target Audience

The Role of Research in Market Understanding

Writing a business plan involves comprehensive market research that focuses on three key areas:

- **Industry Analysis**: Understanding the broader industry trends, growth rates, and future outlook to determine where your business fits in.
- **Competitor Analysis**: Identifying direct and indirect competitors, assessing their strengths and weaknesses, and finding ways to outperform them.
- **Target Audience Research**: Studying your ideal customers—who they are, what they need, and how to reach them effectively.

Through this process, you gather actionable data that helps you make informed decisions about marketing, pricing, product development, and positioning.

Example: A New Café in a Competitive Market

An entrepreneur planning to open a specialty coffee shop conducts in-depth research as part of their business plan:

- **Industry Insight**: They discover that demand for premium coffee is growing as consumers seek unique experiences.
- **Competitor Analysis**: Existing coffee chains dominate on price and convenience but lack personalization and specialty offerings.
- **Target Audience**: Surveys reveal a niche market of remote workers and students looking for comfortable spaces to work and socialize.

Outcome: Armed with this research, the entrepreneur positions the café as a premium offering with artisanal coffee, cozy workspaces, and high-speed internet, addressing unmet needs in the market.

Benefits of In-Depth Research:

- Reduces guesswork by providing data-driven insights.
- Ensures your products/services align with real market demands.
- Enables better decisions about pricing, marketing, and operations.

2. Identifies Opportunities: Uncovering Untapped Niches and Market Gaps

Finding New Opportunities Through Market Analysis

By thoroughly examining your market, you can identify opportunities that may have otherwise gone unnoticed. These could include underserved customer segments, emerging trends, or gaps in the competition. Market research allows you to capitalize on these opportunities early, giving you a competitive edge.

- **Key Methods for Identifying Opportunities:**
    - **Trend Analysis**: Monitoring shifts in consumer behavior, technology, and industry practices.
    - **Customer Surveys**: Asking potential customers about their needs and frustrations.
    - **Competitor Gaps**: Identifying areas where competitors underperform or fail to meet customer expectations.

Example: A Subscription Box Business

An entrepreneur exploring subscription box services discovers a gap: while food and beauty boxes are saturated, there is a growing demand for eco-friendly, zero-waste household products. Through their research, they identify:

- An audience of environmentally conscious consumers.
- A lack of competitors offering curated zero-waste items.
- Trends showing increased interest in sustainability and reusable products.

Outcome: The business launches a monthly subscription box for sustainable household goods, filling a niche market and positioning itself as a unique offering.

Benefits of Identifying Opportunities:

- Allows you to address underserved customer needs.
- Positions your business in untapped or emerging markets.
- Creates innovative solutions that differentiate your offerings.

3. Analyzes Competition: Finding Your Competitive Edge

Why Competitor Analysis Matters

A business plan provides a framework for analyzing competitors, helping you identify their strengths, weaknesses, and market positioning. By understanding your competition, you can develop strategies to differentiate your business and offer more value to customers.

- **Key Elements of Competitor Analysis:**
  - **Identify Competitors**: Who are the key players in your industry? Include both direct (same product/service) and indirect competitors (alternatives).
  - **Analyze Strengths and Weaknesses**: What are competitors doing well, and where are they falling short?
  - **Understand Their Positioning**: How do competitors market themselves, and what value do they offer customers?
  - **Benchmark Performance**: Compare their pricing, customer base, marketing efforts, and product quality.

Example: A New Fitness Studio

A fitness entrepreneur developing a business plan analyzes local competitors:

- **Strengths**: Established gyms offer low-cost memberships and a wide variety of classes.
- **Weaknesses**: These gyms lack personalized coaching and community-building.
- **Opportunity**: By offering small group classes with personalized attention, the fitness studio can fill a gap in the market.

Outcome: The business positions itself as a boutique fitness studio focusing on individual results and building a sense of community, differentiating it from larger competitors.

Techniques to Analyze Competition Effectively

1. **SWOT Analysis**: Analyze competitors 'Strengths, Weaknesses, Opportunities, and Threats.
2. **Customer Reviews**: Assess competitor reviews to understand customer pain points and preferences.
3. **Competitive Benchmarking**: Compare prices, features, and marketing strategies against competitors.
4. **Mystery Shopping**: Experience competitors 'services or products firsthand to identify gaps and opportunities.

Benefits of Competitor Analysis:

- Helps you develop a unique value proposition to stand out in the market.
- Allows you to capitalize on competitors 'weaknesses and gaps.

- Guides pricing, branding, and marketing strategies to appeal to your target audience.

Practical Steps to Increase Market Understanding with a Business Plan

1. **Conduct Market Research**
   - Use tools like Google Trends, industry reports, and surveys to gather insights.
   - Identify your target market's size, demographics, and behavior.

2. **Segment Your Audience**
   - Divide your audience into segments (e.g., age, location, interests) to better understand and target their needs.

3. **Perform Competitor Analysis**
   - Identify direct and indirect competitors.
   - Research their pricing, marketing, and customer satisfaction levels.

4. **Identify Trends and Opportunities**
   - Stay updated on industry reports, emerging technologies, and consumer shifts to spot new opportunities.

5. **Develop a Competitive Advantage**
   - Use your research to determine what sets your business apart (e.g., superior quality, niche focus, better pricing).

Case Study: A Specialty Ice Cream Brand

Scenario: A new business plans to launch a premium ice cream brand. Through market research:

1. **Industry Analysis**: Premium, artisanal ice cream is growing in popularity among health-conscious and experience-driven consumers.
2. **Competitor Analysis**: Large chains dominate the market but lack unique flavors and healthier options.
3. **Target Audience**: Surveys reveal that consumers want dairy-free, low-sugar options with unique flavors.

Outcome: The brand positions itself as a provider of small-batch, dairy-free ice cream with creative flavors like lavender honey and matcha coconut. Market understanding allows them to stand out in a crowded industry and appeal directly to consumer preferences.

Key Takeaways for Readers

1. **In-depth Research Drives Better Decisions**: Market research helps you understand your industry, competitors, and target audience, ensuring you make informed strategic choices.

2. **Identify Untapped Opportunities**: By analyzing trends and customer needs, you can uncover new niches and gaps in the market to capitalize on.

3. **Gain a Competitive Edge**: Understanding your competition enables you to position your business effectively, offering unique value to customers.

4. **A Data-Driven Approach Wins**: By combining research, analysis, and creativity, you ensure your strategies align with market demands.

Final Thought on Understanding Your Market

Market understanding is the cornerstone of a successful business. A detailed business plan not only forces you to study your industry but also equips you with the insights needed to identify opportunities, outperform competitors, and meet customer needs effectively. When you truly understand the market, your business gains the strategic advantage needed to thrive and grow.

Reflection Thoughts

Operations:

- Outline one operational process you could streamline to save time or money.

- What technology or tool could improve your business operations?

Chapter 7: Professionalism and Communication

Builds Confidence and Professionalism

A well-structured business plan is not just a roadmap for success; it is also a reflection of your commitment, preparedness, and professionalism. It helps build confidence in yourself as an entrepreneur and inspires trust and enthusiasm in others, such as investors, employees, and business partners, by demonstrating your dedication, strategic clarity, and attention to detail, a strong business plan positions you as a serious professional capable of turning ideas into reality.

1. Encourages Commitment: Demonstrating Dedication to Your Venture

Why Commitment Matters

Writing a comprehensive business plan is a deliberate act of dedication. It shows that you are willing to invest time, energy, and effort into understanding every aspect of your business. This process not only demonstrates to others—investors, employees, or stakeholders—that you are serious about your venture, but it also solidifies your own commitment.

- **Key Signals of Dedication in a Business Plan:**
    - Thorough research on the market, competition, and customer needs.
    - Realistic financial projections show how you plan to achieve profitability.
    - Detailed operational plans that outline how the business will run day-to-day.

Example: A Start-Up Founder

A tech entrepreneur crafting a business plan for a mobile app includes in-depth research on user behavior, detailed milestones for product development, and financial projections for the first two years. By doing so, they not only demonstrate their dedication to potential investors but also clarify their own level of commitment to the venture.

Benefits of Encouraging Commitment:

- Reinforces personal belief in the business's viability.
- Demonstrate to others that you are serious and prepared to follow through.
- Builds resilience in facing challenges by providing a clear path forward.

2. Professionalism: Reflecting Your Seriousness and Credibility

The Importance of Professionalism

A well-prepared business plan is a mark of professionalism. It shows investors, partners, employees, and even customers that you are credible, organized, and serious about the venture. Professionalism in a business plan helps you stand out from competitors and gain the trust of stakeholders.

- **Key Elements of Professionalism in a Business Plan:**
  - **Clarity**: Clear goals, strategies, and action steps.
  - **Attention to Detail**: Accurate financial data, realistic projections, and thoughtful risk analysis.
  - **Polished Presentation**: A well-organized, visually appealing document with no errors or inconsistencies.

Example: Pitching to Investors

An entrepreneur seeking funding for a sustainable food business presents a polished, data-driven business plan. It includes financial forecasts, supply chain details, and sustainability practices, all neatly organized and supported with visuals and research. This level of professionalism earns the respect and confidence of investors, increasing the likelihood of funding.

Benefits of Professionalism:

- Enhances your credibility and trustworthiness.
- Makes it easier to secure support from investors, employees, and advisors.
- Positions you as a capable leader who can execute the plan effectively.

3. Builds Self-Assurance: Gaining Confidence Through Clarity and Preparation

How a Business Plan Builds Confidence

Clarity breeds confidence. The process of creating a business plan requires you to think critically about every aspect of your business—its goals, strategies, potential challenges, and opportunities. This level of preparation equips you with the knowledge and tools to move forward with confidence.

- **The Confidence Boost of a Strong Business Plan:**
  - Knowing your market and audience inside-out removes uncertainty.
  - Detailed financial projections provide reassurance that the business is financially viable.
  - Clear milestones allow you to track progress and celebrate wins along the way.

Example: Launching a New Product

A business owner preparing to launch a new product feels uncertain about market demand. Through research for the business plan, they identify a strong target audience and an unmet need in the market. Armed with data, they proceed with confidence, knowing their product has real potential for success.

Benefits of Building Self-Assurance:

- Reduces doubt and hesitation, helping you make bold, informed decisions.
- Equips you with a well-reasoned plan to counter challenges or skepticism.
- Provides a clear vision and action steps that increase personal confidence.

4. Inspires Others: Attracting Partners, Employees, and Investors Who Share Your Vision

Inspiring Through Vision and Preparation

A professional business plan is not just about facts and figures—it's about conveying your passion, vision, and dedication in a way that inspires others. By presenting a clear and well-reasoned strategy, you can attract like-minded partners, employees, and investors who believe in your goals and are willing to help bring your vision to life.

- **What Inspires Others in a Business Plan:**
    - **A Clear Vision**: A compelling explanation of the problem your business solves and the impact it will have.
    - **Strategic Roadmap**: A practical, step-by-step plan for achieving success.
    - **Evidence of Viability**: Data-driven projections, realistic targets, and risk mitigation strategies.

Example: Attracting Key Stakeholders

A founder creating a business plan for an eco-friendly construction company outlines a clear mission to reduce carbon footprints in the housing industry. The plan includes innovative building methods, sustainability metrics, and financial projections. By presenting a well-prepared plan, the founder inspires environmentally conscious investors and employees to join the project and contribute their skills and resources.

Benefits of Inspiring Others:

- Attracts talented team members who align with your mission.
- Builds trust and enthusiasm among potential investors and partners.
- Creates momentum by fostering a shared commitment to the business's success.

Key Tips to Build Confidence and Professionalism in Your Business Plan

1. **Focus on Structure and Clarity**
    - Organize your plan with clear sections: executive summary, market analysis, financial projections, and strategies.

- Use visuals like graphs, charts, and tables to enhance understanding.

2. **Be Thorough and Data-Driven**

    - Support claims with data, such as market research, customer insights, and financial forecasts.
    - Address risks and provide realistic mitigation strategies to show you are prepared.

3. **Polish the Presentation**

    - Use professional formatting and eliminate typos or errors.
    - If presenting the plan in person, practice delivering it with confidence and enthusiasm.

4. **Show Your Passion**

    - Use the business plan to articulate not just what you're doing but **why** you're doing it.
    - Inspire others with a compelling story of how your business solves real problems and creates value.

5. **Seek Feedback**

    - Share your plan with mentors, advisors, or trusted colleagues to get constructive feedback. Their insights can improve your plan and build your confidence.

Case Study: A Tech Start-Up Pitching to Investors

Scenario:
A start-up founder developing an AI-powered productivity tool prepares a professional business plan for investors.

Steps Taken:

1. Conducts extensive market research to demonstrate the demand for AI-driven tools.
2. Prepares detailed financial projections and user acquisition goals.
3. Articulates a clear vision of how the product will solve workplace inefficiencies.
4. Polishes the plan's presentation with engaging visuals and a compelling executive summary.

Outcome:
The professional and well-prepared plan inspires confidence in investors, who see the founder's commitment, strategic foresight, and clarity. The start-up secures funding and attracts top-tier advisors who align with the company's mission.

Key Takeaways for Readers

1. **Commitment Drives Success**: The effort you put into crafting a business plan demonstrates your dedication to the venture and builds trust with others.
2. **Professionalism Builds Credibility**: A polished, well-researched business plan reflects seriousness and inspires confidence in stakeholders.
3. **Clarity Creates Confidence**: Preparing a business plan equips you with the knowledge and tools to move forward boldly.
4. **Inspiration Attracts Support**: A clear and compelling vision can inspire partners, employees, and investors to join you on your journey.

Final Thought on Professionalism

A business plan is more than a document—it's a reflection of your commitment, professionalism, and confidence in your vision. By presenting a clear, detailed, and polished plan, you not only inspire trust and enthusiasm in others but also equip yourself with the clarity and self-assurance needed to take your venture forward. With a strong plan, you prove that you're not just dreaming about success—you're building it.

Plan Facilitates Adaptability

In today's dynamic business environment, adaptability is crucial for success. A well-crafted business plan serves as a living document that can evolve and grow alongside your business. It allows you to remain flexible and respond effectively to **shifting market conditions**, unforeseen challenges, or emerging opportunities. By encouraging regular updates and supporting strategic pivots, a business plan ensures that you stay aligned with your long-term goals while maintaining the agility to adjust your strategies and operations when necessary.

1. Encourages Regular Updates: A Living Document for Changing Conditions

Why Regular Updates Matter

A business plan is not meant to be written once and left on a shelf. The most successful businesses treat their plans as **living documents**—resources that are reviewed, refined, and updated regularly to reflect changes in the market, industry, or business operations. This adaptability ensures that the plan remains relevant and actionable, helping you navigate change with confidence.

Key Reasons to Update Your Business Plan

1. **Market Shifts**: Trends, technology, or consumer preferences may evolve, requiring updates to your strategies.
2. **Internal Changes**: Growth milestones, new hires, funding rounds, or operational shifts impact your priorities.
3. **External Factors**: Economic changes, new regulations, or unexpected events like a global crisis necessitate adjustments.
4. **Performance Analysis**: Reviewing key performance indicators (KPIs) allows you to compare your progress to projections and refine your plan.

How to Update Your Plan

- **Schedule Regular Reviews**: Revisit the business plan monthly, quarterly, or annually to assess progress and identify necessary changes.
- **Incorporate Data**: Use real performance data—like financial statements, customer feedback, and market research—to guide updates.
- **Adjust Goals and Milestones**: Modify your short-term or long-term goals to reflect new priorities or market realities.
- **Communicate Changes**: Share updates with stakeholders—team members, investors, or partners—to ensure alignment and support.

Example: An E-Commerce Business

An e-commerce retailer specializing in luxury products updates its business plan quarterly. During one review, the team identifies a growing trend sustainably. By integrating this insight:

- The retailer updates its plan to include eco-friendly product lines.
- Marketing strategies shift to emphasize sustainability, targeting environmentally conscious consumers.

- Financial projections are adjusted to reflect anticipated demand and investment in new inventory.

Outcome: Regular updates allow the business to capitalize on an emerging trend and maintain relevance in the market.

Benefits of Regular Updates:

- Keeps the plan aligned with current business and market realities.
- Allows businesses to respond proactively to challenges and opportunities.
- Builds resilience by enabling quick decision-making and adjustments.

2. Supports Pivoting: Adapting Strategies to New Opportunities or Challenges

The Need for Flexibility

No matter how well you plan, unexpected challenges or opportunities will arise. A strong business plan provides the foundation for a **strategic pivot**—the ability to shift directions or adapt strategies without losing sight of your long-term goals. Instead of reacting impulsively, you can use your plan to make data-driven decisions and maintain focus during times of change.

What Is a Pivot?

A **pivot** involves a fundamental shift in one or more aspects of your business to improve outcomes or address a new reality. This could mean:

- Changing your target audience.
- Altering your product or service offerings.
- Exploring new markets or revenue streams.
- Adjusting your pricing, distribution, or business model.

How a Business Plan Supports Pivoting

1. **Clear Baseline**: The business plan provides a reference point, enabling you to compare where you are now versus where you need to go.

2. **Data for Decision-Making**: Financial projections, market analysis, and performance metrics help you evaluate the potential impact of the pivot.

3. **Risk Management**: By identifying potential risks and creating contingency plans, the business plan helps you pivot without compromising stability.

4. **Focused Execution**: The plan ensures that pivots are intentional and aligned with your long-term mission, preventing unnecessary distractions.

Example: A Tech Start-Up Pivoting During a Crisis

A tech start-up specializing in in-person event management software experiences a sudden decline in business during the COVID-19 pandemic. Instead of shutting down, the founders use their business plan to pivot:

- **New Opportunity**: They identify a growing need for virtual event platforms.
- **Strategic Adjustment**: The start-up shifts its focus to developing virtual conferencing tools, integrating video streaming and interactive features.
- **Updated Projections**: The financial section of the plan is revised to reflect new pricing structures and expected revenue streams.
- **Execution**: Marketing strategies are adjusted to target corporate clients needing virtual event solutions.

Outcome: By using their business plan to guide the pivot, the company successfully transitions into a new market, retaining clients and securing new revenue streams.

3. Practical Steps for Adaptability

1. Monitor Market Trends

Regularly track industry changes, consumer behavior, and technological advancements. Tools like **Google Trends**, customer surveys, and industry reports help you stay informed and anticipate shifts.

2. Establish Performance Checkpoints

Use key performance indicators (KPIs) to measure progress against your business plan. If actual performance deviates significantly from projections, evaluate the reasons and adjust accordingly.

- **Example**: If a restaurant notices declining in-person sales, it may adjust to focus on online delivery and meal kits.

3. Build Contingency Plans

Incorporate alternative strategies into your business plan to prepare for uncertainties or challenges. Outline "Plan B" scenarios to respond quickly to unexpected events.

- **Example**: A manufacturer facing potential supply chain disruptions identifies alternative suppliers in advance.

4. Reallocate Resources as Needed

Adaptability requires shifting resources (time, money, personnel) to areas that offer the most value or opportunity.

- **Example**: A company reallocates its marketing budget to focus on social media campaigns as consumer habits shift online.

5. Communicate Changes Clearly

When adapting or pivoting, communicate updates to your stakeholders, including employees, investors, and partners. Transparency builds trust and ensures alignment.

- **Example**: A start-up informs investors of a pivot to a new product backed by updated projections and research.

4. Case Study: A Restaurant Embracing Adaptability

Scenario: A popular dine-in restaurant faces declining revenue due to changing consumer habits and increased competition from food delivery apps.

Steps Taken:

1. **Market Analysis**: The owner reviews the business plan and identifies a growing demand for takeout and delivery services.
2. **Pivot Strategy**:
   - Launches an online ordering system.
   - Develop a special "family meal package" for delivery.
   - Partners with food delivery platforms to expand reach.
3. **Updated Financial Projections**: Revises revenue targets and adjusts expenses to account for delivery fees.
4. **Resource Reallocation**: Staff shifts focus to delivery prep and online customer service.

Outcome: The restaurant adapts its business model, maintains profitability, and builds a new revenue stream through delivery services.

Key Takeaways for Readers

1. **Business Plans Evolve**: A business plan is a living document that should be updated regularly to reflect new challenges, opportunities, and realities.
2. **Supports Strategic Pivots**: A well-maintained plan provides clarity and structure when you need to shift strategies or explore new opportunities.
3. **Adaptability Requires Flexibility**: Regular reviews, performance tracking, and market monitoring allow businesses to pivot quickly and effectively.

4. **Informed Decisions Are Key**: Use the data and insights within your business plan to guide changes and ensure they align with your long-term goals.

Final Thought on Flexibility

Adaptability is a competitive advantage in today's fast-changing world. A business plan provides the foundation for flexibility, enabling you to adapt strategies, seize new opportunities, and overcome challenges without losing focus. By regularly revisiting your plan and using it to guide pivots, you can remain resilient, agile, and prepared for whatever the market brings.

Conclusion

A business plan is much more than a document; it's a dynamic tool that drives success. A well-crafted business plan is an essential instrument for transforming an idea into a thriving business. It equips you with a strategic guide to overcome obstacles, seize opportunities, measure success, and inspire confidence in your vision. Without one, you will find yourself operating in a reactive rather than proactive manner— a risk no entrepreneur should take.

Chapter 8: Implement and Adapt Your Business Plan

Once you have a business plan, the real challenge lies in effectively implementing and adapting it to ensure your business grows and thrives. Here's how you can put your plan into action and adjust it as circumstances evolve:

Best Ways to Implement and Adapt Your Business Plan

Creating a business plan is a critical step in laying the foundation for success, but its true value lies in how effectively you implement and adapt it over time. A solid plan must become a living document, guiding your day-to-day actions, tracking your progress, and evolving as circumstances change. Below is a detailed framework for implementing and adapting your business plan to ensure consistent growth and resilience.

1. Create a Timeline for Achieving Key Milestones

Why It Matters

A timeline provides a **roadmap** for achieving short- and long-term goals. It helps you prioritize tasks, maintain momentum, and measure progress, ensuring your business stays organized and focused. Without a timeline, it's easy to lose sight of priorities, become overwhelmed, or miss critical deadlines.

Steps to Create an Effective Timeline

1. **Break Down Goals into Milestones**: Divide large goals into smaller, actionable steps. Each milestone should be specific, measurable, and time-bound.

    - Example: Instead of "launch a product," set milestones such as:
        - Month 1: Complete product design and testing.
        - Month 2: Finalize suppliers and production schedules.
        - Month 3: Launch the product and implement marketing campaigns.

2. **Assign Deadlines**: Set realistic timeframes for each milestone to create urgency and accountability. Use tools like **Gantt charts**, calendars, or project management software to track progress visually.

3. **Prioritize Tasks**: Identify critical tasks that need immediate attention and allocate resources accordingly. Use frameworks like the **Eisenhower Matrix** to distinguish between urgent and important activities.

4. **Monitor Progress**: Regularly review your progress against the timeline to identify delays or challenges early. Adjust your schedule as needed without losing sight of the ultimate goal.

Example: A Tech Start-Up's Product Launch

- **Milestone 1**: Conduct market research (2 months).
- **Milestone 2**: Develop a prototype and test it with beta users (3 months).
- **Milestone 3**: Finalize production and launch marketing campaigns (6 months).
- **Milestone 4**: Achieve 1,000 product sales within the first 90 days.

By following this structured timeline, the start-up ensures tasks are completed on time, maintaining momentum toward its larger goals.

2. Assign Responsibilities to Team Members

Assigning responsibilities is a key step in effectively implementing your business plan. By clearly defining roles, matching tasks to strengths, and establishing accountability, you ensure that your team operates efficiently, reduces overlap, and stays aligned with your business objectives. Proper delegation not only boosts productivity but also enhances team morale and encourages ownership of outcomes.

Why It Matters

1. **Reduces Redundancy**: Clearly defined roles eliminate confusion and duplication of efforts, ensuring that team members are not working on the same tasks unknowingly.
2. **Boosts Accountability**: When everyone knows what they are responsible for, it is easier to track progress, evaluate performance, and hold individuals accountable for results.
3. **Improves Efficiency**: Matching tasks to skills ensures that team members work on what they do best, leading to higher-quality outcomes and faster results.
4. **Encourages Ownership**: When team members understand their responsibilities and how their work contributes to overall success, they are more motivated and committed.

How to Do It

1. Define Roles and Tasks

Clearly outline the tasks that need to be completed and the roles that will oversee those tasks. Be specific about the scope of work, timelines, and expected outcomes to avoid ambiguity.

- **Steps to Define Roles:**
    - Break down your business plan into actionable tasks (e.g., marketing, sales, operations, customer service).
    - Identify the specific skills and expertise needed for each task.
    - Assign roles that align with each area of responsibility.
- **Example:**
    - **Marketing Team**: Tasked with developing and executing social media campaigns, designing email newsletters, and running paid ads.
    - **Operations Team**: Focuses on inventory management, supply chain coordination, and quality assurance.
    - **Sales Team**: Handles client outreach, follow-ups, and closing deals.

By segmenting the business plan into functional areas, team members can specialize and execute their responsibilities without overlap.

2. Match Tasks to Strengths

Assign tasks based on team members' **skills, strengths, and capacity**. Effective delegation ensures that the right people handle the right tasks, which improves productivity and performance.

- **Steps to Match Tasks to Strengths:**
    - Assess your team's skills, expertise, and interests.
    - Consider workload capacity to avoid burnout.
    - Provide opportunities for growth by aligning tasks with career development goals.
- **Example:**
    - A tech-savvy team member with web development experience takes ownership of creating and maintaining the company website.
    - A sales-driven team member with excellent interpersonal skills is tasked with client outreach and relationship management.
    - An organized team member with attention to detail manages administrative tasks like scheduling and documentation.

Benefits of Matching Tasks to Strengths:

- Reduces errors and inefficiencies by utilizing the right expertise.
- Increases team satisfaction as individuals can leverage their strengths.
- Accelerates progress as team members work confidently within their area of expertise.

3. Establish Accountability

Assigning tasks is only effective when clear accountability is in place. Accountability ensures that team members understand the importance of their role, meet deadlines, and deliver results.

- **How to Establish Accountability:**
    - **Use Communication and Task Management Tools**: Platforms like **Slack**, **Microsoft Teams**, **Asana**, or **Trello** allow you to assign tasks, set deadlines, and monitor progress.
    - **Define Deliverables**: Clearly state what needs to be achieved and by when. Ensure expectations are understood.
    - **Schedule Regular Check-Ins**: Hold weekly or bi-weekly meetings to discuss progress, address obstacles, and provide feedback.

- - **Track Performance**: Monitor progress against key milestones and KPIs (Key Performance Indicators).

- **Example: Marketing Campaign**

  - The marketing lead assigns specific tasks to the team:
    - **Designer**: Create visuals for social media ads (due in 1 week).
    - **Copywriter**: Write ad copy for Facebook and Instagram (due in 3 days).
    - **Digital Marketer**: Launch the ad campaigns and track performance metrics.
  - Progress is monitored through a project management tool like **Monday.com**, and weekly team meetings address any delays or obstacles.

Benefits of Establishing Accountability:

- Creates transparency and ownership among team members.
- Allows leaders to identify and resolve bottlenecks quickly.
- Encourages timely completion of tasks and consistent follow-through.

Tips for Effective Task Delegation

1. **Avoid Overloading Team Members**

   - Be mindful of workloads to prevent burnout. Prioritize tasks and allocate resources based on capacity.
   - Example: If your marketing team is stretched thin, delay less critical projects or hire temporary support.

2. **Outsource Specialized Tasks**

   - For tasks requiring niche expertise, consider outsourcing to freelancers or agencies. This is particularly helpful for technical tasks like graphic design, legal documentation, or software development.
   - Example: A small business might outsource video editing for their YouTube ads or hire a legal consultant to draft contracts.

3. **Use SMART Goals**

   - Assign tasks using the **SMART framework** (Specific, Measurable, Achievable, Relevant, Time-bound). This provides clarity and helps team members stay on track.

4. **Provide Resources and Support**

    - Ensure team members have access to the tools, information, and training needed to succeed in their roles.
    - Example: Provide software licenses, training sessions, or access to mentors for upskilling.

5. **Foster Open Communication**

    - Encourage team members to share challenges, ask for help, and collaborate. Open communication minimizes misunderstandings and keeps tasks moving forward.

Example: Delegating Responsibilities in a Product Launch

Scenario: A company launching a new product assigns responsibilities as follows:

1. **Product Development**:

    - Task: Finalize prototype and ensure quality testing.
    - Assigned to: Product Manager and Engineering Team.

2. **Marketing and Branding**:

    - Task: Develop promotional content, design ads, and create launch materials.
    - Assigned to: Marketing Lead, Graphic Designer, and Copywriter.

3. **Sales and Outreach**:

    - Task: Build relationships with distributors, engage potential customers, and drive pre-orders.
    - Assigned to: Sales Manager and Sales Team.

4. **Logistics and Operations**:

    - Task: Manage inventory, shipping, and fulfillment processes.
    - Assigned to: Operations Lead and Logistics Coordinator.

5. **Accountability**:

- Progress is tracked using Trello, and weekly meetings ensure milestones are being met.
- Each team lead reports on their team's progress, challenges, and next steps.

Key Takeaways for Readers

1. **Clearly Define Roles**: Outline tasks, expectations, and deliverables to avoid confusion and redundancy.

2. **Match Tasks to Strengths**: Assign responsibilities based on team members' expertise, interests, and capacity for better results.

3. **Establish Accountability**: Use tools, deliverables, and regular check-ins to ensure tasks are completed on time and to a high standard.

4. **Be Realistic About Workloads**: Avoid overloading team members and consider outsourcing specialized or time-consuming tasks.

5. **Foster Open Collaboration**: Encourage communication and provide the support needed for teams to excel.

Final Thought on Team Expectations

Delegating tasks effectively is about balancing clarity, accountability, and teamwork. When team members understand their roles, play to their strengths, and have clear expectations, your business plan transforms from theory into action. Through regular check-ins, tracking tools, and open communication, you can ensure your team works efficiently and collaboratively toward achieving your business goals.

3. Remain Flexible and Ready to Adapt

Why It Matters

No business environment remains static. Changes in markets, competition, customer needs, or economic conditions often require businesses to pivot or adjust their strategies. A rigid plan can limit your ability to respond to these shifts. A flexible approach ensures resilience and keeps your business moving forward.

Steps to Adapt Your Business Plan

1. **Reassess Your Plan Regularly**: Update financial projections, marketing strategies, and goals as circumstances change. Schedule quarterly reviews to evaluate the relevance of your plan.

2. **Identify Early Warning Signs**: Monitor key market indicators, customer feedback, and performance metrics to detect trends or challenges that require action.

3. **Create Contingency Plans**: Develop alternative strategies to address unexpected disruptions, such as supply chain issues, economic downturns, or changes in regulations.

4. **Experiment and Pivot Strategically**: Use small-scale experiments to test new strategies before fully committing to a major pivot. Gather data, analyze results, and scale successful approaches.

Example: A Restaurant Adapting to Market Conditions

A dine-in restaurant experiences declining foot traffic. By analyzing market conditions, the owners pivot to:

- Offering online ordering and home delivery.
- Adding virtual cooking classes to engage customers.
- Launching a loyalty program to increase repeat business.

By remaining adaptable, the restaurant maintains revenue streams and builds a stronger customer base.

4. Communicate and Share the Plan with Stakeholders

Why It Matters

Transparency and alignment are key to effective implementation. Sharing your business plan ensures that stakeholders—including employees, investors, and partners—are aware of the business's goals, milestones, and strategies.

Steps to Communicate Effectively

1. **Share the Vision**: Communicate the company's mission, goals, and strategy to all stakeholders.

2. **Provide Regular Updates**: Keep stakeholders informed about progress, challenges, and adjustments to the plan.

3. **Encourage Feedback**: Invite team members and advisors to provide input. Their perspectives can help refine strategies and uncover blind spots.

4. **Celebrate Milestones**: Recognize progress and achievements to keep teams motivated and engaged.

Example: Aligning a Growing Team

A tech start-up shares its business plan with new hires to ensure they understand the company's goals, priorities, and individual roles. Regular progress updates foster a shared sense of ownership and commitment to success.

5. Use Technology to Streamline Implementation

Why It Matters

Leveraging technology simplifies the implementation and monitoring of your business plan, saving time and improving efficiency. Modern tools allow for better collaboration, tracking, and adaptability.

Key Tools to Implement and Adapt Your Plan

1. **Project Management Tools**: Platforms like Trello, Asana, and Monday.com keep teams organized and focused on tasks.
2. **Financial Tools**: Tools like QuickBooks and FreshBooks help track budgets, expenses, and financial performance.
3. **Data Analytics**: Use tools like Google Analytics or CRM systems to track customer data and market trends.
4. **Collaboration Tools**: Platforms like Slack or Microsoft Teams facilitate communication across teams and stakeholders.

Key Takeaways for Readers

1. **Create a Clear Timeline**: Break down goals into milestones, set deadlines, and track progress to maintain focus and momentum.
2. **Assign Roles and Responsibilities**: Clarify who is responsible for what to ensure accountability and efficiency.
3. **Monitor Progress Regularly**: Use KPIs, reviews, and tools to assess performance and make timely adjustments.
4. **Stay Flexible**: Adapt your plan as circumstances change while keeping long-term goals in focus.

5. **Communicate Clearly**: Share your plan and updates with stakeholders to align efforts and foster collaboration.

6. **Leverage Technology**: Use modern tools to streamline tracking, collaboration, and data-driven decision-making.

Final Thought on Remaining Flexible

The real power of a business plan lies in its implementation and adaptability. By creating clear timelines, tracking progress, and remaining flexible, you ensure your business can thrive in a changing market. Treat your plan as a living document—one that guides your decisions while providing the agility to pivot when necessary—so you can build a resilient, focused, and successful business.

6. Develop a Budget Aligned with Financial Forecasts

Creating a budget that aligns with your financial forecasts is essential for executing your business plan effectively. It ensures you allocate resources wisely, avoid overspending, and prepare for unexpected challenges. A well-structured budget serves as both a financial roadmap and a control mechanism, helping you stay on track and measure progress toward your business goals.

Why It Matters

1. **Resource Allocation**: A budget helps you distribute your financial resources effectively across key areas such as operations, marketing, staffing, and product development.

2. **Prevents Overspending**: By setting clear spending limits, you can control costs and avoid draining cash reserves unnecessarily.

3. **Supports Strategic Decisions**: A budget ensures that spending aligns with priorities, enabling you to focus on activities that drive growth and profitability.

4. **Mitigates Risk**: Planning for contingencies prepares you for unexpected costs and keeps your business resilient during challenges.

A well-aligned budget bridges the gap between financial projections and day-to-day decision-making, ensuring your financial goals are achievable.

How to Develop a Budget

1. Review Financial Projections

Start by reviewing the financial forecasts in your business plan, which include:

- **Expected Revenue**: Projected income over a specific period (e.g., monthly, quarterly, or yearly).
- **Expenses**: Estimated costs required to operate the business (fixed and variable).
- **Cash Flow**: The expected inflow and outflow of money, ensuring you have enough cash to cover operations.
- **Example**: If your financial projection estimates $100,000 in revenue in Year 1:
    - $50,000 may go toward product development and inventory.
    - $20,000 for marketing and advertising campaigns to drive sales.
    - $15,000 for staffing and operational costs.
    - $10,000 for logistics and delivery expenses.
    - $5,000 for a contingency fund to cover unexpected issues.

2. Break Down Costs into Categories

Categorize your budget into key segments to allocate funds and manage spending. This segmentation helps you prioritize and track costs efficiently.

- **Common Budget Categories:**
    1. **Marketing**: Advertising, promotions, social media campaigns, trade shows, and content creation.
    2. **Product Development**: Research, prototyping, manufacturing, and quality testing.
    3. **Operations**: Rent, utilities, software subscriptions, and administrative costs.
    4. **Staffing**: Salaries, benefits, and freelancer or contractor fees.
    5. **Logistics**: Shipping, warehousing, and inventory management.
    6. **Miscellaneous**: Legal fees, licenses, insurance, or unexpected smaller expenses.
- **Example**: For a new e-commerce business with a $20,000 annual budget:
    1. $5,000 for social media advertising (Facebook, Instagram, Google Ads).
    2. $2,000 for trade show participation.
    3. $8,000 for inventory purchases and warehousing.
    4. $3,000 for website development and hosting fees.

5. **$2,000** reserved for contingency funds.

Tips for Breaking Down Costs

- Prioritize areas that directly contribute to revenue generation, such as marketing and product quality.
- Monitor high-cost categories closely to identify opportunities for savings.
- Be conservative with revenue forecasts and generous with expense estimates to create a buffer.

3. Track Spending in Real Time

Monitoring your spending regularly ensures you stay within budget and avoid overspending. Tools and systems help you track cash flow, analyze spending patterns, and make adjustments as needed.

- **Budget Tracking Tools:**
  - **QuickBooks**: Great for expense tracking, invoicing, and cash flow management.
  - **Wave Accounting**: A free option for small businesses to manage income and expenses.
  - **Mint** or **Expensify**: Useful for categorizing expenses and setting spending alerts.
  - **Excel/Google Sheets**: Simple, customizable spreadsheets for budget tracking and expense management.

How to Monitor Spending:

1. Set up **spending limits** for each category to control costs. For example, allocate no more than $5,000 for monthly marketing expenses.
2. Review expenses **weekly or monthly** to identify overspending early.
3. Use automated tools to generate reports on where your money is going and adjust spending as necessary.
4. **Flag deviations**: If expenses exceed a category's budget, investigate and take corrective action.

- **Example**: A marketing campaign exceeds its allocated $5,000 budget due to rising ad costs. By catching this early, you can pause the campaign, optimize spending, or shift funds from another category (e.g., miscellaneous expenses).

4. Plan for Contingencies

Unforeseen costs are inevitable in business. A contingency fund ensures you're prepared for unexpected events without derailing your budget.

- **How Much to Set Aside**:
    - Aim to allocate **10–20% of your total budget** for contingencies.
    - Adjust the percentage based on your industry and risk factors (e.g., businesses with seasonal demand may require larger buffers).

- **Common Unexpected Expenses:**
    - Supply chain delays or price increases.
    - Emergency equipment repairs.
    - Unexpected marketing or legal costs.

- **Example**:
  A food truck business sets aside $3,000 as a contingency fund. When a key piece of equipment breaks down mid-year, the contingency covers repair costs without affecting cash flow.

Tips for Developing and Managing Your Budget

1. **Be Realistic**: Base your budget on conservative revenue projections and realistic cost estimates to avoid financial strain.
2. **Revisit the Budget Regularly**: Adjust the budget if your financial forecasts or business priorities change. Major updates may occur quarterly or annually.
3. **Separate Fixed and Variable Costs**: Fixed costs (e.g., rent, salaries) are predictable, while variable costs (e.g., marketing spending, raw materials) need more flexibility. Prioritize controlling variable costs.
4. **Prioritize ROI**: Focus spending on areas that will generate the greatest return on investment, such as marketing, product innovation, and customer service.
5. **Communicate the Budget**: Share the budget with team members to ensure everyone is aware of financial constraints and priorities.

Example: Developing a Budget for a Fitness Studio

Scenario: A new fitness studio estimates $80,000 in revenue for its first year. Here's how they break down their budget:

1. **Marketing ($12,000)**:

- $5,000 for social media ads and Google Ads.
- $3,000 for influencer partnerships.
- $4,000 for opening day events and promotions.

2. **Operations ($24,000):**

   - $18,000 for rent and utilities.
   - $6,000 for gym software subscriptions and maintenance.

3. **Staffing ($30,000):**

   - Salaries for trainers and support staff.

4. **Miscellaneous ($6,000):**

   - Legal fees, licenses, and insurance.

5. **Contingency Fund ($8,000):**

   - Reserved for unexpected repairs, slower-than-expected revenue, or emergency costs.

Execution: Using QuickBooks to track spending, the studio ensures they remain within budget while reviewing expenses monthly. The owner reallocates funds as needed to prioritize high-impact marketing efforts that drive membership growth.

Key Takeaways for Readers

1. **Start with Financial Projections**: Use your revenue and expense forecasts as the foundation for your budget.

2. **Break Down Costs**: Categorize your budget into clear, trackable segments to align spending with priorities.

3. **Track Spending in Real Time**: Use tools like QuickBooks or Wave Accounting to monitor your expenses and avoid overruns.

4. **Plan for the Unexpected**: Set aside a contingency fund (10–20% of your budget) to cover unforeseen expenses.

5. **Revisit Regularly**: Review and adjust your budget as business conditions and financial projections change.

Final Thought on Financial Contingencies

A well-aligned budget is essential for turning your business plan into reality. By carefully reviewing projections, breaking down costs, tracking spending, and planning for contingencies, you create a financial roadmap that keeps your business on course. Regular monitoring and adjustments ensure that your resources are allocated where they matter most, allowing your business to grow sustainably and thrive in changing conditions.

7. Break Tasks into Manageable Increments

Breaking large tasks into smaller, actionable increments is one of the most effective strategies for achieving big goals. By dividing complex projects into **smaller, well-defined steps**, you make progress more manageable, reduce overwhelm, and create momentum toward success. This approach helps teams maintain focus, track progress, and celebrate small wins along the way, which motivates them to keep moving forward.

Why It Matters

1. **Reduces Overwhelm**: Large tasks can feel intimidating and lead to procrastination. Smaller tasks make starting easier.
2. **Improves Actionability**: Breaking goals into clear, actionable steps helps clarify what needs to be done and by when.
3. **Builds Momentum**: Completing smaller tasks creates a sense of accomplishment and motivates you to tackle the next step.
4. **Enhances Focus**: Smaller increments allow you to prioritize critical tasks and avoid distractions.
5. **Facilitates Tracking**: It's easier to monitor progress and identify roadblocks when tasks are broken into measurable steps.

How to Do It

1. Create Subtasks for Each Milestone

To break large tasks into increments, first, identify the **key milestones** of your project or goal. Then, break those milestones into **bite-sized subtasks** that can be completed step by step.

- **Steps to Create Subtasks:**

    1. Identify the overall goal or milestone (e.g., "Launch a website").
    2. Break the goal into stages or phases.
    3. Define the actionable tasks needed to complete each phase.
    4. Set deadlines for each subtask to maintain momentum.

- **Example: Launching a Business Website**

    1. **Milestone 1**: Plan the website
        - Research hosting platforms and purchase a domain.
        - Decide on the website structure and key pages.
        - Develop wireframes for layout and user experience.

    2. **Milestone 2**: Create website content
        - Write content for the homepage, about page, and services page.
        - Source or design images, logos, and graphics.

    3. **Milestone 3**: Develop and Test the Website
        - Choose a website builder (e.g., WordPress, Squarespace).
        - Build pages based on wireframes and content.
        - Test functionality (links, forms, mobile responsiveness).

    4. **Milestone 4**: Launch the website
        - Optimize for SEO and loading speed.
        - Conduct a final quality check.
        - Go live and promote the website.

By dividing the larger task of "launching a website" into smaller, manageable increments, the project becomes actionable and less overwhelming.

2. Prioritize Tasks for Impact

Not all tasks carry the same weight or urgency. Prioritize the tasks that **drive the greatest impact early** in the process. This ensures you are making progress on what matters most and prevents wasted effort.

- **How to Prioritize Tasks**:

    - Use the **Pareto Principle (80/20 Rule)**: Focus on the 20% of tasks that deliver 80% of the results.
    - Determine dependencies: Complete tasks that must be finished before others can start (e.g., secure funding before hiring staff).

- Assess urgency and importance: Use tools like the **Eisenhower Matrix** to prioritize high-impact, time-sensitive tasks.

- **Example: Prioritizing Tasks for a Product Launch**
  - Secure product prototypes (critical for testing and marketing).
  - Conduct market research to validate product demand.
  - Develop a marketing strategy and secure pre-orders.
  - Finalize production and prepare for distribution.

Focusing on these high-priority tasks ensures that the product launch progresses efficiently, with each step building on the last.

3. Set Weekly or Monthly Goals

Breaking tasks into weekly or monthly goals creates **consistent progress** and a clear sense of direction. Smaller time-bound goals prevent procrastination and provide measurable checkpoints for tracking progress.

- **How to Set Weekly or Monthly Goals:**
  - Use your milestones to create a timeline with weekly or monthly targets.
  - Set **specific, measurable goals** that can be completed within a set timeframe.
  - Track progress using tools like **Trello**, **Asana**, or even a simple to-do list.
  - Regularly review and adjust goals to stay on track.

- **Examples of Weekly Goals**:
  - For customer validation: "This week, complete five customer interviews and document feedback."
  - For branding: "By Friday, finalize the company's logo design and color scheme."
  - For marketing: "This month, create and schedule 10 social media posts to promote the product launch."

By assigning weekly or monthly goals, tasks remain actionable, and progress can be celebrated in smaller, motivating increments.

Practical Tools to Break Tasks into Manageable Steps

1. **Project Management Tools**:

- **Trello**: Visual task boards to break down goals into subtasks and track progress.
- **Asana**: Create projects, assign tasks, set deadlines, and monitor completion.
- **Monday.com**: A versatile tool for tracking goals, subtasks, and timelines.

2. **Time Management Frameworks**:
   - **Time Blocking**: Schedule time in your calendar to focus on specific subtasks.
   - **Pomodoro Technique**: Break work into 25-minute intervals with short breaks, focusing on one small task at a time.

3. **Simple Lists and Checkpoints**:
   - Break tasks into to-do lists categorized by priority (e.g., daily, weekly, monthly).
   - Use checklists to mark off completed tasks and visualize progress.

Tips for Breaking Tasks Into Increments

1. **Start with Quick Wins**: Begin with small, easily achievable tasks to build momentum and confidence.
2. **Avoid Overloading Yourself**: Assign only 2–3 significant tasks per day to avoid burnout.
3. **Set Deadlines**: Add due dates to each subtask to maintain a sense of urgency and accountability.
4. **Review and Adjust Regularly**: Reassess progress weekly or monthly to identify roadblocks and refine tasks.
5. **Focus on Actionable Steps**: Break tasks down until they are clear, concrete, and immediately actionable.
   - **Example**: Instead of "build marketing strategy," break it into:
     - Identify target audience demographics.
     - Create a list of marketing channels (social media, email, ads).
     - Draft key messaging and campaign goals.

Case Study: Launching a Small Business Podcast

Goal: Launch a small business podcast within 2 months.

1. **Milestone 1**: Plan the Podcast (Week 1–2)

- Research competitors and define the target audience.
- Decide on podcast format, episode length, and topics.
- Choose a podcast name and create branding elements (logo, theme music).

2. **Milestone 2**: Prepare Content and Guests (Week 3–4)
   - Outline the first five episodes, including talking points.
   - Reach out to guest speakers and schedule interviews.
   - Write introductory and outro scripts for each episode.
3. **Milestone 3**: Record and Edit (Week 5–6)
   - Record episodes using recording software like Audacity or GarageBand.
   - Edit audio for clarity, adding music and transitions.
4. **Milestone 4**: Launch and Promote (Week 7–8)
   - Upload episodes to podcast hosting platforms (Spotify, Apple Podcasts).
   - Promote the podcast on social media and through email newsletters.

Outcome: By breaking the larger goal into weekly subtasks, the podcast launch becomes manageable, organized, and less overwhelming.

Key Takeaways for Readers

1. **Divide Goals into Subtasks**: Break large goals into smaller, actionable tasks to reduce overwhelm and improve clarity.
2. **Prioritize Impactful Work**: Focus on tasks that drive significant progress early in the process.
3. **Set Weekly or Monthly Goals**: Assign time-bound goals to ensure consistent progress and accountability.
4. **Use Tools to Stay Organized**: Leverage project management tools and time management frameworks to track tasks effectively.
5. **Review and Adjust**: Regularly reassess progress, adjust tasks, and celebrate milestones to maintain motivation.

Final Thought on Breaking Down Goals

Breaking tasks into manageable increments transforms ambitious goals into achievable steps. By planning smaller, actionable tasks, prioritizing critical work, and setting clear deadlines, you reduce overwhelm and create a clear path to success. Whether you're launching a product, running a campaign, or managing daily operations, this approach helps you move forward steadily and confidently while celebrating progress along the way.

8. Monitor Progress Regularly

Monitoring progress regularly is critical to ensuring that your business plan stays on track and achieves its objectives. It allows you to identify obstacles early, make informed adjustments, and celebrate achievements, keeping the team motivated and focused. Regular tracking provides transparency, accountability, and opportunities to optimize strategies to achieve your goals efficiently.

Why It Matters

1. **Identifies Roadblocks Early**: By regularly checking progress, you can detect issues before they escalate and address them proactively.
2. **Facilitates Adjustments**: Tracking progress allows you to adapt plans and strategies based on real-time data, ensuring agility in changing circumstances.
3. **Increases Accountability**: Regular reviews encourage team members to stay committed to their responsibilities and deadlines.
4. **Keeps Momentum and Motivation High**: Celebrating small wins provides a sense of accomplishment and encourages continued effort and engagement.
5. **Provides Data-Driven Insights**: Monitoring KPIs ensures that decisions are based on measurable progress rather than assumptions.

How to Monitor Progress

1. Schedule Regular Progress Reviews

Set up **consistent intervals** for reviewing progress to keep the team aligned, track milestones, and evaluate performance. Frequency will depend on your project timeline and the nature of your goals.

- **Weekly Reviews**: Suitable for fast-moving projects or short-term tasks. Use these to discuss daily challenges, progress, and immediate next steps.

- **Monthly Reviews**: Evaluate progress toward medium-term goals, identify trends, and analyze KPIs. These reviews allow you to address roadblocks and adjust strategies if needed.
- **Quarterly Reviews**: Assess performance against larger milestones or financial targets. Use these reviews to evaluate progress, refine long-term strategies, and set new goals.

Steps for an Effective Progress Review:

1. **Assess Progress**: Compare actual performance to the goals and milestones outlined in your business plan.
2. **Identify Issues**: Discuss challenges, delays, or underperformance and determine root causes.
3. **Adjust Plans**: Based on insights, update strategies, reallocate resources, or redefine timelines.
4. **Set Actionable Next Steps**: Define tasks and responsibilities for the upcoming period.

- **Example**: A retail store holds weekly check-ins to assess sales, stock levels, and marketing efforts. A monthly review evaluates customer traffic, revenue, and expenses to fine-tune marketing campaigns or inventory management.

2. Use Dashboards or Tracking Systems

Dashboards and tracking systems provide **real-time visibility** into performance, making it easier to monitor progress and share updates across the team.

- **What to Track**: Focus on Key Performance Indicators (KPIs) aligned with your goals.

    - **Financial Metrics**: Revenue, expenses, profit margins, and cash flow.
    - **Operational Metrics**: Project completion rates, production efficiency, or customer fulfillment rates.
    - **Sales and Marketing Metrics**: Customer acquisition, website traffic, lead conversion rates, and return on investment (ROI).
    - **Customer Metrics**: Satisfaction scores, retention rates, or repeat purchases.

- **Tools for Monitoring Progress**:

    - **Project Management Software**: Tools like **Asana**, **Trello**, or **Monday.com** track tasks, deadlines, and team performance.

- **Data Dashboards**: Platforms like **Google Analytics**, **Tableau**, or **Power BI** visualize KPIs and performance trends.
- **Financial Tools**: Use **QuickBooks** or **Xero** to monitor expenses, revenue, and budgets.
- **Spreadsheets**: A simple Google Sheet or Excel dashboard can track tasks, deadlines, and KPIs.

- **Example**: A marketing agency uses a **project management tool** like Trello to monitor campaign milestones and deadlines. Simultaneously, they use **Google Analytics** to track website traffic and conversion rates, ensuring campaigns deliver measurable results.

3. Celebrate Small Wins

Recognizing and celebrating small achievements builds momentum, keeps morale high, and fosters a positive, motivated team culture. Breaking down large goals into smaller milestones allows you to celebrate progress at regular intervals.

- **Why Celebrating Wins Is Important**:
  - Reinforces a sense of accomplishment and progress.
  - Keeps the team motivated and engaged in reaching larger goals.
  - Provides opportunities for reflection and learning.

- **How to Celebrate Small Wins:**
  - **Acknowledge Achievements**: Publicly recognize team members for meeting milestones or exceeding expectations.
  - **Incentivize Success**: Offer rewards such as bonuses, team lunches, gift cards, or time off.
  - **Share Results**: Use meetings, emails, or dashboards to share progress and highlight the impact of the team's efforts.
  - **Set the Next Goal**: Tie small wins to the larger vision, reinforcing how achievements contribute to the big picture.

- **Example**: A start-up aiming to acquire 1,000 customers celebrates reaching its first 100 customers with a team lunch. This acknowledgment motivates the team to push toward the next milestone.

Tips for Monitoring Progress Effectively

1. **Set Clear Metrics**: Define KPIs and milestones that align with your overall goals. Avoid tracking too many metrics; focus on what matters most.

2. **Document Progress**: Use reports, dashboards, and meeting notes to document progress over time. This provides a clear historical record for future reviews.
3. **Stay Flexible**: Use progress reviews as opportunities to pivot or adjust strategies when goals aren't being met. Be open to revisiting timelines and priorities.
4. **Maintain Consistency**: Stick to a regular schedule for progress reviews to ensure accountability and sustained focus.
5. **Encourage Feedback**: Invite team members to share insights, concerns, and suggestions during reviews to improve processes and outcomes.

Case Study: A Start-Up Monitoring Progress Toward Launch

Scenario: A SaaS start-up preparing for a product launch sets measurable milestones and monitors progress weekly.

1. **Weekly Goals**:
   - Complete beta testing and collect user feedback.
   - Address bugs identified in the testing phase.
   - Finalize the product's pricing model and marketing strategy.

2. **Tools Used**:
   - **Asana**: Tracks task assignments, deadlines, and completion rates.
   - **Google Sheets**: Logs user feedback and prioritizes changes.
   - **Financial Dashboard**: Monitors spending against the pre-launch budget.

3. **Celebrating Wins**:
   - When beta testing is completed, the team holds a short celebration to recognize their efforts and prepare for the next phase.

4. **Progress Adjustments**:
   - Delays in bug resolution prompt the team to adjust the timeline for launch by two weeks.

Outcome: By regularly monitoring progress, the start-up addresses challenges proactively, adapts timelines realistically, and keeps team morale high, resulting in a smoother product launch.

Key Takeaways for Readers

1. **Set Regular Progress Reviews**: Schedule weekly, monthly, or quarterly check-ins to evaluate progress, address issues, and adjust plans.
2. **Track KPIs and Metrics**: Use tools like dashboards, project management software, and financial trackers to monitor performance in real-time.
3. **Identify and Resolve Roadblocks**: Detect challenges early and take proactive steps to keep goals on track.
4. **Celebrate Small Wins**: Acknowledge achievements to boost team morale and motivation.
5. **Remain Flexible**: Be prepared to adapt strategies and timelines based on your findings.

Final Thought on Tracking Progress

Monitoring progress regularly is essential for turning your business plan into actionable results. By scheduling reviews, tracking KPIs, and celebrating small wins, you ensure your team stays aligned, motivated, and focused on achieving your goals. Progress monitoring not only keeps you on track but also enables you to adapt and optimize your strategies as circumstances evolve, ensuring sustained success.

9. Monitoring Progress with Key KPIs

Key Performance Indicators (KPIs) are essential tools for tracking progress, measuring performance, and ensuring your business stays aligned with its strategic objectives. By focusing on the right KPIs, you gain **data-driven insights** that allow you to evaluate success, identify areas for improvement, and adapt strategies as needed. When implemented effectively, KPIs provide clarity, accountability, and measurable benchmarks that drive business growth.

1. Setting Measurable Goals

Before selecting KPIs, you must establish clear, measurable goals that align with your business plan. These goals act as **benchmarks** to identify the KPIs most relevant to your success. Goals should follow the **SMART framework**: Specific, Measurable, Achievable, Relevant, and Time-bound.

- **Example Goals with Corresponding Focus Areas**:
    - **Financial Goal**: Increase revenue by 20% within the next year.
        - **Relevant KPIs**: Monthly revenue growth, profit margins, average transaction value.

- **Marketing Goal**: Acquire 1,000 new customers in six months.
    - **Relevant KPIs**: Customer acquisition cost (CAC), website conversion rates, and lead generation metrics.
- **Operational Goal**: Reduce production costs by 15% over the next quarter.
    - **Relevant KPIs**: Cost per unit, production efficiency, inventory turnover.
- **Customer Satisfaction Goal**: Achieve a Net Promoter Score (NPS) of 75 within three months.
    - **Relevant KPIs**: Customer retention rate, NPS, customer feedback scores.

Why Measurable Goals Matter:

- Goals provide **clarity** on what success looks like.
- They help you determine which KPIs are most meaningful to track.
- They establish a timeline for progress evaluation.

2. Choosing the Right KPIs

Not all KPIs are created equal. Choosing the most impactful KPIs depends on your business type, goals, and industry. The right KPIs should provide actionable insights into performance, enabling you to make informed decisions.

Criteria for Selecting KPIs:

1. **Aligned with Goals**: KPIs must directly connect to the specific objectives you want to achieve.
2. **Measurable**: The KPI should be quantifiable (e.g., a percentage, ratio, or number).
3. **Actionable**: Tracking the KPI should enable you to take specific actions to improve outcomes.
4. **Time-Bound**: KPIs should track performance over a set period (e.g., monthly, quarterly).
5. **Relevant to Your Business**: Choose KPIs that suit your industry and business model.

Examples of KPIs for Common Business Objectives:

1. **Financial Performance**:

- **Revenue Growth Rate**: Measures the percentage increase in revenue over a given period.
- **Profit Margin**: Percentage of revenue that remains as profit after expenses.
- **Cash Flow**: Tracks inflow and outflow of cash to ensure operational stability.

2. **Marketing and Sales**:

   - **Customer Acquisition Cost (CAC)**: Average cost of acquiring a new customer.
   - **Conversion Rate**: Percentage of leads that convert into paying customers.
   - **Return on Investment (ROI)**: Revenue generated compared to marketing spend.

3. **Operational Efficiency**:

   - **Cost Per Unit**: Total production cost divided by the number of units produced.
   - **Inventory Turnover**: How frequently inventory is sold and replaced.
   - **Production Downtime**: Measures time lost due to operational interruptions.

4. **Customer Satisfaction and Retention**:

   - **Net Promoter Score (NPS)**: Measures customer loyalty based on satisfaction surveys.
   - **Customer Retention Rate**: Percentage of customers who continue doing business with you.
   - **Customer Lifetime Value (CLV)**: Total revenue a business can expect from a single customer.

3. Implement Tools to Monitor KPIs

Tracking KPIs efficiently requires the right tools and systems. Leveraging technology enables real-time monitoring, simplifies data analysis, and ensures your team stays aligned with goals.

Recommended KPI Tracking Tools:

1. **Google Analytics**: For tracking website metrics like traffic, conversions, and user behavior.
2. **CRM Software (e.g., HubSpot, Salesforce)**: Monitors customer acquisition, sales performance, and client relationships.
3. **Project Management Tools (e.g., Asana, Trello)**: Tracks team progress and task completion.
4. **Financial Tools (e.g., QuickBooks, Xero)**: Monitors cash flow, revenue growth, and expenses.
5. **Dashboard Software (e.g., Tableau, Power BI, Google Data Studio)**: Visualizes KPIs in an easy-to-digest format with charts and reports.

Example: E-Commerce Store Monitoring KPIs

- **Sales and Revenue Metrics**: Tracked using Shopify and Google Analytics.
- **Customer Satisfaction**: Measured through post-purchase surveys and NPS tools.
- **Inventory Efficiency**: Monitored using inventory management software like TradeGecko.

4. Analyze and Adjust Regularly

Monitoring KPIs isn't just about gathering data—it's about analyzing it to identify trends, spot issues, and take corrective actions when needed. Regular analysis ensures that you're progressing toward your goals and adapting to any changes in performance or the market.

Steps to Analyze KPIs Effectively:

1. **Schedule Regular Reviews**: Set monthly or quarterly meetings to review KPI data.
2. **Compare Performance**: Assess current results against benchmarks or previous periods.
3. **Identify Patterns**: Look for trends or anomalies (e.g., sudden drops in website traffic or spikes in production costs).
4. **Adjust Strategies**: Based on KPI insights, refine your business plan, allocate resources differently, or pivot strategies where necessary.
- **Example**: If a marketing campaign shows low ROI, you might adjust ad targeting, change messaging, or reallocate the budget to a different channel.

Benefits of Regular Analysis:

- Keeps the team focused on priorities.
- Highlights underperforming areas for improvement.
- Enables proactive decision-making to stay on course.

5. Celebrate Progress and Wins

Monitoring KPIs provides an opportunity to **celebrate achievements**, even small ones. Recognizing progress motivates teams, builds momentum, and reinforces positive behaviors.

- **Examples of Celebrating Wins**:
  - When you hit a milestone (e.g., achieving a 10% increase in revenue), acknowledge team efforts with rewards, shoutouts, or team events.
  - Share KPI success during team meetings to highlight individual contributions.

Celebrating wins keeps morale high and maintains momentum as you work toward larger goals.

Case Study: Monitoring KPIs for a Growing SaaS Company

Scenario: A SaaS company aiming to grow revenue by 30% over the next year sets clear KPIs:

1. **Revenue KPIs**: Monthly Recurring Revenue (MRR) and Average Revenue Per User (ARPU).
2. **Marketing KPIs**: Lead conversion rate and customer acquisition cost (CAC).
3. **Customer KPIs**: Churn rate and Net Promoter Score (NPS).

Tools Used:

- **HubSpot CRM**: Tracks lead conversions and customer acquisition costs.
- **QuickBooks**: Monitors cash flow and revenue metrics.
- **NPS Software**: Collects and analyzes customer satisfaction scores.

Progress Monitoring:

- Monthly KPI reviews reveal a high churn rate among new users.
- The company uses this insight to improve onboarding processes, reducing churn by 20% within three months.

Outcome: By monitoring KPIs consistently and taking targeted actions, the company achieves its growth targets while improving customer retention.

Key Takeaways for Readers

1. **Set Clear, Measurable Goals**: Use SMART goals as benchmarks to identify the KPIs that matter most to your business.

2. **Choose Relevant KPIs**: Select KPIs that align with your goals, are measurable, and provide actionable insights.

3. **Use Tools to Track KPIs**: Leverage software and dashboards for real-time tracking and easy analysis.

4. **Analyze and Adjust**: Regularly review KPI data, identify trends, and refine strategies to stay on track.

5. **Celebrate Wins**: Recognize progress and achievements to motivate the team and maintain momentum.

Final Thought on Monitoring KPIs

Monitoring progress with KPIs is the cornerstone of effective business management. By setting clear goals, tracking meaningful metrics, and analyzing performance regularly, you gain the insights needed to make informed decisions and keep your business on track. KPIs turn abstract objectives into measurable outcomes, empowering you to identify successes, overcome challenges, and drive sustainable growth.

10. Types of KPIs to Monitor

A. Financial KPIs

Financial health is a cornerstone of any business. Monitor these metrics to ensure profitability and sustainability:

1. **Sales Revenue**: Total income from sales during a specific period.
   - Example: "Achieve $100,000 in sales this quarter."
   - Tool: Track using accounting software like QuickBooks.

2. **Net Profit Margin**: Percentage of revenue left after all expenses.
   - Formula: Net Profit Margin = Net Income Revenue × 100
   - Example: Aim for a 15% margin by reducing operational expenses.

3. **Cash Flow**: Measure inflows and outflows to ensure liquidity.
   - Tool: Use cash flow statements to track monthly trends.

B. Marketing KPIs

Marketing performance determines how effectively you attract and retain customers:

1. **Customer Acquisition Cost (CAC)**: The cost of acquiring a single customer.
    - Formula: CAC = Total Marketing Costs / Number of New Customers
    - Example: Aim for a CAC under $50 for digital ad campaigns.
2. **Customer Lifetime Value (CLV)**: The total revenue a customer generates over their lifetime.
    - Formula: CLV = Average Purchase Value × Frequency of Purchases × Customer Lifespan
    - Example: Target a CLV of $500 for recurring subscription models.
3. **Conversion Rate**: Percentage of leads that turn into customers.
    - Formula: Conversion rate = (number of conversions / total audience) x 100
    - Example: Improve conversion rates from 3% to 5% via optimized landing pages.

C. Operational KPIs

Efficiency metrics measure how well your business operates:

1. **Turnaround Time**: Time taken to complete a specific process (e.g., order fulfillment).
    - Example: Reduce turnaround time from 48 hours to 24 hours.
2. **Production Costs**: Total costs incurred to produce goods or services.
    - Tool: Use cost-tracking software to identify inefficiencies.
3. **Inventory Turnover**: The rate at which inventory is sold and replaced.
    - Formula: Inventory Turnover

    Inventory Turnover=Average InventoryCost of Goods Sold
    - Example: Aim for an inventory turnover ratio of 5 per quarter.

D. Customer Satisfaction KPIs

Happy customers drive long-term success. Use these metrics to monitor satisfaction:

1. **Net Promoter Score (NPS)**: Measures customer loyalty.
    - Question: "How likely are you to recommend our business?"
    - Scoring: -100 (all detractors) to 100 (all promoters).
    - Example: Improve NPS from 50 to 70 by enhancing customer support.

2. **Customer Retention Rate**: Percentage of customers retained over a specific period.
    - Formula: Retention Rate = (Total Customers - New Customers) Starting Customers × 100

    $$\text{Retention Rate} = \frac{\text{(Total Customers - New Customers)}}{\text{Starting Customers}} \times 100$$

    - Example: Increase retention rate by 10% through loyalty programs.

Tools for Monitoring KPIs

Tracking KPIs is easier with the right tools:

- **Google Analytics**: Monitor website traffic, bounce rates, and conversion metrics.
- **CRM Systems (e.g., HubSpot, Salesforce)**: Track customer acquisition, retention, and CLV.
- **Accounting Software (e.g., Xero, QuickBooks)**: Automate financial reports and cash flow tracking.
- **Project Management Tools (e.g., Asana, Monday.com)**: Track operational efficiency and milestone progress.

4. Regularly Review and Analyze KPIs

A. Set Review Cadence

- Weekly: For operational KPIs, like production costs and turnaround times.
- Monthly: For financial KPIs, like cash flow and profit margins.
- Quarterly: For long-term goals, like revenue growth and customer retention.

B. Adjust Strategies Based on Insights

- **Underperforming Metrics**: Identify areas lagging and implement corrective measures.
    - Example: If CAC is too high, optimize ad targeting or switch to lower-cost marketing channels.
- **Overperforming Metrics**: Allocate additional resources to areas showing high ROI.
    - Example: If CLV exceeds expectations, focus on upselling or cross-selling strategies.

5. Share Progress with Your Team

- Create **visual dashboards** to make KPI data accessible and understandable for your team.

- Use team meetings to discuss progress and brainstorm solutions for challenges.
- Celebrate hitting milestones to keep morale high.

Conclusion on KPIs to monitor

By selecting the right KPIs, using tools to monitor them, and regularly analyzing their performance, you can maintain a clear picture of your business's health and progress. This proactive approach ensures that your business remains adaptable, efficient, and focused on achieving its objectives.

11. Secure Resources and Build a Team

Implementing a business plan effectively requires a strong foundation of resources, including capital, talent, and technology. Without the right resources in place, even the most well-thought-out plan can falter. By aligning your resource allocation with the priorities in your business plan, you can ensure smooth operations, effective execution, and sustainable growth.

1. Capital: Ensure Adequate Funding to Cover Startup or Operational Expenses

Why It Matters

Capital is the lifeblood of any business. Securing sufficient funding ensures you can:

- Cover startup costs (e.g., equipment, inventory, marketing).
- Manage day-to-day expenses (e.g., rent, salaries, utilities).
- Invest in growth opportunities (e.g., product development, market expansion).
- Mitigate financial risks and cash flow challenges during the early stages.

How to Secure Funding

1. **Assess Funding Needs**: Use your business plan to estimate your capital requirements for both short-term (startup) and long-term operations. Factor in fixed costs, variable costs, and contingencies.

2. **Explore Funding Options**:
    - **Bootstrapping**: Self-fund the business using personal savings.
    - **Small Business Loans**: Secure loans from banks, credit unions, or government-backed programs (e.g., SBA loans).
    - **Investors**: Seek venture capital or angel investors who align with your vision.

- **Crowdfunding**: Use platforms like Kickstarter or GoFundMe to raise capital from the public.
- **Grants and Competitions**: Apply for business grants or startup competitions for non-dilutive funding.

3. **Create a Financial Plan**: Include revenue forecasts, expense projections, and funding needs in your financial plan to show investors or lenders that your business is financially viable.

Example:

A food truck business needs $50,000 to launch. They break it down as follows:

- $25,000 for purchasing and outfitting the truck.
- $10,000 for inventory and supplies.
- $5,000 for marketing and branding.
- $5,000 for permits and insurance.
- $5,000 for a contingency fund.

The owner secures funding by combining personal savings and a small business loan.

2. Talent: Hire Employees or Contractors with the Necessary Skills

Why It Matters

Your team is one of the most valuable resources in implementing your business plan. Skilled, motivated individuals help you execute tasks, drive innovation, and grow the business. Building the right team ensures:

- Critical tasks are handled efficiently.
- Roles and responsibilities align with your priorities.
- The business can adapt to challenges and opportunities.

How to Build the Right Team

1. **Identify Key Roles**: Review your business plan to determine the roles and skills necessary for execution. Divide roles into core areas, such as:

   - **Operations**: Production, logistics, quality control.
   - **Sales and Marketing**: Lead generation, customer acquisition, and branding.
   - **Finance and Administration**: Managing budgets, payroll, and legal compliance.
   - **Technology**: Website development, IT infrastructure, or software management.

2. **Hire Strategically**:
   - **Full-Time Employees**: Hire for roles critical to daily operations or long-term strategy.
   - **Contractors/Freelancers**: Outsource specialized tasks, like graphic design, copywriting, or legal work, on a project basis.
   - **Advisors and Consultants**: Bring in experts to address knowledge gaps and offer strategic guidance.
3. **Focus on Skills and Culture**: Look for individuals who not only have the technical expertise but also align with your company's values, mission, and vision.
4. **Leverage Recruitment Channels**:
   - Post job ads on platforms like **LinkedIn**, **Indeed**, or industry-specific boards.
   - Use freelancer websites like **Upwork** or **Fiverr** for specialized tasks.
   - Tap into your network or consider referrals to find reliable talent.
5. **Develop Training and Onboarding**: Once hired, provide clear training, tools, and goals to ensure your team can perform effectively.

Example:

A tech start-up building an e-commerce platform identifies three key roles:

- **Web Developer**: Responsible for coding and maintaining the website.
- **Digital Marketer**: Handles SEO, social media, and paid ads.
- **Operations Manager**: Manages inventory, order fulfillment, and customer support.

Instead of hiring full-time staff initially, the start-up outsources development to a freelance web developer and focuses on building a lean, scalable team.

3. Technology: Invest in Tools and Software to Streamline Operations

Why It Matters

Technology helps businesses operate efficiently, automate repetitive tasks, and make data-driven decisions. Investing in the right tools enables you to scale effectively and compete in a modern business environment.

How to Choose the Right Technology

1. **Identify Key Needs**: Refer to your business plan to determine areas where technology can improve efficiency, such as:

   - Project management.
   - Customer relationship management (CRM).
   - Financial tracking and accounting.
   - Marketing automation.
   - E-commerce and sales tracking.

2. **Choose Scalable Tools**: Invest in solutions that can grow with your business. Start with essential tools and add advanced features as needed.

3. **Popular Tools by Category**:

   - **Project Management: Asana, Trello,** or **Monday.com** for task tracking and collaboration.
   - **Accounting and Finance: QuickBooks, Xero,** or **FreshBooks** for budgeting, invoicing, and financial management.
   - **Customer Relationship Management (CRM): HubSpot, Salesforce,** or **Zoho CRM** for managing customer data and sales pipelines.
   - **Marketing Automation: Mailchimp** or **Hootsuite** for email campaigns, social media scheduling, and analytics.
   - **Communication Tools: Slack, Zoom,** or **Microsoft Teams** for seamless team communication.

4. **Integrate Tools for Efficiency**: Ensure the tools you choose to integrate to avoid data silos and redundancies.

Example:

An online retailer uses the following tools to streamline operations:

- **Shopify** for managing the online store and inventory.
- **QuickBooks** for financial tracking and expense management.
- **HubSpot CRM** for managing customer relationships and tracking sales.
- **Hootsuite** for automating social media campaigns.

By integrating these tools, the retailer simplifies operations, tracks financial performance, and scales marketing efforts efficiently.

4. Align Resources with Business Priorities

Securing resources is only part of the process. To maximize effectiveness, ensure that resource allocation matches your **business priorities**. Review your business plan regularly to evaluate whether resources are being directed toward high-impact areas.

How to Align Resources:

1. **Prioritize Critical Functions**: Focus funding, talent, and technology on tasks that are essential for achieving milestones.
    - Example: For a product launch, allocate more resources to marketing and product development rather than expanding administrative overhead.
2. **Track Resource Utilization**: Use project management tools to monitor how resources are being used and ensure efficiency.
3. **Reallocate as Needed**: Adjust resource allocation based on progress and emerging priorities.
4. **Plan for Contingencies**: Allocate 10-20% of your budget as a contingency to address unexpected expenses or resource shortages.

Example: Building a Team and Securing Resources for a Marketing Agency

Scenario: A small marketing agency aims to scale its operations and expand services.

1. **Capital**: Secures $100,000 in funding through a combination of bootstrapping and a small business loan.
2. **Talent**:
    - Hires a **project manager** to coordinate campaigns and manage client accounts.
    - Contracts a **graphic designer** and **content writer** for specialized tasks.
3. **Technology**: Invests in tools like:
    - **Trello** for managing campaign tasks.
    - **Mailchimp** for email marketing.
    - **QuickBooks** for tracking revenue and expenses.
4. **Resource Alignment**: Allocates 40% of funding toward client acquisition and 30% to hiring talent, prioritizing activities that directly impact growth.

Outcome: By securing the right mix of funding, tools, and talent, the agency successfully expands its services and acquires new clients.

Key Takeaways for Readers

1. **Secure Capital**: Assess funding needs and explore options like loans, investors, or bootstrapping to cover costs.
2. **Build a Strong Team**: Identify key roles and hire talent with the skills needed to execute your business plan.
3. **Invest in Technology**: Use tools and software to automate tasks, improve collaboration, and track progress efficiently.
4. **Align Resources with Priorities**: Allocate funding, talent, and tools to high-impact areas that drive progress.
5. **Monitor and Adjust**: Regularly evaluate resource usage and reallocate as needed to adapt to challenges or opportunities.

Final Thought on Securing Funding

Securing the right resources and building a capable team is vital for implementing your business plan. By strategically aligning capital, talent, and technology with your priorities, you lay the groundwork for efficiency, scalability, and success. A well-resourced business has the tools, people, and financial support needed to thrive in a competitive environment.

12. Communicate the Plan to Stakeholders

A business plan is only as effective as its ability to align and engage the people who are responsible for its execution or have a vested interest in its success. Clear communication of the plan ensures that all stakeholders—employees, investors, partners, and suppliers—understand their roles, how they contribute to achieving the goals, and how the business will evolve over time. Providing regular updates and encouraging feedback fosters transparency, collaboration, and commitment, helping everyone stay invested and aligned with the company's vision.

Why Communication Matters

1. **Creates Alignment**: Ensures everyone is working toward the same goals with a unified understanding of priorities and expectations.
2. **Builds Trust and Confidence**: Investors, partners, and employees are more likely to trust your leadership and support your business when they understand your plan and progress.
3. **Fosters Engagement**: When stakeholders understand their role in the plan, they feel valued and motivated to contribute to its success.
4. **Encourages Collaboration**: Open communication invites input, builds stronger relationships, and improves teamwork among stakeholders.

5. **Allows for Adaptation**: Stakeholder feedback can provide insights that help refine and improve your strategies.

How to Effectively Communicate Your Business Plan

1. Tailor the Message to Each Stakeholder Group

Each stakeholder group has different interests, priorities, and levels of involvement. Tailor your communication to focus on the aspects of the plan that matter most to each group.

- **Employees**:
  - **What to Share**: Company goals, specific team objectives, individual responsibilities, timelines, and how their role contributes to success.
  - **Why It Matters**: Employees need clarity on their roles to perform effectively and feel connected to the company's mission.
  - **How to Share**: Present the plan during team meetings, onboarding sessions, or in company-wide newsletters. Use visuals like charts and milestones to make the plan easier to digest.
  - **Example**: A tech start-up introduces its growth plan during a team meeting, explaining how the development, marketing, and sales teams will collaborate to acquire 10,000 new users within a year.

- **Investors**:
  - **What to Share**: Financial projections, growth milestones, market analysis, and risk mitigation strategies.
  - **Why It Matters**: Investors need confidence that your business has a clear direction, growth potential, and strategies to achieve profitability.
  - **How to Share**: Use formal presentations, pitch decks, and quarterly updates. Highlight data-driven insights and key achievements.
  - **Example**: A small manufacturing business provides quarterly investor reports summarizing revenue growth, production metrics, and plans for expansion into a new market.

- **Partners and Suppliers**:
  - **What to Share**: Operational plans, supply chain needs, collaboration expectations, and timelines.

- **Why It Matters**: Partners and suppliers need visibility into your operations and growth plans to align their services and resources effectively.
- **How to Share**: Use meetings, contracts, or partnership reviews to outline expectations and timelines.
- **Example**: A food distributor shares its expansion plan with suppliers, outlining anticipated order volumes and delivery schedules for the upcoming year to secure commitments and streamline operations.

2. Use Clear and Simple Language

Make the business plan easy to understand, avoiding unnecessary jargon or overly complex data. Use visuals and summaries to make the information more digestible.

- **Use Visual Tools**: Graphs, timelines, charts, and dashboards simplify data and make it easier to grasp goals and performance metrics.
- **Highlight Key Takeaways**: Focus on critical objectives, milestones, and responsibilities rather than overwhelming stakeholders with every detail.
- **Create an Executive Summary**: A one-page overview of the plan can quickly communicate the most important elements to busy stakeholders.

3. Provide Regular Updates

A business plan isn't a one-time document; it evolves as the business grows and changes. Keeping stakeholders informed with regular updates ensures they stay engaged and aligned.

- **Frequency**: Schedule updates consistently (e.g., weekly team meetings, monthly partner reviews, quarterly investor reports).
- **What to Share**: Progress toward milestones, changes to the plan, challenges, and successes.
- **How to Share**:
    - **Employees**: Weekly or monthly team meetings, company-wide emails, or virtual dashboards.
    - **Investors**: Quarterly reports, progress emails, or formal meetings with updates on KPIs.
    - **Partners/Suppliers**: Regular check-ins to share timelines, upcoming needs, and potential adjustments.
- **Example**: A start-up shares monthly updates with investors highlighting progress toward growth targets, customer acquisition metrics, and revenue performance.

4. Encourage Two-Way Communication

Communication should not be one-sided. Invite feedback and input from stakeholders to foster collaboration and improve the plan.

- **Ways to Encourage Feedback**:
    - Host Q&A sessions after presenting the plan.
    - Conduct surveys or one-on-one meetings to gather opinions.
    - Create open communication channels (e.g., Slack, feedback forms) for ongoing input.

- **Why Feedback Matters**:
    - Employees often identify practical challenges or process improvements.
    - Partners and suppliers can offer better solutions for collaboration or resource management.
    - Investors may provide strategic advice to overcome obstacles or unlock new opportunities.

- **Example**: A small business holds quarterly all-hands meetings where employees are encouraged to ask questions and offer suggestions for improving operations.

5. Use Technology to Enhance Communication

Leverage tools and software to share the business plan and updates efficiently. This ensures consistent messaging and access to up-to-date information.

- **Tools for Effective Communication**:
    - **Presentations**: Use PowerPoint, Google Slides, or Canva to present the plan visually.
    - **Project Management Tools**: Platforms like **Asana**, **Monday.com**, or **Trello** help teams track progress toward milestones.
    - **Dashboards**: Tools like **Tableau**, **Power BI**, or Google Data Studio visualize KPIs for investors or team members.
    - **Collaboration Tools**: Use Slack, Microsoft Teams, or email to share updates, gather feedback, and maintain ongoing communication.

Example: Communicating a Business Plan for a Fitness Studio

Scenario: A new fitness studio shares its business plan with stakeholders.

1. **Employees**:

- Team meeting presents the company's vision, growth goals (e.g., acquiring 500 new members in Year 1), and individual roles in achieving success.
- Weekly updates track class schedules, marketing campaigns, and client retention rates.

2. **Investors**:
   - A detailed pitch deck outlines financial projections, growth strategies, and risk management plans.
   - Quarterly reports track revenue growth, new member sign-ups, and marketing ROI.

3. **Suppliers**:
   - Regular check-ins ensure that equipment suppliers can meet demand as the studio expands.

Outcome: Clear communication ensures that employees feel motivated, investors remain confident, and suppliers can align resources to meet the studio's needs.

Key Takeaways for Readers

1. **Tailor the Message**: Adjust communication for different stakeholder groups, focusing on what matters most to them.
2. **Keep It Clear and Simple**: Use visuals, summaries, and straightforward language to make the plan easy to understand.
3. **Provide Regular Updates**: Schedule consistent progress reports to keep stakeholders informed and engaged.
4. **Encourage Feedback**: Foster two-way communication to improve the plan and build stronger collaboration.
5. **Use Technology**: Leverage tools like dashboards, presentations, and project management software for efficient communication.

Final Thought on Communicating with Stakeholders

Effectively communicating your business plan ensures that all stakeholders—employees, investors, partners, and suppliers—are aligned, engaged, and committed to its success. By sharing regular updates, encouraging feedback, and tailoring your message, you build trust, foster collaboration, and create momentum that drives your business forward. Clear communication turns your plan from a static document into a dynamic blueprint for growth and success.

13. Be Flexible and Adapt to Changes

In today's fast-paced and dynamic markets, adaptability is critical for long-term business success. While a business plan provides a clear roadmap, it must remain flexible to adjust to changing circumstances, market conditions, and unforeseen challenges. The ability to review, identify trends, and pivot strategies as needed ensures your business stays relevant and competitive while maintaining alignment with your long-term vision.

Why Adaptability Matters

1. **Responds to Market Dynamics**: Consumer needs, technologies, and market trends are constantly evolving. Flexibility allows you to adjust strategies quickly to meet changing demands.
2. **Improves Resilience**: Businesses that adapt efficiently can survive challenges like economic downturns, new competition, or shifts in customer behavior.
3. **Optimizes Performance**: Regular reviews of business performance help you identify what's working and what isn't so you can focus on the most impactful strategies.
4. **Seizes New Opportunities**: Staying flexible enables you to pivot toward emerging opportunities that align with your vision and goals.
5. **Maintains Competitive Advantage**: Companies that adapt faster than competitors can gain an edge, responding to trends and disruptions ahead of others.

How to Adapt Your Business Plan Effectively

1. Conduct Regular Reviews

To ensure your business plan remains relevant, it's crucial to schedule regular reviews and assessments. These reviews allow you to measure progress, evaluate performance, and identify areas that need adjustment.

- **How Often to Review**:
    - **Quarterly Reviews**: Assess short-term performance metrics, sales goals, and project milestones. Adjust tactics if needed.
    - **Semi-Annual or Annual Reviews**: Analyze the broader picture, including market conditions, competition, and financial health.
- **What to Evaluate During Reviews**:

- **Key Performance Indicators (KPIs)**: Are you meeting your revenue targets, operational goals, and marketing objectives?
- **Resource Allocation**: Are you directing time, money, and manpower toward the most effective areas?
- **Market Trends**: Are new competitors emerging, or is customer behavior shifting?
- **Risks and Challenges**: Identify obstacles that have arisen and develop strategies to address them.

Example: A small retail store holds quarterly reviews to analyze sales performance. After noticing a drop in sales for a particular product category, they adjust their inventory to prioritize higher-performing products.

2. Identify Trends and Stay Informed

Staying ahead of market trends and competitor activities ensures your business can anticipate changes and respond effectively. Keeping a pulse on external factors helps you adapt proactively rather than reactively.

- **How to Identify Trends**:
    - **Monitor Industry Reports**: Regularly review research from industry analysts, trade publications, and market reports.
    - **Analyze Customer Preferences**: Use customer surveys, reviews, and purchasing data to understand shifting behaviors.
    - **Track Competitor Activity**: Keep an eye on competitors 'product launches, marketing strategies, and innovations.
    - **Leverage Technology**: Tools like Google Trends, social listening platforms, and analytics dashboards can reveal emerging patterns.

Example: A coffee shop owner notices through social media trends that customers increasingly seek plant-based alternatives. The owner adapts by adding oat milk and vegan pastries to the menu, attracting a growing market segment.

Benefits of Identifying Trends:

- Allows you to anticipate customer needs before competitors.
- Helps identify new growth opportunities (e.g., emerging technologies or market gaps).
- Prevents stagnation by ensuring your offerings remain relevant.

3. Pivot Strategies When Necessary

Pivoting means making strategic shifts to aspects of your business that aren't performing well while staying true to your long-term vision. A pivot can involve changing your product offerings, targeting a new market, or adopting a new business model.

- **When to Pivot**:

  - If performance metrics show a persistent decline in revenue, leads, or customer satisfaction.
  - When market conditions shift due to external factors (e.g., economic changes, new competitors).
  - If customer feedback reveals dissatisfaction or changing preferences.

- **How to Pivot Strategically**:

  - **Identify the Problem**: Use data to pinpoint where your current strategy is falling short (e.g., low ROI from a marketing campaign).
  - **Test New Ideas**: Before fully committing to a new direction, test changes on a smaller scale (e.g., run a pilot campaign).
  - **Communicate Changes**: Keep employees, investors, and customers informed about why the pivot is necessary and how it aligns with your vision.
  - **Stay True to Your Core Vision**: A pivot should address a short-term challenge while still aligning with your long-term mission.

Example: A SaaS company focused on software for gyms experiences declining sales during the COVID-19 pandemic. They pivot their strategy to target virtual fitness classes, offering software tailored for trainers hosting online workouts. This shift helps the company maintain revenue and expand its customer base.

Key Steps to Build a Culture of Adaptability

1. **Encourage Open Communication**: Foster a culture where employees and stakeholders feel comfortable suggesting changes or improvements.
2. **Invest in Data-Driven Decision-Making**: Use real-time analytics to identify performance gaps and opportunities.
3. **Train for Flexibility**: Equip your team with problem-solving skills and encourage creative thinking to adapt to challenges.
4. **Create Contingency Plans**: Incorporate "Plan B" options into your business plan to address potential risks or disruptions.
5. **Stay Customer-Centric**: Prioritize customer feedback and market needs when making changes to products, services, or strategies.

Real-World Example: Netflix's Pivot to Streaming

Scenario: Netflix initially operated as a DVD rental-by-mail business. As internet speeds improved and on-demand viewing became popular, Netflix recognized a trend toward digital streaming.

- **Identifying the Trend**: They saw customer demand for convenient, on-demand content.
- **Pivoting Strategy**: Netflix shifted its business model to focus on online streaming while still offering DVDs initially.
- **Staying True to the Vision**: Netflix's core mission of providing convenient access to entertainment remained intact.

Outcome: Netflix successfully adapted to changes in technology and consumer behavior, becoming the global leader in digital streaming.

Tips for Remaining Flexible and Adapting to Changes

1. **Regularly Update Your Plan**: Treat your business plan as a living document. Reassess goals, strategies, and resources quarterly or semi-annually.
2. **Track Key Metrics**: Use KPIs to measure performance and identify areas for improvement. Be quick to act on what the data reveals.
3. **Stay Alert to Market Changes**: Monitor industry trends, economic shifts, and competitor moves.
4. **Test Changes Before Scaling**: Pilot new strategies or products on a smaller scale to minimize risk.
5. **Embrace Innovation**: Stay open to experimenting with new ideas, technologies, or business models.

Key Takeaways for Readers

1. **Conduct Regular Reviews**: Schedule quarterly or semi-annual assessments to measure progress and update the plan based on data.
2. **Monitor Market Trends**: Stay informed about changes in customer preferences, competitor activities, and industry shifts.
3. **Be Ready to Pivot**: If a strategy isn't working, adjust your approach while staying aligned with your core vision.
4. **Use Data to Guide Decisions**: Leverage performance metrics and market research to make informed, adaptable changes.
5. **Foster a Flexible Culture**: Encourage open communication, creativity, and problem-solving within your team to navigate change effectively.

Final Thought on Adaptability

Adaptability is a hallmark of successful businesses. While your business plan provides the framework, its strength lies in its ability to evolve alongside market trends, challenges, and opportunities. Regular reviews, a keen eye on trends, and the willingness to pivot when needed to ensure your business remains agile, resilient, and positioned for long-term success.

14. Test and Validate Assumptions

A business plan often relies on assumptions about customer behavior, pricing, and market demand. While assumptions help form the foundation of your strategies, it is essential to test and validate them before committing resources or scaling operations. By systematically gathering real-world data, conducting market tests, and refining your offerings based on feedback, you can ensure that your strategies are grounded in reality and aligned with actual market needs. Validating assumptions reduces risk, improves decision-making, and increases the likelihood of success.

Why Testing and Validation Matters

1. **Reduces Risk**: Testing assumptions early allows you to identify flaws or inaccuracies before scaling operations, saving time, money, and resources.
2. **Improves Decision-Making**: Real-world data provides concrete evidence to support business decisions, minimizing reliance on guesswork.
3. **Aligns with Market Reality**: Validating assumptions ensures your products, services, and strategies match customer needs and preferences.
4. **Optimizes Resources**: By testing and refining ideas, you avoid overcommitting resources to unproven concepts.
5. **Increases Confidence**: Testing gives stakeholders (investors, employees, and partners) confidence that your strategies are well-informed and viable.

How to Test and Validate Assumptions

1. Identify Key Assumptions

Start by identifying the assumptions in your business plan that are critical to your success. These often include:

- **Customer Behavior**: Who are your target customers? Will they pay for your product or service?
- **Market Demand**: Is there a sufficient demand for your product or service to support growth?

- **Pricing Strategy**: Will customers accept the price you've set, or do you need to adjust it?
- **Sales Channels**: Will your chosen distribution channels effectively reach your audience?
- **Operational Costs**: Are your cost estimates realistic for production, marketing, or logistics?

Example: A subscription box company assumes that its target audience (young professionals) will pay $30/month for a curated collection of premium snacks.

- **Key Assumption**: Young professionals are willing to pay a premium for convenience and quality.
- **What to Test**: The price point, perceived value, and overall demand for the offering.

2. Conduct Market Tests

Before fully launching a product or strategy, conduct small-scale tests to gather real-world feedback and validate assumptions. Market tests allow you to test hypotheses with minimal investment and refine your approach based on the results.

Types of Market Tests:

1. **Pilot Programs**: Introduce your product or service to a small group of customers to observe how they interact with it.

    - **Example**: A fitness app runs a beta test with 50 users to evaluate features, pricing, and user engagement before a full release.

2. **Minimum Viable Product (MVP)**: Launch a simplified version of your product that delivers core features to test customer interest.

    - **Example**: A software company launches a basic version of a new CRM tool to see if businesses find it valuable enough to adopt.

3. **A/B Testing**: Compare two versions of a product, price point, or marketing message to determine which performs better.

    - **Example**: An e-commerce store tests two landing pages with different product descriptions to see which one drives more conversions.

4. **Pre-Orders and Waitlists**: Gauge interest by offering pre-orders or sign-ups to validate demand.

    - **Example**: A tech gadget company opens pre-orders to confirm market interest before beginning full-scale production.

Benefits of Market Testing:

- Provides measurable feedback from actual customers.
- Helps identify weaknesses or unexpected challenges early.
- Minimizes the cost of failure by testing on a smaller scale.

3. Gather Customer Feedback

Direct customer feedback is one of the most effective ways to validate assumptions. Engaging with potential customers allows you to refine your offerings and understand their needs more accurately.

How to Gather Feedback:

1. **Surveys and Interviews**: Ask targeted questions to potential customers to validate assumptions about pricing, features, and demand.

    - **Example**: A survey asks customers how much they would pay for a meal delivery service and what features they value most (e.g., speed, variety, price).

2. **Focus Groups**: Bring together a small group of customers to test products or services and share their opinions.

    - **Example**: A cosmetic brand invites 10 people to test a new skincare product and provide feedback on effectiveness and packaging.

3. **User Behavior Analytics**: Analyze how customers interact with your website, app, or product to understand their preferences and pain points.

    - **Example**: An online retailer uses heatmap tools to identify which sections of a webpage attract the most attention and where users drop off.

4. **Customer Reviews and Testimonials**: Use feedback from early adopters to identify areas for improvement and validate demand.

Key Questions to Ask Customers:

- What problem does this product/service solve for you?
- How much would you pay for this product/service?
- How likely are you to recommend it to others?
- What improvements would you like to see?

4. Analyze Real-World Data Against Projections

Compare your initial assumptions and projections with real-world results to validate their accuracy. This ensures your strategies are grounded in evidence, not speculation.

Steps to Analyze Data:

1. Collect key metrics, such as sales figures, user engagement, or cost data.
2. Compare results against your assumptions. Identify areas where projections align and where discrepancies exist.
3. Determine the root causes of any discrepancies. Were your assumptions inaccurate, or were external factors at play?
4. Refine your business plan based on insights from the data. Adjust pricing, target markets, or marketing tactics as needed.

Example:

- **Assumption**: A food truck business assumes it will sell 100 meals per day at $12 each.
- **Reality**: During the first two weeks, the average daily sales are only 60 meals, and customers suggest that the price feels too high.
- **Adjustment**: Lower the price to $10, introduce combo deals to increase perceived value, and target locations with higher foot traffic.

5. Iterate and Refine Based on Insights

Testing and validating assumptions is an ongoing process. Use the feedback and data gathered to iterate, refine, and improve your strategies before scaling further.

- **Refine Offerings**: Make product or service improvements based on customer feedback.
- **Adjust Pricing**: Test different pricing models to find the sweet spot that balances affordability with profitability.
- **Rethink Target Markets**: If demand is lower than expected, explore other customer segments that might find value in your offering.
- **Improve Messaging**: Tailor marketing campaigns to address customer concerns or highlight key benefits.

Example: Validating Assumptions for a New SaaS Product

Assumption: Small businesses will pay $50/month for software that automates their accounting processes.

Validation Steps:

1. Conduct surveys to confirm interest and understand pricing expectations.
2. Launch a Minimum Viable Product (MVP) with core features to a beta group.
3. Collect user feedback on usability, pricing, and value.

4. Analyze data: How many users sign up, how long they use the product, and what features they request.

Outcome: Feedback reveals that customers prefer a tiered pricing model based on usage. The business adjusts its pricing strategy and focuses on adding features that increase value for small businesses.

Key Takeaways for Readers

1. **Identify Assumptions**: Recognize critical assumptions about customers, pricing, and demand in your business plan.
2. **Test Small-Scale**: Conduct market tests, such as pilot programs, MVPs, or A/B tests, to gather real-world data.
3. **Engage with Customers**: Use surveys, focus groups, and direct feedback to validate assumptions and refine offerings.
4. **Analyze Results**: Compare actual data against projections to identify discrepancies and make evidence-based decisions.
5. **Iterate and Adjust**: Use insights to refine your strategies, improve offerings, and align your plan with market realities.

Final Thought on Checking Assumptions

Validating assumptions is a crucial step in turning your business plan into a successful reality. By testing strategies, engaging customers, and analyzing data, you ensure your decisions are rooted in evidence rather than guesswork. This approach not only reduces risk but also positions your business to adapt, innovate, and thrive in a dynamic market.

15. Use Technology for Automation and Scalability

Leveraging technology is essential for streamlining operations, reducing manual effort, and ensuring your business can scale efficiently. By implementing tools for **project management**, **finance tracking**, and **customer relationship management (CRM)**, you enable your team to focus on strategic, high-value tasks rather than routine activities. Automation improves productivity, enhances accuracy, and allows businesses to grow without significant increases in operational complexity or resource demands.

Why Technology and Automation Matter

1. **Efficiency**: Technology automates repetitive tasks, saving time and freeing up team members to focus on strategy and innovation.
2. **Scalability**: Automation tools allow businesses to handle increasing workloads and customers without a proportional rise in resources.

3. **Accuracy**: Automated systems minimize human error, ensuring tasks like finance management or order processing are handled reliably.
4. **Improved Collaboration**: Digital tools enhance communication and task tracking, keeping teams aligned, even across locations.
5. **Data-Driven Decisions**: Technology provides real-time analytics, enabling smarter, faster decision-making.

How to Leverage Technology for Automation and Scalability

1. Project Management Software

Purpose: Helps teams organize, assign, and monitor tasks while tracking progress toward business goals.

Key Tools:

- **Asana**: Organizes projects into tasks, deadlines, and team assignments with visual dashboards.
- **Trello**: Uses boards, lists, and cards to manage workflows and track task progress in an easy-to-understand format.
- **Monday.com**: Combines project tracking with collaboration tools and customizable workflows.
- **ClickUp**: Offers task management, time tracking, and goal-setting features for more comprehensive project control.

Benefits:

- Keeps projects organized and team members accountable.
- Reduces miscommunication with centralized task lists and updates.
- Allows managers to monitor progress in real-time and identify bottlenecks.

Example: A marketing agency uses **Trello** to manage campaigns. Each card on the board represents a task, such as writing content, designing visuals, or scheduling ads. Team members update progress, and project managers oversee deadlines seamlessly.

2. Accounting and Financial Management Tools

Purpose: Simplifies budgeting, bookkeeping, expense tracking, and financial reporting.

Key Tools:

- **QuickBooks**: Automates invoicing, expense tracking, and financial reporting, ideal for small and medium businesses.
- **Xero**: Cloud-based accounting tool that simplifies accounts payable, invoicing, and cash flow monitoring.

- **FreshBooks**: User-friendly software for freelancers and small businesses to handle billing, expenses, and time tracking.
- **Wave**: Free accounting software that includes invoicing, expense management, and receipt scanning.

Benefits:

- Saves time on manual data entry and calculations.
- Ensures financial records are accurate and up to date.
- Provides real-time visibility into cash flow, expenses, and revenue.
- Simplifies tax preparation and reporting.

Example: A small retail store uses **QuickBooks** to automate daily financial tasks such as tracking sales, managing supplier invoices, and generating monthly profit-and-loss reports. This allows the owner to make quick financial decisions without getting bogged down by manual paperwork.

3. Customer Relationship Management (CRM) Systems

Purpose: Centralizes customer data, improves interactions, and streamlines sales and marketing processes.

Key Tools:

- **HubSpot**: Provides free CRM functionality, including lead tracking, email marketing automation, and pipeline management.
- **Salesforce**: A robust CRM for managing sales, marketing automation, and customer support at scale.
- **Zoho CRM**: Affordable and customizable software with features for small-to-medium businesses.
- **Pipedrive**: Focuses on pipeline management and sales tracking for growing teams.

Benefits:

- Provides a 360-degree view of customer data and interactions.
- Automates follow-ups, reminders, and email campaigns to nurture leads and retain customers.
- Tracks sales pipelines and customer journeys, improving conversion rates.
- Enhances team collaboration by centralizing customer information.

Example: A SaaS company uses **HubSpot** to track potential leads, automate follow-up emails, and analyze customer behavior. The system alerts the sales team when a lead takes significant action, such as opening an email or requesting a demo, ensuring timely engagement.

4. Marketing Automation Tools

Purpose: Automates marketing workflows, campaigns, and customer engagement.

Key Tools:

- **Mailchimp**: Automates email campaigns, audience segmentation, and performance tracking.
- **Hootsuite**: Schedules and automates social media posts while providing analytics to optimize engagement.
- **ActiveCampaign**: Combines email automation, CRM, and sales automation for comprehensive marketing support.
- **Buffer**: Allows small businesses to schedule posts and measure social media performance.

Benefits:

- Saves time by automating content distribution and follow-ups.
- Personalizes marketing efforts through segmentation and targeted messaging.
- Improves campaign performance with real-time data analytics.

Example: A boutique store uses **Mailchimp** to send automated emails promoting new arrivals and special offers. They track open rates and conversions to refine their messaging for better results.

5. E-Commerce and Inventory Management Tools

Purpose: Streamlines online sales, inventory tracking, and fulfillment processes.

Key Tools:

- **Shopify**: An all-in-one e-commerce platform for building and managing online stores.
- **WooCommerce**: A WordPress plug-in that enables customizable online sales.
- **TradeGecko (now QuickBooks Commerce)**: Manages inventory, order fulfillment, and multi-channel sales.
- **Square**: Integrates point-of-sale systems with online stores for seamless inventory and sales tracking.

Benefits:

- Simplifies order management and ensures accurate inventory tracking.
- Automates fulfillment processes, saving time and improving customer satisfaction.
- Provides analytics to optimize product availability and pricing strategies.

Example: A clothing brand uses **Shopify** to manage its online store, track inventory, and automate customer order notifications. This ensures efficient order fulfillment while maintaining accurate inventory levels.

6. Communication and Collaboration Tools

Purpose: Enhances team collaboration and ensures efficient communication.

Key Tools:

- **Slack**: A messaging platform for teams to share updates, files, and discussions in organized channels.
- **Zoom**: A popular video conferencing tool for virtual meetings, especially with remote teams.
- **Microsoft Teams**: Combines chat, video meetings, and file sharing in one platform.
- **Google Workspace**: Provides collaborative tools like Google Docs, Sheets, and Calendar for seamless team collaboration.

Benefits:

- Facilitates remote work and real-time collaboration.
- Keeps teams aligned and informed with centralized communication.
- Improves efficiency with quick file sharing and task updates.

Example: A tech start-up uses **Slack** to centralize project updates and communication. Remote team members can share files, ask questions, and receive feedback in real-time.

Benefits of Technology for Automation and Scalability

1. **Streamlined Workflows**: Reduces manual effort, eliminates redundancies, and improves team productivity.

2. **Improved Accuracy**: Automation minimizes human error, ensuring data consistency and reliability.

3. **Cost Savings**: Automating repetitive tasks reduces the need for additional personnel.

4. **Scalable Operations**: Technology allows businesses to handle growth without increasing complexity or overhead costs.

5. **Real-Time Analytics**: Provides data-driven insights to improve decision-making and optimize performance.

Key Takeaways for Readers

1. **Adopt Project Management Tools**: Use platforms like **Asana** or **Trello** to manage tasks, track progress, and keep teams aligned.
2. **Automate Financial Processes**: Tools like **QuickBooks** and **Xero** simplify accounting, invoicing, and expense tracking.
3. **Use CRM Systems**: Invest in tools like **HubSpot** or **Salesforce** to improve customer relationships and automate follow-ups.
4. **Streamline Marketing Efforts**: Leverage tools like **Mailchimp** or **Hootsuite** to automate campaigns and track performance.
5. **Enhance Communication**: Platforms like **Slack** and **Microsoft Teams** keep teams connected and collaborative.
6. **Ensure Scalability**: Implement tools that can grow with your business, providing flexibility and efficiency as demands increase.

Final Thought on Technology

Technology and automation are vital for modern businesses looking to scale efficiently and remain competitive. By adopting the right tools for project management, finance, CRM, and marketing, you can streamline operations, enhance collaboration, and focus your team's energy on strategic growth initiatives. Automation saves time, reduces manual effort, and provides the foundation needed to scale your business sustainably and successfully.

16. Seek Mentorship and Advice

Seeking mentorship and advice from experienced professionals, industry experts, or business advisors is a powerful way to refine and strengthen your business plan. Mentors can offer insights, guidance, and valuable feedback based on their knowledge and experience, helping you avoid common pitfalls and develop more effective strategies. By tapping into a network of advisors and utilizing available resources, you gain clarity, validation, and support to move your business forward with confidence.

Why Mentorship and Advice Matter

1. **Access to Experience and Knowledge**: Mentors have often faced similar challenges and can share practical solutions, strategies, and lessons learned.
2. **Objective Feedback**: Mentors provide constructive criticism that can uncover blind spots or weaknesses in your plan.
3. **Network Expansion**: Advisors can introduce you to valuable connections, such as investors, partners, or industry peers.
4. **Risk Mitigation**: Gaining advice from experienced mentors helps you anticipate challenges and make informed decisions to reduce risks.
5. **Motivation and Confidence**: Having a trusted mentor provides emotional support and encouragement as you work toward your goals.

How to Seek Mentorship and Advice

1. Engage with Industry Experts and Mentors

Connecting with professionals who have experience in your field provides targeted advice tailored to your industry's challenges and opportunities.

- **Where to Find Industry Mentors**:
    - **Networking Events**: Attend local and national industry conferences, trade shows, and business networking events to meet experts.
    - **Industry Associations**: Join trade organizations or associations specific to your industry (e.g., Chamber of Commerce, National Retail Federation).
    - **Mentorship Platforms**: Use platforms like **SCORE**, **MicroMentor**, or **Clarity.fm** to connect with volunteer mentors and business advisors.
    - **LinkedIn**: Reach out to professionals in your network or industry leaders whose experience aligns with your business goals.
- **Example**: A food entrepreneur connects with a mentor who owns a successful chain of restaurants. The mentor provides insights on supply chain optimization, cost management, and customer acquisition strategies.

Tips for Working with Mentors:

- Be clear about the areas where you need guidance (e.g., financial planning, marketing strategy).
- Respect their time and come prepared with specific questions.

- Implement their suggestions and share updates on progress to show appreciation for their input.

2. Join Networking Events and Entrepreneurial Groups

Participating in networking events and entrepreneurial communities exposes you to a wealth of experience, advice, and new perspectives. These groups foster collaboration, brainstorming, and shared learning.

- **Benefits of Networking Groups**:
    - Share challenges and solutions with other business owners.
    - Get real-world advice from peers who have faced similar struggles.
    - Form partnerships, collaborations, and connections that benefit your business.

- **Where to Participate**:
    - **Local Networking Events**: Check platforms like **Meetup.com** or Eventbrite for industry-specific meetups.
    - **Small Business Communities**: Join local groups such as Chamber of Commerce meetings, Rotary Club events, or SCORE workshops.
    - **Entrepreneurship Programs**: Participate in programs run by **Startup Grind**, **WeWork Labs**, or local incubators and accelerators.
    - **Online Communities**: Platforms like Reddit's r/Entrepreneur, LinkedIn Groups, or Facebook business communities provide virtual networking opportunities.

- **Example**: A tech start-up founder joins a local entrepreneurship group where other start-up owners share tips on securing funding, hiring talent, and navigating legal requirements.

3. Use Small Business Administration (SBA) Resources and Business Accelerators

The **Small Business Administration (SBA)** and business accelerators offer valuable resources, mentorship, and structured programs for entrepreneurs. These resources can help refine your business plan, secure funding, and provide long-term guidance.

- **Small Business Administration (SBA)**:
    - Offers free mentorship through programs like **SCORE**.
    - Provides educational resources, workshops, and templates for business planning.

- Assists with funding opportunities, including grants and SBA-backed loans.

- **Business Accelerators and Incubators**:

  - These programs provide mentorship, funding, office space, and access to networks in exchange for equity or participation fees.
  - Examples: **Y Combinator**, **Techstars**, or local university accelerators.
  - Often include structured workshops, pitch training, and one-on-one guidance to refine strategies.

- **Example**: A start-up founder participates in a Techstars program, receiving mentorship from industry leaders, refining their pitch to investors, and gaining access to funding opportunities.

4. Stay Open to Constructive Criticism

Constructive criticism from mentors or advisors is essential for improving your business plan. While it may feel uncomfortable at times, honest feedback helps you identify weaknesses, improve strategies, and validate ideas before committing resources.

- **How to Accept and Apply Feedback**:

  - **Listen Actively**: Pay attention to the feedback without becoming defensive.

  - **Ask Clarifying Questions**: Understand the reasoning behind suggestions to gain deeper insights.

  - **Prioritize Improvements**: Focus on areas that align with your business goals and have the biggest impact.

  - **Test Suggestions**: Implement advice on a small scale to see if it drives results before fully adopting it.

- **Example**: After presenting a business plan to a mentor, a SaaS company founder learns their pricing model is too complex. They simplify the tiers based on mentor feedback, resulting in higher customer acquisition.

Practical Steps to Build a Mentorship Network

1. **Identify Your Needs**: Define which aspects of your business require guidance (e.g., financial planning, scaling operations, marketing strategy).

2. **Seek Out Multiple Perspectives**: Build relationships with a mix of mentors, advisors, and peers to gain well-rounded insights.
3. **Be Proactive**: Take the initiative to reach out to potential mentors or join mentorship programs.
4. **Build Trust and Respect**: Show appreciation for mentors 'time and advice by following up and sharing progress.
5. **Offer Value in Return**: Mentorship is a two-way relationship—offer to share your expertise or help mentors in areas they need.

Example: Building a Support Network for a Small E-Commerce Business

Scenario: A small e-commerce business owner aims to scale their online store but struggles with marketing and logistics.

1. **Mentor Outreach**: The owner connects with a mentor through SCORE, who provides insights on inventory management and supply chain optimization.
2. **Networking Events**: The owner attends Chamber of Commerce events to meet local marketers who share tips on running effective Facebook ad campaigns.
3. **SBA Resources**: They use SBA templates to refine their financial projections and funding strategy.
4. **Applying Feedback**: After receiving criticism about their website's user experience, the owner works with a freelancer to simplify the checkout process, improving sales conversions.

Key Takeaways for Readers

1. **Engage with Mentors**: Reach out to experienced professionals through platforms like SCORE, LinkedIn, or mentorship programs to gain personalized advice.
2. **Join Networking Groups**: Attend local or virtual networking events to connect with other entrepreneurs, share challenges, and exchange solutions.
3. **Use SBA and Accelerator Programs**: Leverage resources like the SBA, incubators, and business accelerators to gain mentorship, funding, and business training.
4. **Be Receptive to Feedback**: Stay open to constructive criticism to identify blind spots and refine your strategies.
5. **Build a Support Network**: Surround yourself with mentors, peers, and advisors who can provide guidance, validation, and connections.

Final Thought on Finding a Mentor

Mentorship and advice are invaluable tools for refining your business plan, overcoming challenges, and accelerating growth. By actively seeking input from experienced mentors, participating in entrepreneurial networks, and using structured resources like SBA programs, you gain access to knowledge and feedback that can elevate your business. Stay receptive to advice, test suggestions, and continuously improve your strategies to build a resilient and successful business.

17. Celebrate Milestones and Iterate

Celebrating milestones and continuously iterating on your strategies are essential for keeping your team motivated, maintaining momentum, and fostering a culture of improvement. Recognizing small wins boosts morale and reinforces progress while analyzing successes and failures allows you to refine your processes and business plan for greater efficiency and effectiveness. Combining celebration with reflection ensures sustained growth and adaptability.

Why Celebrating Milestones and Iterating Matter

1. **Motivates the Team**: Recognizing achievements—no matter how small—reinforces a sense of accomplishment and encourages continued effort.
2. **Builds Momentum**: Celebrating small wins creates a feeling of progress, motivating the team to tackle the next milestone with energy and focus.
3. **Strengthens Culture**: Acknowledging contributions fosters a positive, collaborative work environment where people feel valued and appreciated.
4. **Provides Opportunities for Reflection**: Analyzing what worked (or didn't) helps refine strategies and improve performance over time.
5. **Drives Continuous Improvement**: Learning from successes and failures allows you to iterate and align your business plan with real-world results.

How to Celebrate Milestones

1. Define Key Milestones

Milestones are measurable achievements that reflect progress toward your larger business goals. Identify specific, clear milestones that are both meaningful and achievable.

- **Examples of Key Milestones**:
  - **Sales Targets**: Achieving $10,000 in monthly revenue or reaching a 20% increase in sales over a quarter.
  - **Customer Acquisition**: Reaching 1,000 new customers, hitting a high retention rate, or reducing customer acquisition costs.
  - **Product Development**: Launching a new product, completing a software MVP, or reaching a prototype approval phase.
  - **Operational Goals**: Reducing production time, improving delivery efficiency, or optimizing inventory management.
  - **Team Achievements**: Onboarding new employees, finishing a major project, or reaching a training certification.

Tip: Break larger milestones into smaller, actionable goals to ensure progress is measurable and frequent.

2. Celebrate Small Wins

Celebrating milestones doesn't always require a major investment. Recognizing achievements can take simple but meaningful forms, reinforcing a sense of pride and progress.

- **Ways to Celebrate Milestones**:
  - **Public Recognition**: Acknowledge achievements in team meetings, newsletters, or company-wide announcements.
  - **Rewards and Incentives**: Offer bonuses, gift cards, or team lunches to celebrate significant wins.
  - **Personalized Celebrations**: Tailor rewards to your team's preferences, such as an off-site event, a day off, or team outings.
  - **Highlight Contributions**: Recognize individual or team efforts in achieving milestones.

Examples:
- A sales team that exceeds its quarterly revenue goal celebrates with a team dinner or outing.
- After successfully launching a new product, the company sends out a congratulatory email to all employees, highlighting the efforts of the development, marketing, and operations teams.

3. Track and Share Progress

Use tools to monitor progress toward milestones and share updates regularly with the team. Transparent communication about progress builds trust and keeps everyone focused.

- **Tools for Tracking Progress**:
    - **Project Management Software**: Use tools like Asana, Trello, or Monday.com to track milestones and tasks.
    - **Dashboards**: Tools like Tableau, Google Data Studio, or Power BI visualize progress with charts and real-time metrics.
    - **KPI Reports**: Regularly update key performance indicators (KPIs) to show how milestones are being met.

Example: A project manager uses **Asana** to show how the team has hit 90% of project milestones ahead of schedule and publicly acknowledges contributors during a weekly team meeting.

How to Iterate and Improve

Celebrating milestones is only part of the process. To maintain growth, it's essential to analyze results, learn from both successes and failures and refine your business plan or processes accordingly.

1. Conduct Post-Milestone Reviews

After reaching a milestone, review what contributed to success and what could have been improved. A structured evaluation provides insights to refine your strategies moving forward.

- **Steps for Post-Milestone Analysis**:
    1. **Assess Performance**: Compare actual results to initial goals or projections.
    2. **Identify Success Drivers**: What strategies or actions contributed to success?
    3. **Analyze Challenges**: What obstacles or inefficiencies did you encounter?
    4. **Gather Feedback**: Involve team members, customers, or stakeholders to get multiple perspectives.
    5. **Document Learnings**: Create a record of takeaways to inform future milestones.

Example: A software start-up launching an MVP assesses that early adopters liked the product's core features but found onboarding confusing. They refine their onboarding process for the next iteration based on this feedback.

2. Use Data to Refine Strategies

Data-driven insights help validate what worked and guide future decisions. Use metrics and analytics to identify patterns, trends, and areas for improvement.

- **Metrics to Analyze**:
    - **Sales Metrics**: Revenue growth, conversion rates, and customer lifetime value.
    - **Customer Metrics**: Retention rates, Net Promoter Score (NPS), and customer acquisition cost (CAC).
    - **Operational Metrics**: Productivity, turnaround time, and resource utilization.

Example: A marketing team reviews campaign analytics and notices that a specific ad format performed better than others. They allocate a larger budget to similar ads in future campaigns.

3. Incorporate Feedback for Continuous Improvement

Feedback from employees, customers, and stakeholders is crucial for identifying blind spots and making meaningful improvements.

- **Ways to Collect Feedback**:
    - **Customer Surveys**: Send post-launch surveys to understand customer satisfaction and suggestions.
    - **Team Debriefs**: Host retrospective meetings to discuss what worked, what didn't, and how processes can improve.
    - **Performance Reviews**: Analyze team or individual performance data to highlight strengths and areas for growth.

Example: After a product launch, a business gathers customer feedback that pricing feels slightly high. The team evaluates options and tests a tiered pricing structure to improve customer adoption.

Tips for Celebrating Milestones and Iterating

1. **Celebrate Frequently**: Don't wait for massive wins—small victories deserve recognition, too.
2. **Tie Wins to Larger Goals**: Remind the team how each milestone contributes to the company's vision and long-term success.
3. **Be Transparent**: Share successes and failures openly, fostering a culture of learning and trust.
4. **Keep Improving**: Use milestone reviews and feedback to refine processes, address challenges, and set clearer goals.

5. **Document Learnings**: Keep a record of lessons learned so the team can avoid repeating mistakes and replicate successes.

Example: Achieving and Iterating on Milestones in an E-Commerce Business

Scenario: An e-commerce business sets a goal to achieve $50,000 in monthly sales within six months.

1. **Celebrate Milestones**: When the company hits $25,000 in Month 3, the leadership team publicly recognizes the marketing and operations teams' contributions. A team lunch is organized to celebrate the halfway point.
2. **Analyze Progress**: The team reviews sales data and identifies that Facebook ads drove most conversions, while email marketing lagged behind expectations.
3. **Iterate for Improvement**:
    - Increase Facebook ad spending to capitalize on what's working.
    - Refine the email strategy by testing new messaging and targeting abandoned cart customers.
4. **Set Next Milestone**: The team sets a new goal: $40,000 in sales by Month 5, refining strategies to improve further.

Key Takeaways for Readers

1. **Celebrate Small Wins**: Recognize achievements like hitting sales targets, launching products, or reaching operational milestones to keep morale high.
2. **Track and Share Progress**: Use project management tools and dashboards to monitor and communicate progress transparently.
3. **Conduct Reviews**: After achieving milestones, analyze what worked, identify challenges, and document lessons learned.
4. **Use Data to Improve**: Rely on metrics and feedback to refine strategies and processes for better results.
5. **Build a Culture of Improvement**: Encourage continuous learning, iteration, and celebration of progress to drive long-term growth.

Final Thought on Milestones

Celebrating milestones and iterating on strategies is a balance between recognition and reflection. Celebrating wins keeps teams motivated and engaged while analyzing successes and failures enables continuous improvement. By recognizing achievements, gathering feedback, and refining processes, your business can adapt, innovate, and move steadily toward long-term success.

18. Keep a Long-Term Perspective

While daily execution is vital for driving immediate progress, it's essential to ensure that all actions remain aligned with your **long-term goals, mission, and vision**. A long-term perspective provides a guiding framework for decision-making, ensuring your business grows sustainably and stays on track toward achieving its broader objectives. Balancing short-term flexibility with a clear focus on your overarching vision helps your business remain adaptable without losing sight of its ultimate direction.

Why Maintaining a Long-Term Perspective Matters

1. **Aligns Daily Actions with Strategic Goals**: Ensures that short-term efforts and decisions contribute to long-term objectives.
2. **Provides a Clear Sense of Direction**: Keeps the team focused on the big picture, preventing distractions or reactive decision-making.
3. **Fosters Sustainable Growth**: Long-term planning enables you to build a solid foundation for scalability, innovation, and resilience.
4. **Improves Resource Allocation**: Ensures time, money, and effort are invested in initiatives that align with your vision.
5. **Builds Stability and Adaptability**: While short-term adjustments are important, consistency in long-term goals provides stability during market fluctuations or challenges.

How to Keep a Long-Term Perspective

1. Revisit Your Mission and Vision Periodically

Your **mission** defines your business's core purpose, while your **vision** articulates where you want to be in the future. Revisiting these periodically ensures that your strategies, decisions, and actions remain consistent with your core goals.

- **How to Revisit and Align**:
    - Schedule quarterly or annual strategy sessions to assess how well daily operations align with your mission and long-term vision.
    - Involve team leaders, stakeholders, or advisors in reviewing progress and adjusting long-term priorities if needed.
    - Reflect on your "why"—why the business exists, whom it serves, and what you want to achieve over the next 5–10 years.

- **Example**: A sustainable fashion brand revisits its mission of "reducing textile waste through eco-friendly clothing." When reviewing progress, the company realigns its short-term operations to prioritize materials sourcing and launch a recycling initiative that supports its broader vision.

2. Balance Short-Term Adjustments with Long-Term Goals

Businesses often need to pivot or adjust strategies to address immediate challenges or opportunities. While short-term flexibility is crucial, ensure that these adjustments don't deviate from your long-term goals.

- **How to Maintain Balance**:
    - **Evaluate Trade-offs**: Before making short-term changes, ask: "Does this align with our long-term objectives, or is it a distraction?"
    - **Set Strategic Priorities**: Use a framework like the **Eisenhower Matrix** to focus on important tasks that also align with your vision.
    - **Link Adjustments to Bigger Goals**: If a pivot is necessary, connect it back to how it contributes to achieving broader objectives.

Example: A software company initially focused on small businesses considers shifting toward enterprise clients for short-term profitability. However, leadership decided to retain a strong presence in the small business segment because it aligns with their long-term vision of democratizing access to affordable software solutions.

3. Use Milestones to Measure Long-Term Progress

Breaking down long-term goals into smaller, time-bound milestones ensures you make steady progress without losing sight of the bigger picture. Regularly revisiting these milestones helps you assess whether short-term actions align with long-term goals.

- **How to Set and Track Milestones**:
    - Divide long-term goals into annual, quarterly, and monthly objectives.
    - Use Key Performance Indicators (KPIs) to measure progress at each milestone.
    - Reassess milestones periodically to ensure they remain relevant to your evolving vision.

Example: A tech start-up with a long-term goal of becoming a global leader in virtual education sets annual milestones for user acquisition, platform development, and geographic expansion. Each milestone ensures short-term actions (like marketing campaigns) align with the overarching vision.

4. Regularly Evaluate and Adjust Your Plan

A long-term perspective doesn't mean a rigid plan. Regularly evaluate your business plan to ensure it remains relevant to current realities, emerging trends, and future goals. Stay adaptable while holding firm to your mission and vision.

- **How to Evaluate Your Plan**:
  - Conduct quarterly or annual reviews of your strategies, KPIs, and market conditions.
  - Compare short-term achievements with long-term targets to identify gaps or misalignments.
  - Refine the business plan if new opportunities or challenges arise while ensuring any changes align with your mission.

Example: A renewable energy company evaluates its 10-year plan annually. When advancements in solar technology emerge, the company integrates this innovation into its strategy without straying from its long-term goal of promoting clean energy adoption worldwide.

5. Communicate the Long-Term Vision to Stakeholders

Consistently communicating your long-term vision to employees, investors, and partners fosters alignment and ensures everyone works toward the same goals. When people understand the bigger picture, they can make better day-to-day decisions that support the company's future success.

- **How to Share Your Vision**:
  - **Team Meetings**: Regularly emphasize the company's mission, vision, and long-term goals in team discussions.
  - **Performance Reviews**: Align individual performance goals with long-term objectives.
  - **Investor Updates**: Reinforce how short-term actions are contributing to the company's broader success.

Example: An e-commerce company shares its 5-year plan during a quarterly town hall meeting. The CEO connects current projects (like expanding logistics capabilities) to the long-term goal of becoming a global online marketplace.

Key Tips for Maintaining a Long-Term Perspective

1. **Create a North Star**: Keep your mission and vision as a guiding compass for all decisions. Revisit them frequently to ensure alignment.
2. **Focus on Sustainable Growth**: Prioritize strategies that support consistent, long-term results rather than short-term gains.
3. **Balance Flexibility and Stability**: Be adaptable to market changes without compromising your overarching goals.
4. **Track Long-Term Progress**: Use milestones and KPIs to measure progress toward bigger objectives.
5. **Stay Future-Oriented**: Anticipate industry trends, technological shifts, and customer demands to position your business for long-term success.

Example: Balancing Short-Term and Long-Term Goals in a Retail Business

Scenario: A local bookstore with a long-term vision of becoming a community hub for readers and events sets short-term goals to boost revenue.

- **Short-Term Actions**: Launch online sales to capitalize on e-commerce trends and attract new customers.
- **Alignment with Long-Term Goals**: They invest part of the profits into renovating their space to host book clubs, author talks, and community events.

Outcome: By balancing short-term revenue-generating strategies with long-term objectives, the bookstore grows sustainably while staying true to its mission.

Key Takeaways for Readers

1. **Revisit Your Mission and Vision**: Regularly assess your company's core purpose and future goals to ensure alignment with actions.
2. **Balance Short-Term and Long-Term Goals**: Adapt to short-term needs while keeping your overarching direction intact.
3. **Set and Track Milestones**: Break long-term goals into smaller, achievable steps to maintain momentum and measure progress.
4. **Evaluate and Adjust**: Regularly review and refine your strategies to keep your business plan relevant.
5. **Communicate the Vision**: Share your long-term goals with stakeholders to foster alignment, focus, and purpose.

Final Thought on Perspectives

Maintaining a long-term perspective ensures that your business grows with purpose, consistency, and resilience. By regularly revisiting your mission, balancing short-term flexibility with long-term goals, and tracking milestones, you can implement your business plan effectively while adapting to changes. A clear focus on the future empowers you to make decisions today that will lay the foundation for sustainable success tomorrow.

Reflection:

Tracking Progress:

> What milestones do you want to achieve in the next 3, 6, and 12 months? Write them below:
> 3 months:
>
> 6 months:
>
> 12 months:

Accountability:

- Who can you rely on to hold you accountable for your goals (e.g., mentor, partner, team member)?

- What methods will you use to track your progress (e.g., journal, software, spreadsheets)?

Adapting to Change:

- When was the last time you updated your business plan? Schedule time to review and revise it if it's been more than six months.

- List one external factor (e.g., market trend, technology) that could impact your business. How will you address it?

Case Study: John's Custom Furniture – From Weekend Hobby to Sustainable Business

Background

John, a self-taught woodworker, loved creating rustic and functional furniture. His designs featured intricate details, reclaimed wood, and a blend of modern and vintage styles. Originally, woodworking was an escape from his corporate job, but growing demand from friends, family, and neighbors sparked the idea of monetizing his hobby.

Despite his talent and passion, John faced obstacles in transitioning from hobbyist to business owner. His sporadic production and inconsistent pricing undermined profitability, while his limited marketing efforts left untapped growth opportunities.

Phase 1: Identifying the Challenges

1. **Underpricing Products**:

    - John based his pricing on what he thought people could afford rather than on his costs or the value of his work.
    - This approach resulted in minimal profit margins and limited ability to reinvest in his business.

2. **Lack of Business Processes**:

    - He handled everything himself, from sourcing materials to crafting, selling, and delivering products.
    - Without structured workflows, he often experienced delays and stress from juggling multiple orders.

3. **Limited Market Reach**:

    - John relied solely on word-of-mouth referrals and local markets, which capped his potential customer base.

4. **Work-Life Imbalance**:

    - Balancing furniture orders with a demanding full-time job left John overwhelmed and unable to grow his business.

Phase 2: Developing a Strategy for Growth

John decided to formalize his operations and turn his hobby into a profitable business. He created a detailed business plan that focused on three pillars: pricing, marketing, and operations.

1. Crafting a Sustainable Pricing Model

- **Cost Analysis**: John calculated the total cost of materials, labor (including his time), and overhead, such as tools, electricity, and workspace maintenance.
- **Profit Margin**: He aimed for a 50% cost markup to ensure profitability while remaining competitive.
- **Value-Based Pricing**: For custom orders, he emphasized the uniqueness and craftsmanship, allowing for premium pricing.

Example:

- A rustic coffee table:
    - Material cost: $75
    - Labor: $150 (10 hours at $15/hour)
    - Overhead: $25
    - Total cost: $250
    - Selling price: $375 ($250 + 50% markup)

2. Expanding Market Reach

- **Digital Presence**:
    - Built a website featuring professional photos, detailed product descriptions, and an easy-to-use ordering system.
    - Launched an Instagram account showcasing finished pieces, work-in-progress videos, and customer testimonials.
- **Partnerships**:
    - Collaborated with local interior designers who featured his furniture in client projects.
    - Partnered with boutique home decor stores to display select pieces.
- **E-Commerce Expansion**:
    - Added an Etsy shop and joined an online marketplace for handmade goods, reaching a national audience.

Results:

- Instagram followers grew to 15,000 within six months, with direct inquiries increasing by 50%.
- Online sales accounted for 30% of total revenue by the end of the year.

3. Streamlining Operations

- **Workspace Upgrade**:
    - Rented a larger workshop and invested in better tools, increasing productivity.
    - Organized materials and tools to reduce wasted time during production.
- **Batch Production**:
    - Standardized processes for popular items, such as dining tables and coffee tables, to reduce lead times.
- **Team Building**:
    - Hired a part-time assistant for administrative work and a junior craftsman to handle basic tasks.

Impact:

- Production efficiency improved by 40%.
- John reduced order fulfillment times from four weeks to two weeks.

4. Enhancing Customer Experience

- **Custom Order Process**:
    - Created a step-by-step workflow for custom orders, including consultations, design approvals, and milestone updates.
- **Packaging and Delivery**:
    - Introduced eco-friendly, branded packaging and partnered with a reliable local delivery service.
- **Post-Sale Engagement**:
    - Followed up with customers to ensure satisfaction and encouraged reviews on his website and social media.

Phase 3: Overcoming Challenges

1. **Managing Growth**:

    - As orders increased, John struggled to keep up. He implemented a booking system with limited monthly slots for custom work, ensuring manageable workloads.

2. **Competition**:

    - Competitors began replicating his designs. John introduced limited-edition pieces and exclusive collections to maintain uniqueness.

3. **Balancing Creativity and Scalability**:

    - While batch production improved efficiency, it limited John's creative freedom. He dedicated one day a week to experimental designs, which became highly sought after as signature pieces.

Phase 4: Results and Achievements

1. **Financial Success**:
   - Revenue: $150,000 in the first year, exceeding the initial goal of $100,000.
   - Profit Margin: Maintained a 35% profit margin after reinvesting in tools and team expansion.
2. **Brand Growth**:
   - Featured in a national design magazine as a "rising star in handcrafted furniture."
   - Secured partnerships with three boutique home decor stores.
3. **Operational Excellence**:
   - Fulfilled 200+ orders in the first year, with a 95% on-time delivery rate.
4. **Personal Fulfillment**:
   - Transitioned to woodworking full-time, achieving his dream of turning passion into a profession.

Future Goals

1. **Scaling Production**:
   - Explore partnerships with larger retailers to offer a "rustic modern" furniture line.
   - Invest in advanced machinery to increase production without sacrificing quality.
2. **Expanding Product Offerings**:
   - Introduce smaller, more affordable items like cutting boards, wine racks, and coasters to attract new customers.
3. **Workshops and Classes**:
   - Host woodworking classes to build community engagement and diversify income streams.
4. **Sustainability Initiatives**:
   - Commit to using 100% reclaimed or sustainably sourced wood by the end of year two.

Key Takeaways for Readers

1. **Plan for Growth**:
   - Scaling a hobby into a business requires clear goals, structured processes, and strategic investments.

2. **Focus on Branding**:
   - A strong, consistent brand helps differentiate your offerings in a competitive market.

3. **Adapt and Innovate**:
   - Balance efficiency with creativity to maintain uniqueness while scaling operations.

4. **Invest in Customer Relationships**:
   - A seamless, personalized customer experience builds loyalty and generates repeat business.

Step-by-step summary for transitioning from a hobby to a business:

Step 1: Self-Assessment

- Reflect on your hobby's potential as a business. Ask yourself:
  - Is there a demand for your product or service?
  - Are you willing to dedicate consistent time and effort?
  - Do you have the necessary skills, or are you willing to learn?

Step 2: Research and Planning

- Conduct market research to understand your target audience and competitors:
  - Who would buy your product or service?
  - What differentiates your offering from others in the market?
- Write a business plan:
  - Define your mission, vision, and goals.

- Outline the steps to establish and grow your business.
- Include financial projections, marketing strategies, and operational plans.

Step 3: Setting Up Finances

- Separate your personal and business finances:
    - Open a business bank account.
    - Track income and expenses using accounting software or spreadsheets.
- Determine pricing for profitability:
    - Calculate all costs and ensure your pricing includes a healthy profit margin.
- Explore funding options if needed:
    - Use savings or small loans, or seek investors to cover startup costs.

Step 4: Branding and Marketing

- Create a unique and professional brand:
    - Develop a logo, color scheme, and tagline that reflect your business values.
- Build an online presence:
    - Set up social media profiles and a website to showcase your products or services.
    - Engage with your audience through posts, videos, and interactions.
- Market your business:
    - Use strategies like social media ads, email campaigns, partnerships, and word-of-mouth.

Step 5: Launching the Business

- Decide on your launch approach:
    - Start small with soft launches or limited sales to test the market.
    - Promote your launch through an event, online campaign, or special offers.
- Ensure compliance:
    - Register your business and obtain the necessary licenses or permits.
    - Protect your intellectual property if applicable.

Step 6: Growing and Scaling

- Optimize operations:

- - Streamline production or service delivery to improve efficiency and reduce costs.
    - Invest in tools, technology, or personnel to handle increased demand.
- Expand your reach:
    - Explore new sales channels like e-commerce, partnerships, or retail outlets.
    - Introduce additional products or services based on customer feedback.
- Monitor and adapt:
    - Regularly evaluate your progress and adjust strategies to stay competitive.

Chapter 9: Vision and Mission

The Importance of a Clear Vision and Mission

A clear vision and mission are essential elements of a successful business. Together, they define the purpose, direction, and identity of your organization, guiding decision-making and inspiring stakeholders. Below are the reasons why having a well-articulated vision and mission is crucial.

Define the Purpose of the Business

Clearly defining the purpose of your business provides direction, clarity, and motivation for your team and stakeholders. At its core, a business's purpose is communicated through its **vision** and **mission**, which outline its long-term aspirations and the tangible value it aims to deliver. These elements serve as a guiding compass for decision-making, inspire employees, and attract customers and partners who share the same values.

The Role of Vision in Defining Purpose

A **vision statement** describes the long-term aspirations of a business, outlining the ultimate impact it wants to achieve in the future. It is **forward-looking, aspirational, and inspirational**, reflecting what the business strives to become and how it hopes to change the world or its industry.

Why a Vision Statement Matters

1. **Provides a Clear Direction**: Guides strategic decisions and ensures daily actions align with long-term goals.
2. **Inspires and Motivates**: Energizes employees, investors, and partners by communicating a meaningful purpose.
3. **Builds Identity**: Shapes how the business is perceived by customers, investors, and the community.
4. **Attracts Like-Minded Stakeholders**: Draws in employees, customers, and partners who resonate with the company's aspirations.

Key Characteristics of a Vision Statement

A strong vision statement should:

- **Be Future-Oriented**: Describe the long-term goals and aspirations of the company.
- **Be Clear and Concise**: Avoid overly complex or vague language. It should be easy to understand and communicate.
- **Be Inspirational**: Appeal to emotions and motivate people to rally behind a shared purpose.
- **Reflect Ambition**: Set bold goals that push the business beyond its current reality.

Examples of Vision Statements

1. **Sustainable Energy**:

    - *"To make sustainable energy accessible to everyone."*
        - **Purpose**: This statement clearly defines the company's goal of creating a future where clean, renewable energy is available to all, addressing environmental and accessibility challenges.

2. **Technology Innovation**:

    - *"To connect people and ideas through technology that inspires creativity and innovation."*
        - **Purpose**: The company aspires to create technology that enhances connectivity and enables innovation.

3. **Education**:

    - *"To transform education by providing equal learning opportunities to students around the world."*

- **Purpose**: This vision communicates the company's ambition to make education more accessible and impactful on a global scale.

4. **Healthcare**:

    - *"To revolutionize healthcare delivery and improve lives through cutting-edge medical innovation."*
        - **Purpose**: The statement emphasizes improving lives by pushing the boundaries of medical advancements.

5. **Retail and E-Commerce**:

    - *"To make high-quality, affordable products accessible to families everywhere."*
        - **Purpose**: The company defines its mission as creating affordability and accessibility while delivering value to its customers.

How to Craft a Vision Statement That Defines Purpose

1. **Ask Big-Picture Questions**:

    - *What long-term impact do we want to make?*
    - *How will the world or industry change because of our efforts?*
    - *What is our ultimate goal 5, 10, or 20 years down the line?*

2. **Focus on Impact**: Identify the positive difference your business aims to make for customers, society, or the environment.

3. **Think Aspirationally**: Don't limit your vision to where you are today—articulate your boldest ambitions.

4. **Involve Your Team**: Collect input from employees, leaders, and key stakeholders to ensure the vision reflects shared values and aspirations.

5. **Make it Concise and Memorable**: Your vision should be short enough to remember and powerful enough to inspire action.

How the Vision Aligns with Business Purpose

The **vision** provides a clear sense of why the business exists and where it's headed, which directly connects to the company's purpose.

- **Aligning Purpose and Vision**:
  - If the purpose of your business is to promote sustainability, your vision might focus on environmental impact (e.g., "To create a cleaner, greener planet for future generations").
  - If the purpose is innovation, the vision might emphasize pushing boundaries in technology or creativity (e.g., "To redefine the future of smart technology through relentless innovation").

Practical Steps to Implement the Vision Statement

1. **Communicate It Regularly**: Share the vision statement during team meetings, presentations, and onboarding processes. Embed it in all internal and external communications.
2. **Incorporate It into Decision-Making**: Use the vision as a guiding principle when evaluating strategies, opportunities, and challenges.
3. **Tie It to Company Goals**: Break the long-term vision into annual and quarterly goals to ensure steady progress toward achieving it.
4. **Make It Visible**: Display the vision statement on office walls, company websites, marketing materials, and employee handbooks.

Example: A Renewable Energy Company

Business Purpose: To reduce the world's dependence on fossil fuels.

Vision Statement: *"To make sustainable energy accessible to everyone."*

- **Why It Works**:
  - **Clarity**: The vision is clear and understandable—it's about accessibility and sustainability.
  - **Aspirational**: It outlines a bold ambition to make renewable energy a standard for all.
  - **Impact-Focused**: The statement highlights the company's role in driving global environmental change.
  - **Alignment with Purpose**: The vision ties directly to the business's core mission of reducing fossil fuel usage.

Implementation:

- The company uses its vision as a filter for decision-making, such as investing in affordable solar panel technology or expanding into underserved markets to improve energy accessibility.

Benefits of Having a Defined Vision

1. **Strategic Alignment**: A clear vision keeps all business strategies and initiatives aligned with long-term goals.
2. **Motivation for Teams**: Employees understand how their work contributes to a greater purpose, improving morale and engagement.
3. **Competitive Differentiation**: A compelling vision sets your business apart by highlighting what you stand for and aspire to achieve.
4. **Investor and Partner Attraction**: A well-articulated vision appeals to stakeholders who share the same values and goals.

Key Takeaways for Readers

1. **Purpose and Vision Go Hand-in-Hand**: The vision articulates the long-term aspirations that define your business's purpose.
2. **Make It Impact-Driven**: A strong vision statement reflects the difference your business aims to make in the world.
3. **Keep It Clear and Inspirational**: A concise, memorable vision motivates your team, attracts customers, and guides decision-making.
4. **Regularly Revisit and Realign**: Ensure your vision remains consistent with your mission and evolves as needed to reflect changing business priorities.
5. **Communicate It Widely**: Embed the vision in all aspects of your organization to keep it alive and actionable.

Final Thought on Vision

Defining the purpose of your business through a strong vision statement is essential for providing direction, inspiring teams, and achieving meaningful impact. By clearly communicating where your business is headed and the positive change it aims to create, you establish a foundation for sustainable growth and long-term success.

Mission Statement:

Describes the Business's Core Objectives and Approach to Achieving the Vision

A **mission statement** defines the core objectives, values, and approach of a business. While the vision outlines where the business aspires to be in the future, the **mission explains what the business does right now, for whom, and how**. It serves as the foundation for decision-making, day-to-day operations, and long-term strategies, communicating how the business will achieve its vision in tangible, actionable ways.

A well-crafted mission statement inspires employees, attracts customers and partners, and establishes a consistent direction for the business.

Key Elements of a Mission Statement

1. **Purpose**: Communicates what the business exists to do.
2. **Target Audience**: Identifies who the business serves (customers, communities, industries).
3. **Core Offerings**: Describes the products, services, or value the business delivers.
4. **Approach**: Highlights how the business achieves its purpose—whether through innovation, quality, affordability, or other unique approaches.

Why a Mission Statement Matters

1. **Provides Focus and Clarity**: A mission statement ensures every action and decision aligns with the business's objectives.
2. **Guides Strategy**: It serves as a roadmap for operations, marketing, and growth by defining what the business prioritizes.
3. **Inspires Employees**: A clear mission motivates employees by connecting their roles to a meaningful purpose.
4. **Engages Customers and Stakeholders**: It communicates what the business stands for, attracting customers, investors, and partners who share its values.
5. **Builds Brand Identity**: The mission forms the foundation for branding, messaging, and customer perception.

Key Characteristics of a Strong Mission Statement

A good mission statement should:

- **Be Concise**: Ideally, one to two sentences—clear and to the point.
- **Be Specific**: Avoid generic language; focus on what makes your business unique.
- **Be Action-Oriented**: Describe what the business does and how it does it.
- **Be Customer-Focused**: Highlight the value you deliver to your target audience.
- **Reflect Values**: Communicate your business's core principles and approach.

Examples of Mission Statements by Industry

1. Renewable Energy

- *"We provide innovative solar solutions to empower households and businesses with clean energy."*
    - **Purpose**: Providing clean energy solutions.
    - **Target Audience**: Households and businesses.
    - **Approach**: Innovation in solar technology.
    - **How It Supports the Vision**: Enables the company's long-term goal of creating a sustainable energy future.

2. Technology

- "To connect people around the world through seamless, intuitive communication technology."
    - **Purpose**: Connecting people globally.
    - **Target Audience**: Individuals and businesses.
    - **Approach**: Providing seamless, intuitive communication tools.

3. Education

- "We make learning accessible to students everywhere by providing high-quality, affordable online courses."
    - **Purpose**: Making education accessible and affordable.
    - **Target Audience**: Students around the world.
    - **Approach**: Offering online courses focused on quality and affordability.

4. Retail

- "We bring families together by offering high-quality, affordable meals and products that make life easier."
    - **Purpose**: Enhancing family life.
    - **Target Audience**: Families looking for affordability and convenience.
    - **Approach**: Providing high-quality, affordable meals and products.

5. Nonprofit

- "To fight hunger by delivering nutritious meals and resources to underserved communities worldwide."
    - **Purpose**: Fighting hunger.
    - **Target Audience**: Underserved communities.
    - **Approach**: Delivering meals and resources.

How to Create an Effective Mission Statement

1. **Define Your Purpose**: Start by asking:
    - What problem does your business solve?
    - Why does your business exist?

2. **Identify Your Audience**: Consider who benefits from your products, services, or solutions.
    - Examples: Households, businesses, specific industries, or communities.

3. **Describe Your Offering**: Outline what products or services you provide and what makes them unique.
4. **Explain Your Approach**: Highlight how you achieve your purpose—whether through innovation, quality, sustainability, affordability, or customer service.
5. **Keep It Concise and Action-Oriented**: Use clear, straightforward language that focuses on what your business does today. Avoid jargon or vague buzzwords.

Mission vs. Vision: Key Differences

Aspect	Mission Statement	Vision Statement
Focus	Describes the present-day purpose and approach	Outlines long-term aspirations and impact
Timeframe	Immediate, actionable goals	Future-oriented, aspirational goals
Purpose	Guides daily operations and decision-making	Inspires and sets direction for the future
Example	"We provide innovative solar solutions to empower households and businesses with clean energy."	"To make sustainable energy accessible to everyone."

Real-World Example: Tesla

- **Vision**: "To create the most compelling car company of the 21st century by driving the world's transition to electric vehicles."

- **Mission**: "To accelerate the world's transition to sustainable energy through electric vehicles and renewable energy solutions."

- **Breakdown**:
    - **Purpose**: Accelerate the transition to sustainable energy.
    - **Target Audience**: Individuals, businesses, and governments looking for clean transportation and energy.
    - **Approach**: Providing electric vehicles and renewable energy solutions.

How to Use Your Mission Statement Effectively

1. **Communicate It Widely**:

- Include your mission on your website, marketing materials, and employee onboarding programs.
- Ensure team members understand how their roles contribute to fulfilling the mission.

2. **Use It as a Decision-Making Tool**:
   - When evaluating strategies or opportunities, ask: *"Does this align with our mission?"*

3. **Inspire Action**:
   - Use the mission statement to rally your team around a shared purpose and motivate consistent effort.

4. **Refine It Over Time**:
   - Periodically review your mission statement to ensure it aligns with your evolving business priorities and market conditions.

Example: A Small Solar Company

Mission Statement: *"We provide innovative solar solutions to empower households and businesses with clean energy."*

- **Purpose**: Helping customers transition to clean energy.
- **Target Audience**: Households and businesses.
- **Core Offering**: Solar energy solutions.
- **Approach**: Focusing on innovation to make solar energy accessible and effective.

How It Works in Practice:

- Marketing campaigns emphasize the environmental and financial benefits of their solar solutions.
- The company prioritizes research and development to improve solar efficiency and affordability.
- Employees align their roles with the mission—engineers focus on innovation, sales teams emphasize empowerment through clean energy, and customer service prioritizes education and support.

Key Takeaways for Readers

1. **Define Your Purpose**: Clearly articulate what your business does, for whom, and how it does it.

2. **Be Specific and Action-Oriented**: Avoid vague language—describe tangible objectives and approaches.
3. **Focus on Value**: Communicate the unique value your business provides to customers or society.
4. **Align with Your Vision**: Ensure the mission supports the long-term aspirations outlined in your vision.
5. **Inspire and Guide**: Use the mission to motivate your team, attract customers, and guide strategic decisions.

Final Thought on Mission

A strong mission statement serves as the foundation of your business's purpose, providing clarity, focus, and direction. By clearly defining what you do, whom you serve, and how you deliver value, you inspire action, align operations with your core objectives, and set the stage for achieving your long-term vision.

Clarity for Stakeholders:

Providing a Concise Explanation of Why the Business Exists and What It Seeks to Accomplish

Clear and well-articulated **mission** and **vision statements** provide stakeholders—employees, customers, investors, partners, and suppliers—with a strong understanding of the business's purpose, values, and objectives. These statements serve as a foundational **guiding framework**, ensuring everyone is aligned with the company's direction, goals, and reason for existence.

By clearly communicating what the business **does today** (mission) and what it aspires to **achieve in the future** (vision), stakeholders can better understand their roles, build trust, and engage with the business meaningfully.

Who Are the Stakeholders, and Why Do They Need Clarity?

1. **Employees**:
    - Employees look to the mission and vision statements for **motivation** and to understand how their roles contribute to the bigger picture.
    - **Why It Matters**: Clarity fosters alignment, job satisfaction, and a sense of purpose, encouraging employees to work toward shared goals.

2. **Customers**:
   - Customers engage with businesses that have clear values and a compelling purpose, aligning with their personal beliefs or needs.
   - **Why It Matters**: A concise mission and vision build trust, brand loyalty, and emotional connections.

3. **Investors and Lenders**:
   - Investors need to see a clear purpose and direction before committing financial support.
   - **Why It Matters**: Clarity on the business's objectives demonstrates focus, long-term potential, and operational stability.

4. **Partners and Suppliers**:
   - Partners and suppliers seek alignment in purpose, strategy, and priorities to foster collaboration.
   - **Why It Matters**: Understanding the company's mission ensures smoother relationships, shared values, and mutually beneficial partnerships.

5. **The Community and Society**:
   - Businesses often have a broader societal impact, and clear purpose statements help communicate how they contribute to the greater good.
   - **Why It Matters**: Purpose-driven businesses gain goodwill, positive brand perception, and community support.

How Mission and Vision Create Clarity for Stakeholders

1. Explaining Why the Business Exists (Mission)

The **mission statement** outlines the business's **core purpose**—what it does, for whom, and how it creates value. This clarity ensures stakeholders understand what the business offers, its goals, and the problems it solves.

- **Key Points of Clarity in a Mission Statement**:
  - The "What" Describes the core product, service, or offering.
  - The "Who": Identifies the target audience or market the business serves.

- The "How": Highlights the business's unique approach, values, or methods of delivering value.

Example:

- *Mission: "We provide innovative solar solutions to empower households and businesses with clean energy."*
    - **What**: Innovative solar solutions.
    - **Who**: Households and businesses.
    - **How**: Focusing on innovation to deliver clean energy.
    - **Clarity for Stakeholders**: Employees know their focus is clean energy solutions; investors see a commitment to a growing, sustainable industry; customers understand the company's purpose of empowerment through renewable energy.

2. Articulating the Long-Term Impact (Vision)

The **vision statement** communicates the **long-term aspirations** of the business—what it seeks to accomplish in the future. It paints a clear picture of the desired outcome and impact, inspiring stakeholders to work toward achieving that future.

- **Key Points of Clarity in a Vision Statement**:
    - The "Why" Explains the broader purpose or goal of the business.
    - The "Future State": Describes where the company aspires to be in 5, 10, or 20 years.
    - The "Impact": Highlights how the business will positively influence its customers, industry, or the world.

Example:

- *Vision: "To make sustainable energy accessible to everyone."*
    - **Why**: To solve the problem of energy sustainability and accessibility.
    - **Future State**: A world where sustainable energy is widely available.
    - **Impact**: Positive environmental change and greater energy equity.
    - **Clarity for Stakeholders**: Employees understand their work supports a larger, impactful goal; investors see long-term growth potential in a sustainable industry; customers see how their purchase contributes to a cleaner world.

Practical Ways Clear Purpose Benefits Stakeholders

1. **Alignment for Teams**:
    - Employees and leadership stay aligned on priorities and strategies.

- Example: A mission like *"Deliver affordable health care to underserved communities"* ensures all departments—operations, marketing, and finance—prioritize affordability and access.

2. **Confidence for Investors**:

    - A clear purpose helps investors and lenders evaluate the business's focus and viability.
    - Example: A start-up with a mission to *"revolutionize online education"* and a vision of *"becoming the global leader in virtual learning"* reassures investors that the business has a clear path and growth potential.

3. **Trust and Loyalty for Customers**:

    - Customers trust businesses with transparent, value-driven purposes.
    - Example: A sustainable clothing brand with a mission like *"To design high-quality fashion that reduces environmental impact"* attracts eco-conscious buyers.

4. **Collaboration with Partners and Suppliers**:

    - Partners and suppliers align resources and strategies with businesses whose missions complement their own.
    - Example: A food company with a mission to *"source organic, local ingredients to create healthy, affordable meals"* will attract suppliers committed to sustainable practices.

5. **Community Engagement**:

    - A clear mission fosters goodwill and encourages local communities to engage with the business.
    - Example: A construction firm with a mission to *"build resilient, eco-friendly infrastructure to benefit future generations"* earns community support for projects.

How to Ensure Your Mission and Vision Provide Clarity

1. **Be Concise and Specific**: Use simple, actionable language that avoids jargon or vagueness.

2. **Make Them Relatable**: Stakeholders should quickly understand how the mission and vision connect to their role or interest.
3. **Communicate Consistently**: Share your mission and vision across internal documents, websites, marketing materials, and investor presentations.
4. **Reflect Core Values**: Ensure the statements align with your business's culture, principles, and promises.
5. **Revisit Regularly**: Update the mission or vision if the business evolves but ensure consistency in purpose.

Real-World Examples: Clarity for Stakeholders

1. **Google**:
    - **Mission**: "To organize the world's information and make it universally accessible and useful."
    - **Vision**: "To provide access to the world's information in one click."
    - **Clarity**:
        - **Employees**: Know their role is to improve information accessibility.
        - **Users**: Understand Google's purpose to make information useful and quick to find.
        - **Investors**: See a strong focus on innovation and growth in information technology.
2. **Tesla**:
    - **Mission**: "To accelerate the world's transition to sustainable energy."
    - **Vision**: "To create the most compelling car company of the 21st century by driving the world's transition to electric vehicles."
    - **Clarity**:
        - **Employees**: Work toward a clean energy future.
        - **Customers**: Understand Tesla's commitment to sustainability.
        - **Investors**: See long-term growth in a renewable energy market.
3. **Nike**:
    - **Mission**: "To bring inspiration and innovation to every athlete in the world."
    - **Vision**: "To do everything possible to expand human potential."
    - **Clarity**:

- **Employees**: Aim to innovate products that inspire performance.
- **Customers**: See Nike as a brand that helps them reach their full potential.

Key Takeaways for Readers

1. **Mission Defines the Now**: It explains what the business does, for whom, and how it creates value.
2. **Vision Defines the Future**: It articulates the long-term aspirations and the impact the business seeks to achieve.
3. **Provide Clear and Specific Statements**: Ensure stakeholders—employees, investors, customers, and partners—quickly understand the business's purpose and goals.
4. **Reinforce Through Communication**: Consistently share the mission and vision across all platforms to build trust and alignment.
5. **Create Relatable Connections**: Help stakeholders see how their interests, roles, or values align with the business's purpose.

Final Thought on Clarity

Clarity in your mission and vision statements ensures that all stakeholders understand **why your business exists** and **what it seeks to accomplish**. By providing a clear, actionable framework, you inspire employees, build trust with customers, attract investors, and foster stronger partnerships, positioning your business for long-term success.

Making the Leap:
- Write down one action you can take today to treat your hobby like a business (e.g., setting prices, marketing, creating a schedule).
- What's one thing holding you back from transitioning to a business, and how can you overcome it?

Customer Focus:
- What feedback have you received from customers or friends about your product or service? How will you act on it?
- Create a short pitch for your business in 2-3 sentences.

Financial Discipline:

- Do you have separate accounts for your personal and business finances? If not, plan to open one.

- Write down three ways to generate consistent revenue from your business.

Case Study: Lisa's Organic Skincare – Business Plan Implementation for Success

Background

Lisa was passionate about natural skincare and spent years experimenting with organic ingredients to create her lotions, scrubs, and facial oils. She often gifted her products to friends and family, who raved about the results. Motivated by their encouragement, Lisa decided to turn her passion into a business.

However, her initial efforts lacked structure. Without a clear business plan, Lisa struggled to price her products, manage inventory, and attract consistent customers. Recognizing the need for a strategy, she developed and implemented a comprehensive business plan to guide her journey.

Phase 1: Creating the Business Plan

Lisa's business plan focused on five critical areas: market analysis, product offerings, operations, marketing, and financial projections.

1. **Market Analysis**:
    - **Target Audience**: Eco-conscious women aged 25-45 who value sustainability and natural ingredients.
    - **Competitor Research**: Lisa analyzed her competitors and identified gaps, such as affordable organic skincare with sustainable packaging.
2. **Product Offerings**:

- Launched with three core products:
    - Organic Lavender Body Scrub
    - Hydrating Rose Facial Oil
    - Soothing Aloe Vera Lotion
  - Each product highlighted its organic, cruelty-free, and eco-friendly qualities.

3. **Operations Plan**:
   - Sourced certified organic ingredients from local farmers.
   - Set up a production process in a rented commercial kitchen to comply with regulations.
   - Created a system for batching production to minimize waste.

4. **Marketing and Branding**:
   - Developed a brand identity with the tagline: "Nourish Your Skin Naturally."
   - Built an online store with high-quality photos and detailed product descriptions.
   - Focused on social media platforms like Instagram and Pinterest to connect with her audience.

5. **Financial Projections**:
   - Initial funding: $15,000 (savings and a small family loan).
   - Year 1 Goal: Generate $50,000 in revenue with a 30% profit margin.
   - Estimated production cost per unit: $5; selling price: $20, ensuring a 75% markup.

Phase 2: Implementing the Business Plan

1. Streamlining Operations

- **Production**:
    - Lisa scheduled weekly production days, allowing her to create products in batches and maintain a consistent inventory.
    - She invested in simple automation tools, like a filling machine, to reduce manual labor.
- **Packaging**:
    - Sourced biodegradable containers and designed labels with an earthy, minimalist aesthetic.

- Partnered with a local printer to ensure fast and eco-friendly production.
- **Inventory Management**:
  - Used software to track raw materials and finished products, avoiding overproduction or shortages.

2. Building Brand Awareness

- **Website Launch**:
  - Lisa's website featured an e-commerce store, a blog on natural skincare tips, and customer testimonials.
  - Added a subscription option for monthly product deliveries, boosting recurring revenue.
- **Social Media Strategy**:
  - Created engaging Instagram content, including behind-the-scenes production videos, skincare routines, and customer success stories.
  - Partnered with micro-influencers to promote her products, offering free samples in exchange for reviews and exposure.
- **Community Engagement**:
  - Participated in local farmers' markets and eco fairs, building a loyal customer base and generating word-of-mouth referrals.
  - Hosted free online workshops on DIY skincare tips, driving traffic to her website.

3. Pricing and Financial Management

- **Pricing Review**:
  - Adjusted prices based on feedback and cost analysis, ensuring profitability while remaining competitive.
  - Introduced tiered pricing for bundles (e.g., "Glow Kit" with three products at a 10% discount).
- **Budget Allocation**:
  - Invested 40% of her funding in marketing, 30% in raw materials, and 30% in production tools and operational expenses.
- **Monitoring Financials**:
  - Used accounting software to track sales, expenses, and profit margins, regularly reviewing these metrics to guide decisions.

4. Customer Experience

- **Personalized Touch**:
  - Included handwritten thank-you notes with every order, creating a memorable unboxing experience.
- **Customer Feedback**:
  - Sent follow-up emails with surveys to gather insights and improve her products.
- **Loyalty Program**:
  - Launched a rewards system where customers earned points for purchases, referrals, and social media shares.

Phase 3: Overcoming Challenges

1. **Scaling Production**:
   - Initially overwhelmed by high demand, Lisa hired a part-time assistant to help with production and packaging.
   - Outsourced non-core tasks like label design and social media scheduling to freelancers.
2. **Supply Chain Issues**:
   - A delay in raw material deliveries forced Lisa to diversify her suppliers, ensuring a consistent supply chain.
3. **Building Trust Online**:
   - Customers hesitated to purchase skincare online without trying the products first. Lisa addressed this by offering sample-size products and a 100% satisfaction guarantee.

Phase 4: Results and Growth

1. Financial Success:

- Exceeded her first-year goal, generating $65,000 in revenue with a 35% profit margin.
- Subscription sales accounted for 20% of her total revenue, providing a steady monthly income.

2. Brand Recognition:

- Lisa's products were featured in a local eco-living magazine, boosting sales and web traffic.
- Her Instagram account grew to 25,000 followers within a year, with high engagement rates.

3. Operational Efficiency:

- Weekly production runs ensured a steady inventory, reducing waste by 20%.
- Hiring support staff freed Lisa's time to focus on product development and strategy.

4. Customer Loyalty:

- 80% of customers became repeat buyers, and her loyalty program saw a 90% participation rate.

Future Plans

1. **Product Expansion:**
   - Introduce seasonal products, such as summer sunscreens and winter moisturizers.
   - Develop travel-sized versions for customers on the go.
2. **Sustainability Goals:**
   - Transition to refillable packaging options to reduce waste.
   - Partner with an organization to plant a tree for every product sold.
3. **Retail Partnerships:**
   - Expand into eco-friendly boutiques and natural food stores.
4. **Scaling Production:**
   - Lease a larger workspace and invest in advanced equipment to meet growing demand.
   - Hire a full-time production manager to oversee daily operations.

Lessons Learned

1. **A Plan Guides Action:**
   - A well-thought-out business plan provided clarity and direction, helping Lisa make informed decisions.
2. **Flexibility is Key:**
   - Lisa adapted her strategies based on feedback, market trends, and unforeseen challenges.
3. **Customer Experience Drives Loyalty:**
   - Personalized touches, high-quality products, and excellent service turned one-time buyers into loyal advocates.

4. **Data Informs Growth**:
    - Regularly monitoring financial and operational metrics ensured sustainable growth and profitability.

Key Takeaways for Readers

- **A strong business plan is a roadmap**, but **its value lies in execution and adaptation**.
- Prioritize customer relationships to build loyalty and long-term revenue streams.
- Invest in your brand's visibility, whether through social media, partnerships, or community engagement.
- **Operational efficiency and financial discipline are critical** for scaling successfully.

Conclusion: Business or Hobby…

Businesses and Hobbyists navigate a dynamic and ever-changing landscape, and both can make profits. The tools, strategies, and frameworks outlined in this book provide a comprehensive guide to achieving growth, resilience, and success. From crafting detailed business plans to leveraging cutting-edge digital tools, every aspect of business development hinges on a commitment to continuous improvement, strategic foresight, and a deep understanding of customer needs. These principles not only lay the foundation for a thriving enterprise but also foster innovation and adaptability in the face of challenges.

Throughout this journey, we have explored essential concepts such as stakeholder alignment, customer feedback loops, financial planning, and market trend analysis. Each of these elements plays a critical role in creating a business that is both competitive and sustainable. By integrating these practices, businesses can build stronger connections with their audiences, enhance operational efficiency, and ensure that their goals remain aligned with market realities.

However, the true power of this book lies in its focus on practical application. Success is not merely about knowledge but the ability to translate that knowledge into actionable steps. The templates, tools, and examples provided are designed to empower readers to take immediate action, whether launching a new venture, scaling an existing business, or refining internal processes. By taking a proactive approach, readers can position their businesses as forward-thinking, customer-centric, and results-driven organizations.

In closing, the journey of building and growing a business is not a destination but a continuous process of learning and evolution. By embracing the frameworks and tools shared in this book, readers are equipped to tackle uncertainties with confidence, seize opportunities with clarity, and lead their businesses toward a future of sustained success. Let this be a roadmap not only for profitability but also for creating meaningful impact in the markets and communities they serve.

P.S. There is an extensive list of tools near the back of this book that will keep you up-to-date and prepared.

Chapter 10: Worksheets and Templates

Worksheet 1: Business Plan Overview

Business Name and Vision

1. **Business Name:** _____
2. **Tagline or Slogan:** _____
3. **Mission Statement:** What is the purpose of your business?
   - Example: "To create high-quality, sustainable skincare that promotes self-care and eco-conscious living."
   - Your Mission: _____
4. **Vision Statement:** What does success look like in 5 years?
   - Example: "To become the leading brand for organic skincare products in the region."
   - Your Vision: _____

Goals and Objectives

Goal	Timeline	Measure of Success
Example: Launch a product line	6 months	3 products available on the website

Worksheet 2: Market Analysis

Target Market

1. Who is your ideal customer?

    - Age Range: _____
    - Gender (if applicable): _____
    - Location: _____
    - Interests/Values: _____

2. What problem does your product/service solve?

    - Problem: _____
    - Solution: _____

3. Who are your competitors?

    - Competitor 1: _____
    - Competitor 2: _____
    - What sets you apart from these competitors? _____

Worksheet 3: Products or Services

Product/Service Details

Product/Service Name	Description	Price	Unique Selling Point (USP)
Example: Rose Facial Oil	Organic oil for hydration	$25.00	100% organic, sustainable
_____	_____	_____	_____
_____	_____	_____	_____
_____	_____	_____	_____

Revenue Model

1. How will you generate income?
    - Example: Direct sales, subscriptions, wholesale partnerships.
    - Revenue Streams: _____

Worksheet 4: Marketing and Branding

Marketing Strategy

Channel	Action	Frequency
Social Media	Post 3x weekly on Instagram and Facebook	Weekly
Email Marketing	Send monthly newsletters with promotions	Monthly
Influencer Outreach	Partner with 3 influencers in your niche	Quarterly

Brand Identity

1. What are your brand values? (e.g., eco-friendly, innovative, affordable)

    ○ Values: _____
2. What is your brand voice? (e.g., casual, professional, friendly)

    ○ Voice: _____
3. Design Elements:

    ○ Logo: _____
    ○ Color Scheme: _____
    ○ Fonts/Style: _____

Worksheet 5: Operations Plan

Production/Service Workflow

Step	Who is Responsible	Resources Needed
Example: Source Materials	Owner	Local supplier contracts

Inventory Management

Product/Material	Current Stock	Reorder Level	Supplier
Example: Lavender Oil	20 bottles	10 bottles	Local Farms Co.

Worksheet 6: Financial Plan

Startup Costs

Expense	Amount
Equipment	$
Raw Materials	$
Marketing	$
Website Design	$
Legal/Registration Fees	$
	$
Total	$

Revenue Projections

Month	Projected Sales	Projected Expenses	Profit/Loss
January	$	$	$
February	$	$	$

Worksheet 7: Tracking and Adaptation

Milestone Tracker

Milestone	Target Date	Progress Notes

Example: Launch Website	April 1	Content uploaded, testing phase

Feedback and Adjustment

1. What feedback have you received from customers?

    ○ Feedback: _____

2. What adjustments will you make to improve?

    ○ Adjustments: _____

Example Business Plan: Lisa's Gourmet Bakery

Executive Summary

Lisa's Gourmet Bakery specializes in handcrafted, organic baked goods, offering a range of cookies, pastries, and bread made from locally sourced ingredients. Our target market includes health-conscious individuals and families seeking high-quality, preservative-free baked goods. We aim to generate $100,000 in revenue in our first year and expand to three additional farmers 'markets within two years.

Business Description

- **Business Name**: Lisa's Gourmet Bakery
- **Tagline**: "From Our Oven to Your Table – Always Fresh, Always Natural."
- **Mission Statement**: To provide delicious, high-quality baked goods made with love and the finest organic ingredients.
- **Vision Statement**: To become a leading brand for organic baked goods in the region, known for taste, quality, and sustainability.

Market Analysis

Target Market:

- Primary: Health-conscious women aged 25-45.
- Secondary: Families seeking healthy snack options for kids.

Competitor Analysis:

Competitor	Strengths	Weaknesses
Sarah's Sweets	Large variety of baked goods	Uses artificial ingredients
Healthy Bakes Co.	Strong focus on organic options	Higher prices, limited customization

Market Opportunity:

- Growing demand for organic and preservative-free products.
- Increasing consumer preference for locally sourced goods.

Products and Services

Product	Description	Price
Classic Sourdough Loaf	Organic, slow-fermented sourdough bread	$10.00
Chocolate Chip Cookies	Soft, chewy cookies made with dark chocolate	$15.00 (12-pack)
Lemon Poppyseed Muffins	Light, zesty muffins with organic ingredients	$18.00 (6-pack)

Unique Selling Proposition: All products are handcrafted, organic, and made with locally sourced ingredients. Custom orders are available for special occasions.

Marketing and Sales Strategy

Marketing Channels:

- **Social Media**: Instagram, Facebook, and TikTok for product highlights, customer testimonials, and live baking sessions.
- **Local Markets**: Weekly stalls at two popular farmers 'markets.

- **Email Marketing**: Monthly newsletters with product updates and seasonal promotions.

Sales Strategy:

- Offer free samples at farmers' markets to attract new customers.
- Launch an online store with nationwide shipping.
- Partner with local cafes and organic food stores to stock our baked goods.

Operations Plan

Production Workflow:

1. Source organic ingredients from local farms every Monday.
2. Bake products in a certified commercial kitchen.
3. Package baked goods in eco-friendly, biodegradable materials.

Inventory Management:

Ingredient	Current Stock	Reorder Point	Supplier
Organic Flour	50 lbs	20 lbs	Local Grains Co.
Dark Chocolate	20 lbs	5 lbs	Chocolate Farms Direct

Financial Plan

Startup Costs:

Expense	Amount
Kitchen Equipment	$5,000
Ingredients	$1,500
Marketing Materials	$2,000
Legal and Licensing	$1,000
Total	$9,500

Revenue Projections:

Month	Projected Sales	Projected Expenses	Profit/Loss
January	$8,000	$4,000	$4,000
February	$10,000	$5,000	$5,000

Growth Plan

1. **Year 1**: Establish a presence in two farmers 'markets and launch an online store.
2. **Year 2**: Expand to three additional markets and introduce catering services.
3. **Year 3**: Open a flagship bakery location.

Business Plan Templates

Business Plan Structure Template

This template provides a detailed outline for drafting a comprehensive business plan, helping you define your goals, evaluate your market, and map out strategies for success.

1. Executive Summary

Purpose: A concise overview of your business plan. This section is typically written last but appears first in the plan.
Key Elements:

- Business Name, Location, and Mission Statement.
- Description of your product or service.
- Summary of market opportunity and competitive advantage.
- Key financial goals (e.g., revenue targets, funding requirements).
- Vision for the future.

Example: "Our company, EcoBake, produces sustainable, eco-friendly baking supplies. Our mission is to reduce waste in the baking industry by providing compostable and reusable products. With a growing demand for environmentally conscious goods, we aim to achieve $500,000 in annual revenue within three years."

2. Business Description

Purpose: Provide detailed information about your business, including its structure and purpose.
Key Elements:

- Legal structure (e.g., sole proprietorship, LLC, corporation).
- History and background of the business or founder.
- Core mission, vision, and values.
- Unique selling proposition (USP).

Example: "EcoBake was founded in 2023 to address the environmental impact of disposable baking tools. Our innovative product line includes compostable parchment paper and silicone baking mats designed for eco-conscious bakers."

3. Market Analysis

Purpose: Demonstrate your understanding of the market and target audience.
Key Elements:

- **Industry Overview**: Current trends, growth potential, and market size.
- **Target Market**: Detailed description of your ideal customers (demographics, behaviors, needs).
- **Competitive Analysis**:
    - Competitors 'strengths and weaknesses.
    - Your competitive advantage.

Example: "Demand for sustainable kitchen products is projected to grow by 20% annually. Our target market includes eco-conscious consumers aged 25-45 who value sustainability and are willing to invest in quality kitchenware."

4. Products and Services

Purpose: Describe what your business offers and how it fulfills customer needs.
Key Elements:

- Description of products or services.
- Unique features and benefits.
- Product lifecycle or future development plans.
- Pricing strategy.

Example: "Our flagship product is a reusable silicone baking mat designed to replace single-use parchment paper. It's heat-resistant, durable, and easy to clean, offering an affordable alternative for eco-conscious bakers."

5. Marketing and Sales Strategy

Purpose: Outline how you will attract and retain customers.
Key Elements:

- **Marketing Plan**: Channels and tactics (e.g., social media, email marketing, influencer partnerships).
- **Sales Strategy**:
    - Sales funnel or process.

- - Customer retention and loyalty programs.
- Branding and messaging.

Example: "We plan to utilize Instagram and TikTok influencers to showcase our products. Additionally, we'll offer a subscription service for recurring customers, providing discounts on bulk orders."

6. Operations Plan

Purpose: Explain the logistics of running your business.
Key Elements:

- Location and facilities.
- Production processes or supply chain management.
- Technology and tools used.
- Key partnerships or suppliers.

Example: "Our production facility in Austin, Texas, sources materials from certified sustainable vendors. We use automated machinery to streamline production, ensuring consistent quality and minimizing waste."

7. Financial Plan

Purpose: Provide a clear picture of your business's financial health and projections.
Key Elements:

- **Startup Costs**: Initial investments needed to launch the business.
- **Financial Projections**:
  - Income statement (revenue, expenses, profit).
  - Cash flow statement.
  - Break-even analysis.
- **Funding Requirements**:
  - How much funding do you need?
  - How funds will be used.
  - Expected ROI for investors.

Example: "We seek $100,000 in seed funding to cover production equipment ($50,000), marketing expenses ($30,000), and initial inventory ($20,000). We project $250,000 in revenue by the second year, achieving profitability within 18 months."

8. Risk Analysis

Purpose: Identify potential challenges and outline mitigation strategies.
Key Elements:

- Operational risks (e.g., supply chain disruptions).
- Market risks (e.g., changing customer preferences).
- Financial risks (e.g., cash flow shortages).

- Contingency plans.

Example: "To address potential supply chain disruptions, we have partnered with multiple suppliers. Additionally, we maintain a 90-day inventory buffer to ensure uninterrupted operations."

9. Appendix

Purpose: Include supporting documents and additional information.
Key Elements:

- Resumes of key team members.
- Detailed market research data.
- Product photos or prototypes.
- Legal documents (e.g., business licenses, contracts).

Tips for Writing Your Business Plan

1. **Be Clear and Concise**: Use simple language to convey your ideas.
2. **Use Visuals**: Include charts, graphs, and tables to illustrate financial projections and market trends.
3. **Customize for the Audience**: Tailor the plan for investors, partners, or internal use.
4. **Review and Revise**: Regularly update the plan to reflect changes in the market or your business.

This business plan template ensures you cover all critical aspects of your venture, providing a solid foundation for success.

Business Plan Workbook Template

This workbook is designed to help you create a detailed business plan for your venture. Each section contains prompts and tables to guide you through the process.

Section 1: Executive Summary

- **Business Name**: _____
- **Tagline**: _____
- **Mission Statement**: What is the purpose of your business?

- Example: "To create high-quality, sustainable skincare that promotes self-care and eco-conscious living."

- Your Mission: _____

- **Vision Statement**: What does success look like in 5 years?

  - Example: "To become the leading brand for organic skincare products in the region."

  - Your Vision: _____

Section 2: Business Description

1. **What problem does your business solve?**

   - Problem: _____

   - Solution: _____

2. **Key Features of Your Business**:

   - What makes your business unique? _____

   - What value do you provide to your customers? _____

3. **Goals and Objectives**:
   | Goal | Timeline | Measure of Success |

4. Example: Launch a website | 3 months | Website live and taking orders |
   _____ | _____ | _____ |
   _____ | _____ | _____ |

Section 3: Market Analysis

Target Market

- **Who is your ideal customer?**

- Age Range: _____
- Gender (if applicable): _____
- Location: _____
- Interests/Values: _____

- **Competitor Analysis:**

Competitor	Strengths	Weaknesses

Section 4: Products and Services

Product/Service Details

Product/Service Name	Description	Price

Revenue Model

- How will you generate income?
  - Example: Direct sales, subscriptions, wholesale partnerships.
  - Revenue Streams: _____

Section 5: Marketing and Sales Strategy

Marketing Channels

Channel	Action	Frequency
Social Media	Post 3x weekly on Instagram and Facebook	Weekly

Email Marketing	Send monthly newsletters with promotions	Monthly
Influencer Outreach	Partner with influencers in your niche	Quarterly

Brand Identity

- What are your brand values? (e.g., eco-friendly, innovative, affordable)
    - Values: _____
- What is your brand voice? (e.g., casual, professional, friendly)
    - Voice: _____

Section 6: Operations Plan

Production Workflow

Step	Who is Responsible	Resources Needed

Inventory Management

Product/Material	Current Stock	Reorder Level	Supplier

Section 7: Financial Plan

Startup Costs

Expense	Amount

	$
	$
	$
Total	$

Revenue Projections

Month	Projected Sales	Projected Expenses	Profit/Loss
	$	$	$
	$	$	$

Section 8: Tracking and Adaptation

Milestone Tracker

Milestone	Target Date	Progress Notes

Feedback and Adjustment

1. What feedback have you received from customers?

    ○ Feedback: _____

2. What adjustments will you make to improve?

    ○ Adjustments: _____

This workbook provides a structured way to develop your business plan. Complete each section thoroughly and revisit it regularly to update and refine your plan as your business grows.

Tools Used or Suggested in the Book

SWOT Analysis

A SWOT analysis is a strategic planning tool used to evaluate the **Strengths**, **Weaknesses**, **Opportunities**, and **Threats** related to a business, project, or venture. By analyzing these four aspects, businesses can make informed decisions, identify areas for improvement, and plan for potential challenges.

1. Strengths

Strengths are internal factors that give the business an advantage over competitors. These are the areas where the business excels.

Examples:

- Unique products or services.
- Loyal customer base.
- Strong brand reputation.
- Skilled and experienced workforce.
- Efficient processes or technologies.

Questions to Identify Strengths:

- What does your business do well?
- What resources or assets give you an advantage?
- What positive feedback have you received from customers?

2. Weaknesses

Weaknesses are internal factors that place the business at a disadvantage. These are areas that need improvement to stay competitive.

Examples:

- Limited financial resources.
- Lack of online presence or marketing strategy.
- Inefficient operations or outdated technology.
- Gaps in skills or expertise.
- Inconsistent customer service.

Questions to Identify Weaknesses:

- What are the main complaints from customers?
- Where do you lack resources or expertise?
- Which processes or practices are inefficient?

3. Opportunities

Opportunities are external factors that the business can exploit for growth, profitability, or competitive advantage.

Examples:

- Emerging market trends.
- Untapped customer segments.
- Advances in technology can improve efficiency.
- Expansion into new regions or markets.
- Collaborations or partnerships.

Questions to Identify Opportunities:

- What market trends or changes can you leverage?
- Are there unmet needs in your target market?
- Are competitors failing to address certain customer demands?

4. Threats

Threats are external factors that could pose challenges or risks to the business.

Examples:

- Increasing competition.
- Economic downturns or market instability.
- Changes in regulations or compliance requirements.
- Shifting consumer preferences.
- Supply chain disruptions.

Questions to Identify Threats:

- What external factors could harm your business?
- Are there new competitors entering your market?

- How might economic or regulatory changes affect you?

Using SWOT Analysis

Once you've identified strengths, weaknesses, opportunities, and threats, use the findings to make strategic decisions:

1. **Leverage Strengths**: Focus on areas where your business excels to gain a competitive edge.

    - Example: If you have a strong social media presence, use it to engage more customers.

2. **Address Weaknesses**: Develop action plans to improve internal shortcomings.

    - Example: Invest in staff training to overcome skill gaps.

3. **Capitalize on Opportunities**: Take proactive steps to exploit external opportunities.

    - Example: Launch a new product that aligns with an emerging trend.

4. **Mitigate Threats**: Develop contingency plans to reduce the impact of potential risks.

    - Example: Diversify your supply chain to avoid disruptions.

A SWOT analysis is a valuable tool to regularly assess your business environment and adapt strategies for sustained growth and success.

Self-Assessment Quiz

- A structured quiz to determine if your motivation

SMART Goal Setting Framework

The SMART framework is a proven method for setting clear and actionable goals that drive results. By ensuring your goals are Specific, Measurable, Achievable, Relevant, and Time-bound, you can create a roadmap for success and maintain focus on what truly matters.

1. Specific

A goal must be clear and precise, answering the question: Who? What? Where? Why?

Characteristics:

- Clearly defines the objective.
- Avoids vague or ambiguous language.
- Focuses on one key area.

Examples:

- Vague: "Increase sales."
- SMART: "Increase monthly sales revenue by 15% through targeted digital marketing campaigns."

2. Measurable

A goal should have criteria to track progress and measure success.

Characteristics:

- Includes specific numbers or indicators.
- Allows for tracking performance over time.
- Helps evaluate whether the goal has been achieved.

Examples:

- Vague: "Get more customers."
- SMART: "Acquire 50 new customers within the next three months."

3. Achievable

A goal should be realistic and attainable, considering available resources and constraints.

Characteristics:

- Stretches your abilities but remains within reach.
- Accounts for current capabilities, skills, and budget.
- Avoids overly ambitious or unrealistic expectations.

Examples:

- Unrealistic: "Double revenue in one month with no additional resources."
- SMART: "Increase revenue by 20% over the next quarter by expanding product offerings and implementing targeted advertising."

4. Relevant

A goal must align with your overall mission, values, and long-term objectives.

Characteristics:

- Directly contributes to the business's core objectives.
- Addresses current priorities and market opportunities.
- Avoids distractions from unrelated activities.

Examples:

- Misaligned: "Launch a clothing line when the core business is selling software."
- SMART: "Develop a mobile app that complements our existing software suite within six months."

5. Time-Bound

A goal needs a deadline to create urgency and maintain accountability.

Characteristics:

- Includes a specific timeframe or deadline.
- Encourages consistent progress and focus.
- Prevents procrastination or indefinite delays.

Examples:

- Open-ended: "Improve customer service."
- SMART: "Reduce customer complaint resolution time to 24 hours by the end of the next quarter."

Putting It All Together: SMART Goal Example

Goal:
"Acquire 200 new email subscribers by implementing a lead magnet campaign on the website within the next 60 days."

Analysis:

- **Specific**: Focuses on acquiring email subscribers.
- **Measurable**: Set a target of 200 new subscribers.
- **Achievable**: The campaign is realistic, given current resources.
- **Relevant**: Supports the business's goal of growing its audience and engagement.
- **Time-Bound**: Has a 60-day deadline.

Benefits of SMART Goals

- **Clarity**: Breaks down vague aspirations into actionable objectives.
- **Focus**: Prioritizes efforts on what's important.
- **Motivation**: Creates tangible milestones to strive for.
- **Accountability**: Establishes criteria for evaluating progress.
- **Efficiency**: Encourages time-sensitive action and prevents wasted effort.

Tips for Effective SMART Goal Setting

1. **Write Down Your Goals**: Documenting goals increases commitment.
2. **Review Progress Regularly**: Set intervals to evaluate progress and adjust as needed.
3. **Engage Your Team**: Involve stakeholders to ensure alignment and buy-in.
4. **Stay Flexible**: Adapt goals if circumstances change, but keep the SMART framework in mind.

By applying the SMART framework, you can transform broad ambitions into actionable steps, ensuring steady progress toward your business or personal success.

Financial Forecasting Tools

Financial forecasting tools help businesses project future financial performance, providing insights into cash flow, profitability, and return on investment (ROI). These tools are essential for making informed decisions, securing funding, and managing resources effectively. Below is a breakdown of key tools for financial forecasting.

1. Cash Flow Projection Tools

Cash flow projection tools estimate the inflow and outflow of money over a specific period, helping businesses manage liquidity and avoid shortages.

Purpose:

- Track expected income from sales, investments, or loans.
- Forecast expenses such as payroll, rent, and utilities.
- Identify potential cash shortfalls.

Examples:

- **Spreadsheet Software**: Create custom cash flow models using Excel or Google Sheets.
    - Template: Monthly Cash Flow Statement.
- **Accounting Software**: Tools like QuickBooks and Xero provide built-in cash flow forecasting features.

- **Dedicated Platforms**: Float and Pulse specialize in real-time cash flow management and forecasting.

2. Break-Even Analysis Tools

Break-even analysis helps determine when a business will cover its costs and start generating profit.

Purpose:

- Calculate the sales volume needed to cover fixed and variable costs.
- Set pricing strategies and evaluate cost structures.
- Assess the financial viability of new products or services.

Examples:

- **Break-Even Calculators**: Online calculators (e.g., SCORE's Break-Even Calculator) for quick estimates.
- **Spreadsheets**: Build a break-even model with variables like fixed costs, variable costs, and price per unit.
    - Example Formula: Break-Even Point = Fixed Costs ÷ (Price per Unit - Variable Cost per Unit).
- **Business Planning Software**: Platforms like LivePlan include break-even analysis features.

3. ROI Calculation Tools

ROI (Return on Investment) tools measure the profitability of investments, such as marketing campaigns, product launches, or capital expenses.

Purpose:

- Evaluate the efficiency of investments.
- Compare potential opportunities to allocate resources effectively.
- Justify expenditures to stakeholders.

Examples:

- **ROI Formula**: ROI = (Net Profit ÷ Investment Cost) × 100%.
- **Marketing ROI Tools**: Platforms like HubSpot and Google Analytics help calculate ROI for marketing campaigns.
- **Project Management Software**: Tools like Asana and Monday.com include financial tracking for project ROI.

4. Budgeting and Expense Management Tools

These tools help plan and control business expenses, ensuring resources are allocated effectively.

Purpose:

- Create detailed budgets for different departments or projects.
- Track actual expenses against forecasts.
- Identify areas for cost-saving.

Examples:

- **Budgeting Software**: QuickBooks, FreshBooks, and Mint.
- **Expense Tracking Apps**: Expensify and Zoho Expense for managing business spending.
- **Custom Templates**: Build a budget forecast in Excel or Google Sheets.

5. Financial Dashboard Tools

Financial dashboards provide a visual overview of key financial metrics, including cash flow, expenses, revenue, and profitability.

Purpose:

- Centralize financial data for easy analysis.
- Track progress against financial goals.
- Provide insights for strategic decisions.

Examples:

- **Cloud-Based Dashboards**: Platforms like Fathom, Spotlight Reporting, and Tableau offer customizable financial dashboards.
- **Integrated Accounting Tools**: Many accounting platforms (e.g., QuickBooks, Xero) include dashboard features.

6. Scenario Planning and Sensitivity Analysis Tools

Scenario planning tools allow businesses to simulate different financial outcomes based on various assumptions.

Purpose:

- Prepare for best-case, worst-case, and most-likely scenarios.
- Test the impact of changes in sales, expenses, or market conditions.
- Make data-driven decisions under uncertainty.

Examples:

- **Excel Models**: Build dynamic spreadsheets with "what-if" scenarios.
- **Dedicated Tools**: PlanGuru and Quantrix specialize in scenario modeling and sensitivity analysis.

How to Choose the Right Tool

1. **Business Size**: Small businesses may prefer simple spreadsheets, while larger companies benefit from advanced software.
2. **Complexity**: Choose tools that match your financial forecasting needs (e.g., cash flow only vs. comprehensive forecasting).
3. **Integration**: Opt for tools that integrate with your existing accounting or project management systems.
4. **Budget**: Free templates and calculators work for startups, while paid tools offer scalability and additional features.

Benefits of Financial Forecasting Tools

- **Informed Decision-Making**: Predict outcomes and allocate resources effectively.
- **Improved Cash Management**: Avoid cash flow shortages by planning.
- **Strategic Planning**: Align financial goals with operational strategies.
- **Stakeholder Confidence**: Provide clear, data-driven insights to investors or partners.

By using these tools, businesses can gain greater control over their financial future, enhance profitability, and build a strong foundation for long-term growth.

Customer Surveys: Collecting Feedback to Refine Your Business

Customer surveys are a powerful tool for gathering insights from your target audience. They help businesses understand customer needs, preferences, and pain points, enabling them to refine products, services, and overall strategies. Here's a comprehensive guide to designing and implementing effective customer surveys.

Why Use Customer Surveys?

1. **Understand Customer Needs**: Learn what your customers want and expect from your business.
2. **Refine Products and Services**: Use feedback to improve offerings and increase customer satisfaction.
3. **Identify Trends**: Detect patterns in customer behavior or preferences.
4. **Boost Engagement**: Show customers you value their opinions, fostering loyalty.
5. **Evaluate Performance**: Assess the effectiveness of your business strategies and initiatives.

Types of Customer Surveys

1. **Product Feedback Surveys**
   - Gather opinions on specific products or features.
   - Example Questions:
     - "How satisfied are you with [Product]?"
     - "What features would you like to see in future updates?"
2. **Customer Satisfaction (CSAT) Surveys**
   - Measure overall satisfaction with your business or a specific interaction.
   - Example Question:
     - "On a scale of 1-10, how satisfied are you with your recent purchase?"
3. **Net Promoter Score (NPS) Surveys**
   - Assess customer loyalty by asking how likely they are to recommend your business.
   - Example Question:
     - "How likely are you to recommend [Business] to a friend or colleague?"
     - Follow-Up: "What is the main reason for your score?"
4. **Market Research Surveys**
   - Understand customer demographics, preferences, and purchasing behavior.
   - Example Questions:
     - "What factors influence your purchasing decisions?"
     - "Which competitors 'products do you use?"
5. **Post-Purchase Surveys**
   - Evaluate the customer experience immediately after a transaction.
   - Example Questions:
     - "Was the checkout process easy to navigate?"
     - "Did your product meet your expectations?"

Steps to Create an Effective Customer Survey

1. **Define Your Objectives**
   - Be clear about what you want to learn.

- Example Objective: "Understand why customers abandon their shopping carts."

2. **Choose the Right Format**

    - Decide on the survey method:
        - **Online Surveys**: Tools like Google Forms, SurveyMonkey, or Typeform.
        - **Email Surveys**: Sent directly to customers.
        - **In-App or On-Site Surveys**: Embedded in websites or apps.
        - **Phone or In-Person Surveys**: For more detailed, qualitative insights.

3. **Keep It Short and Focused**

    - Limit surveys to 5-10 questions to maintain engagement.
    - Ask only essential questions that align with your objectives.

4. **Use a Mix of Question Types**

    - **Closed-Ended Questions**: Provide specific options (e.g., multiple choice, Likert scale).
    - **Open-Ended Questions**: Allow for detailed responses.
    - **Rating Scales**: Assess satisfaction or likelihood (e.g., 1-10).
    - **Yes/No Questions**: Quickly gather binary data.

5. **Pilot Test the Survey**

    - Share with a small group to ensure clarity and functionality before wider distribution.

6. **Distribute the Survey**

    - Send via email or social media, or integrate it into your website or app.
    - Offer incentives, such as discounts or free samples, to encourage participation.

7. **Analyze the Results**

    - Use data analysis tools to identify trends, pain points, and actionable insights.
    - Segment responses by demographics or other criteria for deeper understanding.

8. **Act on Feedback**

    - Prioritize key findings and implement changes to address customer needs.

- Communicate improvements to show customers their input matters.

Example Customer Survey Questions

1. **Product-Specific Questions**:
   - "What do you like most about [Product]?"
   - "How can we improve this product?"
2. **Experience Questions**:
   - "How would you rate your overall experience with [Business]?"
   - "Was our customer service helpful?"
3. **Demographic Questions**:
   - "What is your age range?"
   - "Where are you located?"
4. **Behavioral Questions**:
   - "How often do you purchase from us?"
   - "What motivates you to choose our products over competitors?"

Best Practices for Customer Surveys

1. **Be Respectful of Time**: Make surveys short and easy to complete.
2. **Ensure Anonymity**: Allow respondents to provide honest feedback without fear of repercussions.
3. **Personalize the Experience**: Use the customer's name or reference recent interactions when possible.
4. **Follow Up**: Thank participants and, if applicable, share how their feedback is being used.

Benefits of Using Customer Surveys

- **Enhanced Customer Satisfaction**: Identify and address areas for improvement.
- **Improved Products and Services**: Tailor offerings to better meet customer needs.
- **Data-Driven Decisions**: Use insights to guide business strategies.
- **Increased Customer Loyalty**: Show customers their input matters, strengthening trust and relationships.

By leveraging customer surveys effectively, businesses can stay attuned to their audience's needs, adapt strategies, and foster growth.

- **Indirect Competitors**: Businesses that provide alternative solutions to the same problem but target different customer needs.
- **Emerging Competitors**: New players entering the market with the potential to disrupt.

Methods to Identify Competitors:

- Online search for similar businesses in your industry.
- Customer feedback and surveys about alternative options.
- Industry reports and market research studies.

Example:
For a sustainable fashion brand, direct competitors are other eco-friendly clothing brands, while indirect competitors might include second-hand stores or fast-fashion brands.

2. Gather Information

Collect data on your competitors to understand their market positioning and strategies.

Key Data Points:

- **Products and Services**: Range, quality, pricing, and unique features.
- **Market Position**: Target audience, branding, and reputation.
- **Marketing Strategies**: Channels used (e.g., social media, email, events) and messaging.
- **Financial Performance**: Revenue estimates, market share, and growth trends.
- **Customer Feedback**: Reviews, ratings, and testimonials to identify strengths and weaknesses.
- **Technology and Operations**: Innovations, tools, and processes that enhance efficiency.

Sources for Data:

- Competitor websites, blogs, and press releases.
- Social media channels and online reviews.
- Tools like SEMrush, SpyFu, and SimilarWeb for digital insights.
- Industry events, trade shows, and networking.

3. Analyze Strengths and Weaknesses

Evaluate what competitors do well and where they fall short.

Strengths:

- What are they known for?
- What unique value do they provide?
- What customer needs are they effectively addressing?

Weaknesses:

- Where do they receive criticism or complaints?
- What gaps exist in their offerings?
- Are there inefficiencies in their operations or delivery?

Example:
A competitor might excel in customer service but have higher prices, creating an opportunity for you to compete on affordability.

4. Evaluate Market Positioning

Understand how competitors differentiate themselves and appeal to their target audience.

Key Questions:

- What is their unique selling proposition (USP)?
- How do they position themselves in terms of price, quality, or innovation?
- What demographics or psychographics do they target?

Example:
A competitor might market itself as a luxury brand, targeting high-income professionals, while your brand could focus on affordability and sustainability for eco-conscious millennials.

5. Compare Marketing and Sales Strategies

Assess how competitors attract and retain customers.

Focus Areas:

- **Marketing Channels**: Which platforms are they active on (e.g., social media, PPC ads, email campaigns)?
- **Customer Engagement**: Do they use loyalty programs, discounts, or personalized offers?
- **Content Strategy**: Analyze blogs, videos, and other content for style and effectiveness.

Example:
If a competitor relies heavily on Instagram ads, you could explore alternative channels like TikTok or partnerships with micro-influencers.

6. Identify Opportunities and Threats

Use your analysis to uncover opportunities for differentiation and assess potential threats.

Opportunities:

- Address unmet customer needs.
- Develop products or services that competitors lack.
- Capitalize on market segments that competitors overlook.

Threats:

- New competitors are entering the market.
- Innovations that may disrupt the industry.
- Shifting customer preferences toward a competitor's offering.

Example:

If customer reviews show dissatisfaction with a competitor's delivery times, you could focus on offering faster, more reliable shipping.

Competitor Analysis Tools

- **SWOT Analysis**: Identify strengths, weaknesses, opportunities, and threats for each competitor.
- **Benchmarking**: Compare your performance metrics (e.g., pricing, customer acquisition rate) with competitors.
- **Porter's Five Forces**: Evaluate competitive forces in your industry, including the threat of substitutes and the bargaining power of buyers and suppliers.
- **Digital Tools**:
    - **SEMrush or Ahrefs**: Analyze competitors 'online traffic and keywords.
    - **Social Mention**: Track competitor mentions on social media.
    - **Glassdoor**: Review employee feedback for insights into company culture and operations.

Competitor Analysis Template

Category	Competitor A	Competitor B	Your Business
Products/Services	High-quality, premium pricing	Wide range, budget-friendly	Sustainable, mid-tier pricing
Target Market	Affluent professionals	Budget-conscious families	Eco-conscious millennials

Marketing Channels	Instagram, email marketing	Facebook, local events	TikTok, influencer partnerships
Strengths	Strong brand reputation	Low prices	Sustainability focus
Weaknesses	Limited product variety	Poor customer service	Smaller online presence

Benefits of Competitor Analysis

1. **Strategic Differentiation**: Identify ways to stand out in the market.
2. **Improved Decision-Making**: Base strategies on data, not assumptions.
3. **Enhanced Customer Understanding**: Learn what customers value from competitors.
4. **Proactive Risk Management**: Prepare for potential competitive threats.

By following this framework, you can gain a comprehensive understanding of your competitors and leverage this knowledge to strengthen your market position and drive growth.

Market Research Platforms

Market research platforms are invaluable tools for gathering insights into industry trends, customer behavior, competitive landscapes, and market opportunities. By leveraging these platforms, businesses can make informed decisions, identify opportunities, and refine strategies.

Top Market Research Platforms

1. Google Trends

- **Purpose**: Analyze search trends over time to identify popular topics, seasonal demand, and geographic interest.
- **Key Features**:
    - Track the popularity of keywords or topics.
    - Compare search interest across regions and periods.
    - Identify seasonal trends for product launches or marketing campaigns.
- **Use Case**:
    - A clothing brand uses Google Trends to determine the peak interest in "summer dresses" to align with marketing efforts.

Website: Google Trends

2. Statista

- **Purpose**: Access comprehensive statistics and industry reports on a wide range of markets.
- **Key Features**:
    - Industry insights and market forecasts.
    - Consumer and business behavior analysis.
    - Global and regional data across various sectors.
- **Use Case**:
    - A technology company uses Statista to research global smartphone adoption rates for product planning.

Website: Statista

3. NielsenIQ

- **Purpose**: Understand consumer behavior, market trends, and product performance.
- **Key Features**:
    - Retail and consumer insights.
    - Performance tracking for products and services.
    - Advanced analytics for market segmentation.
- **Use Case**:
    - A food brand utilizes NielsenIQ to analyze retail sales data and identify high-performing products.

Website: NielsenIQ

4. SEMrush

- **Purpose**: Gain insights into competitors' online strategies and market performance.
- **Key Features**:
    - Traffic analysis for competitor websites.
    - Keyword research for SEO and PPC campaigns.
    - Market trends and content gap analysis.
- **Use Case**:
    - A digital marketing agency uses SEMrush to identify keyword opportunities for a client's content strategy.

Website: SEMrush

5. IBISWorld

- **Purpose**: Access detailed industry research and market analysis reports.
- **Key Features**:

- Comprehensive industry reports with key data and forecasts.
- Competitive landscape analysis.
- Market size and growth trends.
- **Use Case**:
  - A startup uses IBISWorld to analyze the fitness equipment industry for market entry planning.

Website: IBISWorld

6. SurveyMonkey

- **Purpose**: Collect direct feedback from target audiences through customizable surveys.
- **Key Features**:
  - Create and distribute online surveys.
  - Analyze customer preferences and behaviors.
  - Gather insights on product or service satisfaction.
- **Use Case**:
  - A software company uses SurveyMonkey to survey customers about desired features.

Website: SurveyMonkey

7. G2 and Capterra

- **Purpose**: Research customer reviews and ratings for business software and services.
- **Key Features**:
  - User reviews for software tools and platforms.
  - Comparisons of features, pricing, and usability.
  - Trends in software adoption across industries.
- **Use Case**:
  - A business evaluates CRM software options based on user feedback from G2.

Websites:

- G2
- Capterra

8. Crunchbase

- **Purpose**: Analyze business and industry trends, particularly for startups and investments.
- **Key Features**:
  - Information on companies, investors, and funding rounds.

    - Insights into industry growth and emerging players.
    - Track competitors' funding and strategic moves.
- **Use Case**:
    - An entrepreneur uses Crunchbase to study competitors' funding history and strategic partnerships.

Website: Crunchbase

9. Pew Research Center

- **Purpose**: Access social science research and trends in consumer behavior.
- **Key Features**:
    - Studies on consumer habits, preferences, and demographics.
    - Insights into societal trends affecting markets.
    - Free, data-driven reports and visualizations.
- **Use Case**:
    - A nonprofit organization uses Pew Research to understand donor behavior trends.

Website: Pew Research Center

10. Amazon Best Sellers and Reviews

- **Purpose**: Analyze consumer trends and product popularity in various categories.
- **Key Features**:
    - Top-selling products by category.
    - Insights from customer reviews and ratings.
    - Emerging product trends.
- **Use Case**:
    - A retailer uses Amazon data to identify popular products for inventory planning.

Website: Amazon Best Sellers

Choosing the Right Platform

1. **Define Your Goals**: Identify what you want to learn (e.g., customer preferences, market size, competitor performance).
2. **Consider Your Budget**: Some platforms offer free data (Google Trends, Amazon), while others require paid subscriptions (Statista, IBISWorld).
3. **Evaluate Your Needs**: Choose platforms that provide the depth and breadth of data required for your industry.

Benefits of Using Market Research Platforms

- **Informed Decision-Making**: Make data-driven choices for product development, marketing, and operations.
- **Identifying Opportunities**: Discover gaps in the market or emerging trends.
- **Understanding Competition**: Gain insights into competitors 'strategies and positioning.
- **Customer Insights**: Tailor offerings to meet the needs and preferences of your target audience.

By leveraging these platforms, businesses can stay ahead of trends, understand their markets, and refine strategies for sustained growth.

Audience Segmentation Tools

Audience segmentation tools allow businesses to divide their customers into distinct groups based on shared characteristics such as demographics, behavior, psychographics, or geographic location. This segmentation helps tailor marketing efforts, improve product offerings, and enhance customer experiences.

Types of Segmentation

1. **Demographic Segmentation**

   - Dividing customers based on age, gender, income, education, or occupation.
   - **Example**: A luxury brand targeting high-income individuals aged 30-50.

2. **Behavioral Segmentation**

   - Grouping customers by purchase behavior, product usage, or brand loyalty.
   - **Example**: Identifying frequent buyers for exclusive promotions.

3. **Psychographic Segmentation**

   - Segmenting based on lifestyle, values, attitudes, or personality traits.
   - **Example**: Marketing eco-friendly products to environmentally conscious individuals.

4. **Geographic Segmentation**

   - Dividing customers by location, such as city, region, or country.
   - **Example**: Promoting winter gear in colder climates.

5. **Technographic Segmentation**
    - Grouping customers by technology usage and preferences.
    - **Example**: Marketing to mobile-first users for app-based services.

Top Audience Segmentation Tools

1. Google Analytics

- **Purpose**: Analyze website visitors to segment audiences by behavior, location, device, and more.
- **Key Features**:
    - Demographic and geographic insights.
    - Behavior tracking (time on site, pages visited).
    - Custom audience creation for targeted campaigns.
- **Use Case**:
    - An e-commerce store segments users who abandon carts and retargets them with email offers.

Website: Google Analytics

2. HubSpot

- **Purpose**: Segment contacts and leads based on customer relationship management (CRM) data.
- **Key Features**:
    - Advanced segmentation based on lifecycle stage and engagement.
    - Create dynamic lists for targeted email campaigns.
    - Behavioral segmentation from website activity and email interactions.
- **Use Case**:
    - A SaaS company segments leads by industry and sends tailored demos to each segment.

Website: HubSpot

3. Mailchimp

- **Purpose**: Segment email subscribers for personalized email marketing campaigns.
- **Key Features**:
    - Segmentation by demographics, purchase history, and engagement.
    - Behavior-based automations.
    - A/B testing for segmented email campaigns.
- **Use Case**:

- - A retailer segments customers who purchased during a holiday sale and sends them exclusive loyalty discounts.

Website: Mailchimp

4. Salesforce Marketing Cloud

- **Purpose**: Segment customers using data from multiple sources, including CRM and purchase history.
- **Key Features**:
  - AI-powered insights for advanced segmentation.
  - Cross-channel segmentation for email, SMS, and social media campaigns.
  - Custom audience creation based on behavior and preferences.
- **Use Case**:
  - A travel company segments customers by preferred destinations and promotes tailored vacation packages.

Website: Salesforce Marketing Cloud

5. Segment (by Twilio)

- **Purpose**: Collect and unify customer data to create actionable segments.
- **Key Features**:
  - Centralized data from multiple platforms (web, app, CRM).
  - Real-time audience segmentation.
  - Integration with marketing tools for targeted campaigns.
- **Use Case**:
  - A fitness app segments users based on activity levels and sends personalized workout recommendations.

Website: Segment

6. Facebook Ads Manager

- **Purpose**: Create and manage ad campaigns using detailed audience segmentation.
- **Key Features**:
  - Segment audiences by demographics, interests, behaviors, and location.
  - Lookalike audience creation to target similar users.
  - Real-time performance tracking for segmented campaigns.
- **Use Case**:
  - A local business targets Facebook users within a 10-mile radius for a grand opening event.

Website: Facebook Ads Manager

7. Zoho CRM

- **Purpose**: Segment customer data within a CRM for targeted marketing and sales efforts.
- **Key Features**:
  - Create segments based on lead score, location, and behavior.
  - Automate follow-ups for specific segments.
  - Integrate segmentation with email and social media campaigns.
- **Use Case**:
  - A B2B company segments leads by industry size and sends personalized outreach emails.

Website: Zoho CRM

8. Tableau

- **Purpose**: Visualize and analyze customer data for segmentation insights.
- **Key Features**:
  - Customizable dashboards for detailed data analysis.
  - Geographic segmentation maps.
  - Integration with marketing and sales platforms.
- **Use Case**:
  - A retailer uses Tableau to segment customers by purchase frequency and location, optimizing inventory for regional demand.

Website: Tableau

9. Klaviyo

- **Purpose**: Segment e-commerce customers for email and SMS marketing.
- **Key Features**:
  - Advanced segmentation based on purchase behavior and lifecycle stage.
  - Predictive analytics for customer lifetime value (CLV).
  - Automated messaging for each segment.
- **Use Case**:
  - An online store segments high-value customers and sends them exclusive pre-sale access.

Website: Klaviyo

10. Nielsen Claritas

- **Purpose**: Segment audiences using demographic, behavioral, and lifestyle data.
- **Key Features**:

- PRIZM segmentation for detailed customer profiles.
- Insights into consumer preferences and purchase drivers.
- Data-driven strategies for targeting niche audiences.
- **Use Case**:
  - A car dealership uses Claritas to target eco-conscious buyers with electric vehicle promotions.

Website: Nielsen Claritas

Steps to Implement Audience Segmentation

1. **Define Goals**: Identify what you aim to achieve (e.g., improve email open rates, boost sales).
2. **Collect Data**: Use tools to gather demographic, behavioral, and psychographic data.
3. **Analyze Data**: Look for patterns and commonalities among customers.
4. **Create Segments**: Divide your audience into actionable groups based on shared characteristics.
5. **Develop Tailored Strategies**: Design marketing messages, offers, or products specific to each segment.
6. **Monitor and Optimize**: Track performance and refine segmentation over time.

Benefits of Audience Segmentation Tools

- **Personalized Marketing**: Deliver more relevant and impactful campaigns.
- **Improved ROI**: Maximize the effectiveness of marketing efforts.
- **Stronger Customer Relationships**: Address unique customer needs and preferences.
- **Better Resource Allocation**: Focus efforts on high-value segments.

By using these audience segmentation tools, businesses can unlock deeper insights into their customer base and create strategies that resonate with their target audiences, driving engagement and growth.

Milestone Timeline

A milestone timeline is a visual tool that helps businesses track and manage their short- and long-term goals. It provides a clear roadmap of tasks, deadlines, and accomplishments, enabling teams to monitor progress, maintain focus, and ensure accountability.

Purpose of a Milestone Timeline

- **Clarity**: Break down complex goals into manageable steps.
- **Accountability**: Assign responsibilities and deadlines.
- **Motivation**: Celebrate progress as milestones are achieved.
- **Adaptability**: Identify delays or challenges early and adjust plans accordingly.

Key Components of a Milestone Timeline

1. **Milestones**
   - Specific, measurable goals or checkpoints.
   - Examples: Product launch, hitting revenue targets, completing a marketing campaign.
2. **Timeframes**
   - Deadlines or specific time periods for each milestone.
   - Examples: "Q1 2024" or "by March 15, 2024."
3. **Tasks**
   - Action items are required to achieve each milestone.
   - Examples: Conduct market research, design prototypes, finalize marketing materials.
4. **Dependencies**
   - Identify tasks or milestones that rely on the completion of others.
   - Examples: Launching a website depends on completing the design phase.
5. **Stakeholders**
   - Individuals or teams responsible for completing tasks or meeting milestones.
   - Examples: Marketing team, product development team, external vendors.

Steps to Create a Milestone Timeline

1. **Define Your Goals**
   - Clearly articulate short-term and long-term goals.
   - Example: Short-term – Complete product testing by March. Long-term – Launch product by June.
2. **Identify Milestones**
   - Break down goals into smaller, actionable checkpoints.
   - Example: Finalize design → Test prototype → Prepare marketing materials → Product launch.
3. **Assign Deadlines**

- Set realistic timeframes for each milestone based on resources and complexity.
- Example: "Test prototype by February 15, 2024."

4. **Prioritize Tasks**

   - Determine the sequence of activities and identify critical dependencies.
   - Example: Marketing campaign cannot begin until the product logo is finalized.

5. **Create the Timeline**

   - Use a tool or software to visually represent milestones and deadlines.
   - Include progress indicators to show completed milestones.

6. **Track Progress**

   - Regularly update the timeline to reflect changes or completed tasks.
   - Review it during team meetings to ensure alignment.

Tools for Creating Milestone Timelines

1. **Project Management Software**:

   - **Asana**: Visual project timelines with task dependencies.
   - **Trello**: Kanban-style boards for tracking milestones.
   - **Monday.com**: Customizable timelines and progress tracking.

2. **Gantt Chart Tools**:

   - **Microsoft Project**: Comprehensive Gantt chart capabilities.
   - **Smartsheet**: Collaborative Gantt chart timelines.
   - **TeamGantt**: Easy-to-use timeline creation for milestones.

3. **Visual Design Tools**:

   - **Lucidchart**: Create custom timeline diagrams.
   - **Canva**: Design visually appealing milestone timelines.

4. **Spreadsheet Templates**:

   - Excel and Google Sheets offer templates for creating simple milestone timelines.

Example: Milestone Timeline for a Product Launch

Milestone	Deadline	Tasks	Stakeholders
Finalize product design	January 31	Complete sketches, approve prototype	Design team

Test prototype	February 15	Conduct user testing, gather feedback	Product development team
Prepare marketing plan	March 15	Design ads, finalize messaging	Marketing team
Launch pre-sales campaign	April 1	Launch website, activate email campaigns	Sales and marketing teams
Product launch	June 1	Host launch event, ship initial orders	Entire team

Benefits of a Milestone Timeline

- **Enhanced Planning**: Ensures all tasks are accounted for and scheduled effectively.
- **Improved Communication**: Provides a shared reference for all stakeholders.
- **Increased Efficiency**: Helps identify bottlenecks and avoid delays.
- **Boosted Accountability**: Keeps everyone focused on their responsibilities and deadlines.

A milestone timeline is an indispensable tool for keeping projects on track and achieving goals efficiently. Whether it's a spreadsheet, Gantt chart, or software-generated graphic, this tool ensures clear, actionable steps for your team to follow.

Key Performance Indicators (KPIs)

Key Performance Indicators (KPIs) are measurable metrics that businesses use to evaluate success in achieving specific objectives. They provide insights into performance across various areas such as sales, customer acquisition, and operational efficiency, enabling businesses to make data-driven decisions and optimize strategies.

Types of KPIs

1. Sales KPIs

Track the effectiveness of sales strategies and overall revenue generation.

Examples:

- **Revenue Growth**: Measures the increase in revenue over a period.
  Formula: [(Current Period Revenue - Previous Period Revenue) ÷ Previous Period Revenue] × 100.
- **Sales Conversion Rate**: Percentage of leads converted into customers.
  Formula: (Number of Conversions ÷ Number of Leads) × 100.

- **Average Transaction Value (ATV)**: The average amount spent per transaction.
  Formula: Total Revenue ÷ Number of Transactions.
- **Sales Target Attainment**: Measures progress toward meeting sales goals.

2. Customer Acquisition KPIs

Evaluate the success of marketing and customer acquisition efforts.

Examples:

- **Customer Acquisition Cost (CAC)**: The cost of acquiring a new customer.
  Formula: Total Marketing and Sales Costs ÷ Number of New Customers Acquired.
- **Customer Lifetime Value (CLV)**: The total revenue a customer generates during their relationship with the business.
  Formula: (Average Purchase Value × Purchase Frequency) × Customer Lifespan.
- **Lead-to-Customer Conversion Rate**: Percentage of leads that become paying customers.
  Formula: (Number of New Customers ÷ Number of Leads) × 100.
- **Website Traffic-to-Lead Ratio**: Measures the effectiveness of a website in generating leads.
  Formula: (Number of Leads ÷ Website Visitors) × 100.

3. Operational Efficiency KPIs

Measure the efficiency of internal processes and resource utilization.

Examples:

- **Cycle Time**: The time taken to complete a specific process.
  Formula: End Time - Start Time of the Process.
- **Inventory Turnover Rate**: The number of times inventory is sold and replaced over a period.
  Formula: Cost of Goods Sold (COGS) ÷ Average Inventory.
- **Employee Productivity**: Output generated by employees relative to input.
  Formula: Total Output ÷ Total Hours Worked.
- **First Pass Yield (FPY)**: Percentage of processes completed without rework.
  Formula: (Good Units Produced ÷ Total Units Produced) × 100.

4. Customer Satisfaction and Retention KPIs

Gauge the quality of customer experience and loyalty.

Examples:

- **Net Promoter Score (NPS)**: Measures customer loyalty by asking how likely they are to recommend your business.
  Formula: Percentage of Promoters - Percentage of Detractors.
- **Customer Retention Rate**: The percentage of customers retained over a specific period.
  Formula: [(End Period Customers - New Customers) ÷ Start Period Customers] × 100.
- **Churn Rate**: The percentage of customers lost over a specific period.
  Formula: (Number of Lost Customers ÷ Total Customers) × 100.
- **Customer Satisfaction Score (CSAT)**: Measures customer satisfaction with a product or service.
  Formula: (Sum of Positive Responses ÷ Total Responses) × 100.

5. Financial KPIs

Monitor the financial health and sustainability of the business.

Examples:

- **Gross Profit Margin**: Percentage of revenue remaining after deducting the cost of goods sold (COGS).
  Formula: [(Revenue - COGS) ÷ Revenue] × 100.
- **Operating Expense Ratio (OER)**: Percentage of revenue spent on operating expenses.
  Formula: (Operating Expenses ÷ Revenue) × 100.
- **Current Ratio**: Measures liquidity by comparing current assets to current liabilities.
  Formula: Current Assets ÷ Current Liabilities.
- **Return on Investment (ROI)**: The profitability of an investment.
  Formula: (Net Profit ÷ Investment Cost) × 100.

How to Choose the Right KPIs

1. **Align with Goals**: Ensure KPIs are directly linked to your business objectives (e.g., increasing revenue, improving customer satisfaction).
2. **Be Specific and Measurable**: KPIs should be quantifiable and trackable over time.
3. **Focus on Relevance**: Select KPIs that provide actionable insights rather than just data.
4. **Ensure Achievability**: Set realistic targets based on your resources and capabilities.
5. **Time-Bound**: Define a specific timeframe for achieving KPI goals.

Tools for Tracking KPIs

1. **Google Analytics**: For website traffic, conversions, and behavior analysis.
2. **HubSpot**: For tracking sales, marketing, and customer acquisition KPIs.

3. **Tableau**: For creating visual dashboards to track multiple KPIs.
4. **QuickBooks**: For monitoring financial KPIs like profit margins and expenses.
5. **Asana or Monday.com**: For tracking operational efficiency KPIs within projects.

Benefits of Using KPIs

- **Enhanced Decision-Making**: Data-driven insights help prioritize actions.
- **Increased Accountability**: Clear metrics ensure teams stay focused on goals.
- **Improved Performance**: Regular tracking highlights areas for improvement.
- **Goal Alignment**: Keeps every part of the business aligned with overall objectives.

By selecting and monitoring the right KPIs, businesses can measure their success effectively, stay on track to achieve their goals, and adapt strategies as needed.

Operational Checklists

Operational checklists are standardized lists of tasks or procedures designed to streamline business processes, ensure consistency, and minimize errors. They help businesses maintain quality, improve efficiency, and create accountability across teams.

Why Use Operational Checklists?

1. **Consistency**: Ensure tasks are completed the same way every time, reducing variability in outcomes.
2. **Efficiency**: Save time by providing a clear step-by-step guide for recurring tasks.
3. **Accountability**: Assign responsibilities and track progress.
4. **Error Reduction**: Minimize mistakes by providing clear instructions and reminders.
5. **Training**: Serve as a resource for onboarding new employees or cross-training existing staff.

Types of Operational Checklists

1. **Daily Operations Checklist**

    - Ensures routine tasks are completed to keep the business running smoothly.
    - **Examples**:
        - Opening/closing procedures for retail stores.
        - Daily maintenance checks for equipment.

2. **Quality Control Checklist**

    - Ensures products or services meet established quality standards.
    - **Examples**:
        - Inspecting finished goods for defects.

- Verifying customer orders before delivery.

3. **Safety Checklist**

    - Promotes workplace safety and compliance with regulations.
    - Examples:
        - Fire extinguisher and alarm inspections.
        - Equipment safety checks before use.

4. **Project Management Checklist**

    - Tracks tasks and milestones within a project.
    - Examples:
        - Completing initial project planning.
        - Reviewing deliverables before deadlines.

5. **Onboarding Checklist**

    - Standardizes the process of integrating new employees into the company.
    - Examples:
        - Collecting required documents from new hires.
        - Providing training on tools and procedures.

6. **Customer Service Checklist**

    - Ensures consistent and high-quality interactions with customers.
    - Examples:
        - Responding to inquiries within a specific timeframe.
        - Following up with customers after a purchase or support interaction.

7. **Inventory Management Checklist**

    - Tracks inventory levels, orders, and stock handling.
    - Examples:
        - Checking stock levels weekly.
        - Rotating inventory to minimize spoilage.

8. **Marketing Campaign Checklist**

    - Standardizes the planning and execution of marketing efforts.
    - Examples:
        - Creating campaign assets (ads, emails, social posts).
        - Scheduling posts and monitoring performance metrics.

Steps to Create an Effective Operational Checklist

1. **Identify the Process**

    - Define the task or procedure that requires a checklist.

- Example: Daily opening tasks for a retail store.

2. **Break Down Tasks**

   - List all steps needed to complete the process.
   - Example: Unlock doors → Turn on lights → Start POS system → Check cash register float.

3. **Organize Tasks Sequentially**

   - Arrange steps in the order they should be completed.
   - Example: Perform safety checks before starting equipment.

4. **Add Clear Instructions**

   - Include details or tips to clarify tasks.
   - Example: "Ensure cash register has $200 in small bills and coins."

5. **Assign Responsibilities**

   - Specify who is responsible for each task.
   - Example: "Shift manager completes inventory count."

6. **Test the Checklist**

   - Use the checklist in real-world scenarios and make adjustments as needed.

7. **Regularly Review and Update**

   - Keep the checklist relevant by revising it when processes change.

Example: Operational Checklist for Opening a Coffee Shop

Task	Details	Assigned To
Unlock doors and turn on lights	Ensure all lights and signs are on.	Opening manager
Start coffee machines	Preheat espresso machine and grinders.	Barista
Set up the cash register	Verify float and start the POS system.	Shift manager
Check inventory levels	Ensure stock of cups, beans, and milk.	Stock supervisor
Clean tables and restock supplies	Wipe surfaces and refill condiments.	Staff assistant
Review daily specials	Display on the menu board.	Barista

Tools for Managing Checklists

1. **Digital Checklist Apps**:

- **Trello**: Organize tasks visually with drag-and-drop cards.
- **Asana**: Create and track checklists for team collaboration.
- **Monday.com**: Standardize processes with customizable templates.

2. **Project Management Software**:
   - **ClickUp**: Manage recurring checklists for projects or departments.
   - **Wrike**: Create detailed checklists with deadlines and notifications.

3. **Cloud-Based Document Tools**:
   - **Google Sheets/Docs**: Simple and collaborative checklist creation.
   - **Microsoft Excel**: Customizable spreadsheet templates for detailed tasks.

4. **Specialized Apps**:
   - **Checklist.com**: Tailored for creating and managing operational checklists.
   - **Process Street**: Ideal for building repeatable workflows with automation options.

Benefits of Operational Checklists

- **Improved Productivity**: Streamline workflows and reduce wasted time.
- **Error Reduction**: Minimize mistakes by providing step-by-step guidance.
- **Enhanced Training**: Standardized processes make onboarding new employees easier.
- **Consistent Quality**: Maintain high standards across all operations.
- **Greater Accountability**: Assign specific tasks to team members and track progress.

Operational checklists are simple but powerful tools that bring organization, efficiency, and quality to your business processes. Whether in a small team or a large organization, these checklists ensure tasks are done right every time.

Inventory Management Systems

Inventory management systems are tools designed to help businesses track stock levels, manage supplies, streamline operations, and minimize waste. These systems are crucial for ensuring that businesses maintain the right inventory levels to meet customer demand while avoiding overstocking or stockouts.

Key Features of Inventory Management Systems

1. **Real-Time Tracking**

- Monitor stock levels in real-time across multiple locations.
   - Track inventory movement (e.g., sales, returns, transfers).

2. **Stock Alerts**
   - Receive notifications for low stock levels to prevent stockouts.
   - Set reorder points and automate purchase orders.

3. **Barcode and QR Code Integration**
   - Use barcodes or QR codes for easy tracking and inventory updates.
   - Enable faster stock-taking and item identification.

4. **Inventory Forecasting**
   - Predict future stock needs based on historical sales data.
   - Plan for seasonal or promotional demand spikes.

5. **Reporting and Analytics**
   - Generate reports on stock turnover, shrinkage, and profitability.
   - Gain insights into best-selling products and slow-moving inventory.

6. **Waste Reduction**
   - Track expiration dates for perishable goods.
   - Identify overstocked or obsolete items to minimize losses.

7. **Multi-Channel Support**
   - Integrate with e-commerce platforms (e.g., Shopify, WooCommerce).
   - Sync inventory across online and physical stores.

8. **Supplier Management**
   - Manage vendor information and purchase orders in one place.
   - Track delivery schedules and order histories.

Top Inventory Management Systems

1. Zoho Inventory

- **Features**:
  - Multi-channel inventory tracking.
  - Barcode scanning and batch tracking.
  - Integration with platforms like Shopify and Amazon.
- **Best For**: Small to medium-sized businesses (SMBs).
- **Website**: Zoho Inventory

2. TradeGecko (QuickBooks Commerce)

- **Features**:

- Centralized inventory management for multiple locations.
            - Demand forecasting and customizable reporting.
            - Integration with QuickBooks, Shopify, and WooCommerce.
    - **Best For**: Growing businesses with complex inventory needs.
    - **Website**: QuickBooks Commerce

3. Fishbowl Inventory

- **Features**:
    - Barcode tracking and order management.
    - Real-time inventory updates.
    - Integration with QuickBooks and Xero for accounting.
- **Best For**: Manufacturing and warehousing businesses.
- **Website**: Fishbowl Inventory

4. Cin7

- **Features**:
    - Multi-warehouse inventory tracking.
    - Product bundling and kitting support.
    - Advanced analytics and reporting tools.
- **Best For**: Businesses with complex supply chains.
- **Website**: Cin7

5. DEAR Systems

- **Features**:
    - Centralized inventory management and reporting.
    - Batch tracking and expiration date management.
    - Integration with Xero, QuickBooks, and e-commerce platforms.
- **Best For**: Retailers, wholesalers, and manufacturers.
- **Website**: DEAR Systems

6. Square for Retail

- **Features**:
    - POS integration with inventory tracking.
    - Low-stock alerts and reorder management.
    - Sales analytics and inventory performance insights.
- **Best For**: Small businesses and retail stores.
- **Website**: Square for Retail

7. Lightspeed Retail

- **Features**:
    - Inventory tracking with multi-location support.
    - Supplier catalog integration for easy reordering.
    - Built-in reporting and analytics tools.
- **Best For**: Retail and hospitality businesses.
- **Website**: Lightspeed Retail

8. NetSuite ERP

- **Features**:
    - Advanced inventory management with real-time tracking.
    - Automation for supply chain and order management.
    - Comprehensive reporting and forecasting capabilities.
- **Best For**: Large enterprises with complex inventory needs.
- **Website**: NetSuite ERP

How to Choose the Right System

1. **Business Size and Complexity**
    - Small businesses may prefer simpler tools like Zoho Inventory or Square.
    - Larger businesses with multiple warehouses might need advanced systems like NetSuite or Cin7.
2. **Industry Needs**
    - Manufacturing businesses require tools with batch tracking and production scheduling (e.g., Fishbowl, DEAR Systems).
    - Retailers benefit from multi-channel inventory tracking (e.g., TradeGecko, Lightspeed).
3. **Integration Requirements**
    - Ensure the system integrates with existing tools like e-commerce platforms, accounting software, or POS systems.
4. **Scalability**
    - Choose a system that can grow with your business, handling increased inventory and more locations.
5. **Budget**
    - Compare pricing models (subscription vs. one-time payment) and evaluate ROI based on features.

Benefits of Inventory Management Systems

1. **Improved Accuracy**: Minimize manual errors in stock tracking.

2. **Cost Savings**: Avoid overstocking and reduce carrying costs.
3. **Enhanced Efficiency**: Streamline inventory-related processes and reduce time spent on manual tasks.
4. **Better Decision-Making**: Gain insights from data to optimize purchasing and stock levels.
5. **Increased Customer Satisfaction**: Ensure timely product availability and reduce stockouts.

Inventory management systems are essential for businesses aiming to optimize their stock control processes. By selecting the right tool, businesses can improve efficiency, reduce waste, and align inventory levels with customer demand.

Project Management Tools

Project management tools are platforms designed to help teams organize tasks, track progress, and manage milestones efficiently. These tools enhance collaboration, streamline workflows, and provide visibility into project timelines, making them essential for businesses of all sizes.

Key Features of Project Management Tools

1. **Task Management**
   - Assign tasks to team members.
   - Set due dates and track progress.
   - Create subtasks and checklists for detailed tracking.
2. **Collaboration**
   - Enable team communication through comments, file sharing, and integrations with messaging apps.
   - Provide centralized access to project updates.
3. **Milestone Tracking**
   - Define and monitor critical milestones to ensure projects stay on schedule.
   - Visualize timelines through Gantt charts or calendars.
4. **Workflow Automation**
   - Automate repetitive tasks like sending reminders or updating task statuses.
   - Customize workflows to match your team's processes.
5. **Dashboards and Reporting**

- Generate reports on project progress, team performance, and task completion rates.
- Use dashboards to view project summaries at a glance.

6. **Integration**
   - Connect with other tools like Slack, Google Workspace, or Microsoft Office for seamless workflow management.

Top Project Management Tools

1. Trello

- **Features**:
    - Visual Kanban boards for task organization.
    - Drag-and-drop functionality for easy task updates.
    - Checklists, attachments, and due dates within task cards.
- **Best For**: Simple task management and visual organization.
- **Website**: Trello

2. Asana

- **Features**:
    - Task and project management with detailed timelines.
    - Customizable workflows and automation.
    - Reporting features for tracking project progress.
- **Best For**: Teams needing robust task management and reporting.
- **Website**: Asana

3. Monday.com

- **Features**:
    - Customizable boards for task tracking and collaboration.
    - Advanced automation for workflows.
    - Visualizations including Gantt charts, calendars, and dashboards.
- **Best For**: Teams looking for flexibility and scalability.
- **Website**: Monday.com

4. ClickUp

- **Features**:
    - Comprehensive task management with multiple views (list, board, calendar).
    - Time tracking and workload management tools.
    - Extensive customization options.

- **Best For**: Teams seeking an all-in-one solution.
- **Website**: ClickUp

5. Wrike

- **Features**:
    - Real-time updates and task collaboration.
    - Advanced reporting tools and custom workflows.
    - Integration with apps like Salesforce and Microsoft Teams.
- **Best For**: Enterprise teams managing complex projects.
- **Website**: Wrike

6. Basecamp

- **Features**:
    - Simple project management with task lists, schedules, and message boards.
    - Automatic check-ins to keep the team aligned.
    - File sharing and team collaboration tools.
- **Best For**: Small teams and startups.
- **Website**: Basecamp

7. Jira

- **Features**:
    - Agile project management with Scrum and Kanban boards.
    - Backlog management and sprint tracking.
    - Advanced reporting and integration with development tools.
- **Best For**: Software development teams using Agile methodologies.
- **Website**: Jira

8. Smartsheet

- **Features**:
    - Spreadsheet-style project management with automation features.
    - Gantt charts and calendar views for timeline tracking.
    - Collaboration tools for sharing files and tasks.
- **Best For**: Teams familiar with spreadsheets.
- **Website**: Smartsheet

9. Notion

- **Features**:
    - Combines task management with documentation and note-taking.

- Fully customizable templates for projects and workflows.
- Integration with tools like Slack and Google Drive.
- **Best For**: Small teams looking for flexibility in managing tasks and knowledge.
- **Website**: Notion

10. Microsoft Project

- **Features**:
    - Advanced project planning with Gantt charts and resource allocation.
    - Built-in templates for faster setup.
    - Integration with Microsoft Office tools.
- **Best For**: Large organizations managing complex projects.
- **Website**: Microsoft Project

How to Choose the Right Tool

1. **Team Size**

    - Small teams may prefer simpler tools like Trello or Basecamp.
    - Larger teams or enterprises might need advanced tools like Monday.com or Wrike.

2. **Project Complexity**

    - Agile teams benefit from Jira's sprint management features.
    - Spreadsheet enthusiasts may prefer Smartsheet's layout.

3. **Budget**

    - Free tools like Trello and Asana (basic plans) are ideal for startups.
    - Paid platforms like Monday.com or Microsoft Project offer more advanced features.

4. **Integration Needs**

    - Consider tools that integrate seamlessly with your existing software stack (e.g., Slack, Google Workspace).

5. **Customization**

    - Tools like ClickUp and Monday.com offer extensive customization options to match unique workflows.

Benefits of Using Project Management Tools

1. **Improved Collaboration**: Centralized communication and task tracking keep teams aligned.

2. **Enhanced Productivity**: Streamlined workflows reduce time spent on repetitive tasks.
3. **Better Time Management**: Clear deadlines and reminders ensure timely task completion.
4. **Transparency**: Real-time updates provide visibility into project status and team workloads.
5. **Informed Decision-Making**: Reports and analytics help identify bottlenecks and allocate resources effectively.

By leveraging project management tools like Trello, Asana, or Monday.com, businesses can achieve better organization, efficient workflows, and successful project execution.

These platforms cater to diverse needs, ensuring there's a solution for every team size and project complexity.

Budgeting and Expense Tracking Tools

Budgeting and expense tracking tools help businesses monitor income, manage expenses, and ensure financial stability. These tools are essential for maintaining cash flow, planning for future growth, and making informed financial decisions.

Key Features of Budgeting and Expense Tracking Tools

1. **Income and Expense Tracking**
    - Categorize income streams and expenses.
    - Monitor spending habits and identify areas for cost-cutting.
2. **Budget Planning**
    - Set monthly or annual budgets for various categories.
    - Track performance against budgeted amounts.
3. **Invoice and Billing Management**
    - Generate and track invoices.
    - Automate payment reminders for overdue bills.
4. **Financial Reporting**
    - Generate profit and loss statements, cash flow reports, and balance sheets.

- Analyze trends over time for better planning.
5. **Integration**

    - Sync with bank accounts, credit cards, and other financial tools for real-time updates.
6. **Multi-User Access**

    - Enable collaboration among team members or accountants.
    - Set permissions for secure access.

Top Budgeting and Expense Tracking Tools

1. QuickBooks

- **Features**:
    - Comprehensive income and expense tracking.
    - Automatic bank feeds and transaction categorization.
    - Built-in reports for profit and loss, cash flow, and taxes.
- **Best For**: Small to medium-sized businesses.
- **Website**: QuickBooks

2. Microsoft Excel / Google Sheets

- **Features**:
    - Customizable spreadsheets for budgeting and expense tracking.
    - Templates for cash flow analysis and profit tracking.
    - Integration with add-ons for automation (e.g., Google Sheets 'integrations with financial apps).
- **Best For**: Businesses looking for a free or low-cost solution with flexibility.
- **Website**: Microsoft Excel / Google Sheets

3. Wave

- **Features**:
    - Free expense tracking and invoicing.
    - Integration with bank accounts for real-time updates.
    - Simple dashboard for tracking income and expenses.
- **Best For**: Freelancers and small businesses.
- **Website**: Wave

4. Xero

- **Features**:

- - Cloud-based accounting with expense tracking.
    - Multi-currency support for global businesses.
    - Financial reporting and budget tracking.
  - **Best For**: Small businesses with international operations.
  - **Website**: Xero

5. FreshBooks

- **Features**:
  - Expense tracking with receipt scanning.
  - Automated invoicing and payment tracking.
  - Time-tracking integration for service-based businesses.
- **Best For**: Service-based businesses and freelancers.
- **Website**: FreshBooks

6. Mint

- **Features**:
  - Budget tracking and expense categorization.
  - Alerts for bill payments and unusual transactions.
  - Financial goal setting and monitoring.
- **Best For**: Small-scale operations or personal finance tracking.
- **Website**: Mint

7. Zoho Books

- **Features**:
  - Expense tracking, invoicing, and automated payment reminders.
  - Tax calculations and compliance support.
  - Integration with other Zoho apps for complete business management.
- **Best For**: Businesses using the Zoho ecosystem.
- **Website**: Zoho Books

8. Tiller Money

- **Features**:
  - Automated spreadsheets with real-time bank updates.
  - Customizable templates for budgeting and expense tracking.
  - Advanced analytics with personalized dashboards.
- **Best For**: Spreadsheet enthusiasts who want automation.
- **Website**: Tiller Money

9. Expensify

- **Features**:
  - Expense tracking with receipt scanning.
  - Automatic mileage tracking for business trips.
  - Integration with accounting software like QuickBooks and Xero.
- **Best For**: Businesses with frequent travel and expense reimbursement needs.
- **Website**: Expensify

10. PocketGuard

- **Features**:
  - Real-time tracking of income, bills, and spending.
  - Budgeting tools to identify discretionary income.
  - Alerts for overspending and savings opportunities.
- **Best For**: Startups and small businesses managing tight budgets.
- **Website**: PocketGuard

How to Choose the Right Tool

1. **Business Size**
   - Small businesses or freelancers may prefer simpler tools like Wave or Mint.
   - Larger businesses may need more comprehensive solutions like QuickBooks or Xero.
2. **Budget**
   - Free options: Wave, Google Sheets, or Mint.
   - Paid options with advanced features: QuickBooks, FreshBooks, Xero.
3. **Industry Needs**
   - Service-based businesses: FreshBooks for time-tracking and invoicing.
   - International businesses: Xero for multi-currency support.
4. **Integration Requirements**
   - Ensure the tool integrates with existing software (e.g., payroll, invoicing, or CRM tools).
5. **User Friendliness**
   - Look for intuitive interfaces and strong customer support for easier adoption.

Benefits of Budgeting and Expense Tracking Tools

1. **Financial Clarity**: Gain a clear understanding of where money is coming from and where it's going.
2. **Improved Cash Flow Management**: Avoid cash shortages by monitoring income and expenses.
3. **Tax Preparation**: Streamline tax reporting with categorized expenses and automated records.
4. **Informed Decision-Making**: Use reports and insights to allocate resources effectively.
5. **Time Savings**: Automate repetitive tasks like expense categorization and invoicing.

By using budgeting and expense tracking tools like QuickBooks or Excel, businesses can gain better control over their finances, reduce manual errors, and focus on growth opportunities. Whether you need a simple solution or a robust accounting platform, there's a tool suited to your needs.

Funding Proposal Templates

Funding proposal templates are pre-formatted structures designed to help businesses prepare clear, professional, and persuasive funding requests. These templates ensure that all necessary information is presented effectively, increasing the likelihood of securing investment, loans, or grants.

Key Components of a Funding Proposal

1. **Executive Summary**
    - A concise overview of the funding request, summarizing the business, funding needs, and expected outcomes.
    - **Example**:
        - "We are seeking $250,000 to expand our sustainable packaging business, enabling us to scale production, meet growing demand, and achieve projected revenue of $1 million within two years."

2. **Business Description**
    - Introduce your company, its mission, vision, and unique value proposition.
    - **Key Details**:
        - Business name, location, and legal structure.
        - Core products or services.

- Industry overview and market positioning.

3. **Funding Requirements**
    - Clearly state the amount of funding requested and its intended use.
    - **Example Breakdown**:
        - $100,000 for equipment purchases.
        - $50,000 for marketing and sales initiatives.
        - $100,000 for working capital and operational expenses.

4. **Market Analysis**
    - Demonstrate understanding of your industry, target market, and competitive landscape.
    - **Key Points**:
        - Market size and growth trends.
        - Customer demographics and needs.
        - Competitor analysis and differentiation.

5. **Operational Plan**
    - Outline how the business operates and how the funding will improve processes.
    - **Key Elements**:
        - Current operations and supply chain overview.
        - Planned expansions or process improvements.
        - Implementation timelines.

6. **Financial Projections**
    - Provide detailed financial forecasts to demonstrate the business's profitability and sustainability.
    - **Include**:
        - Profit and loss statement.
        - Cash flow projections.
        - Break-even analysis.
    - **Example**:
        - "With the requested funding, we project annual revenue growth of 40%, reaching profitability within 18 months."

7. **ROI and Investor Benefits**

- Highlight what the funder will gain from supporting your business.
- **Examples**:
  - "We anticipate a 20% ROI within three years for investors."
  - "Lenders will be repaid over five years at a 6% interest rate."

8. **Risk Analysis**
   - Address potential risks and how they will be mitigated.
   - **Key Points**:
     - Market competition, regulatory changes, or supply chain disruptions.
     - Contingency plans and risk management strategies.

9. **Supporting Documents**
   - Include appendices with relevant documentation to strengthen your proposal.
   - **Examples**:
     - Business registration and licenses.
     - Detailed financial statements.
     - Customer testimonials or letters of intent.

Sample Templates

1. General Funding Proposal Template

[Template Structure]

- Executive Summary
- Business Description
- Market Analysis
- Funding Requirements
- Operational Plan
- Financial Projections
- ROI and Investor Benefits
- Risk Analysis
- Supporting Documents

2. Loan Proposal Template

[Template Structure]

- Cover Letter: Briefly introduce your funding request.

- Loan Request Summary: Specify the loan amount, term, and purpose.
- Business Overview: Highlight your business's mission and history.
- Financial Data: Include credit history, cash flow statements, and repayment plans.
- Collateral Details: Specify assets offered as loan security.
- Supporting Documents: Tax returns, bank statements, and other financial records.

3. Grant Proposal Template

[Template Structure]

- Cover Letter: Personalized introduction to the grant application.
- Statement of Need: Explain the problem your project addresses.
- Project Description: Detail the scope, objectives, and outcomes.
- Budget Plan: Break down the funding request by category.
- Evaluation Plan: Specify how project success will be measured.
- Appendices: Include letters of support, resumes, and certifications.

4. Startup Investment Proposal Template

[Template Structure]

- Executive Summary
- Problem Statement: Define the market gap or issue your business addresses.
- Solution: Outline your product or service.
- Market Opportunity: Provide market size and growth statistics.
- Financial Forecasts: Include sales projections and ROI for investors.
- Use of Funds: Clearly itemize the funding allocation.
- Team Overview: Highlight the skills and experience of your leadership team.

Tools for Creating Funding Proposals

1. **Microsoft Word/Google Docs**
   - Use pre-formatted templates for professional proposals.
   - Customize to include your business details and goals.
2. **Canva**
   - Create visually appealing funding proposals with customizable templates.
3. **PandaDoc**
   - Use templates designed for funding requests and track proposal approvals digitally.

4. **LivePlan**

    - Comprehensive software for creating business plans and funding proposals.
5. **Template Libraries**

    - Websites like Template.net and Smartsheet offer free and paid proposal templates.

Tips for Writing a Compelling Funding Proposal

1. **Keep It Clear and Concise**

    - Avoid jargon and focus on delivering a straightforward, engaging narrative.
2. **Tailor for the Audience**

    - Adapt the tone and details for investors, lenders, or grant organizations.
3. **Highlight ROI**

    - Emphasize how the funding will benefit the investor or lender.
4. **Provide Data and Evidence**

    - Use credible market research, financial projections, and customer feedback to build trust.
5. **Proofread and Edit**

    - Ensure the proposal is free of errors and professionally formatted.

By using these funding proposal templates and customizing them to your specific needs, you can create professional and persuasive funding requests that resonate with investors, lenders, or grant organizations.

Financial Planning Spreadsheets

1. **Income Tracking**

    - Record all revenue sources (e.g., product sales, services, investments).
    - Categorize income by type and time period.
2. **Expense Tracking**

- Track fixed (rent, salaries) and variable (utilities, raw materials) costs.
- Break down expenses by category and department.

3. **Profitability Analysis**

    - Calculate gross and net profit margins.
    - Identify cost-saving opportunities.

4. **Budget Planning**

    - Set spending limits for various categories.
    - Monitor actual expenses against budgeted amounts.

5. **Cash Flow Management**

    - Forecast inflows and outflows of cash.
    - Identify potential cash shortages or surpluses.

6. **Resource Allocation**

    - Assign funds to different projects, departments, or initiatives.
    - Track utilization to optimize efficiency.

7. **Financial Ratios and Metrics**

    - Calculate key ratios like ROI, debt-to-equity, and break-even points.
    - Use these metrics to assess financial performance.

Templates for Financial Planning Spreadsheets

1. Income and Expense Tracker

- **Purpose**: Monitor revenue streams and track spending to ensure financial balance.
- **Key Features**:
    - Monthly income and expense summary.
    - Automatic calculation of net income.
    - Graphs to visualize spending trends.
- **Example**: Use to manage operational costs and ensure profitability.

2. Budget Planner

- **Purpose**: Create and monitor budgets for specific periods or projects.
- **Key Features**:
    - Budget vs. actual comparison.
    - Alerts for over-budget categories.
    - Customizable for business departments.
- **Example**: Allocate marketing, payroll, and R&D budgets effectively.

3. Cash Flow Forecast

- **Purpose**: Predict and manage cash inflows and outflows to maintain liquidity.
- **Key Features**:
  - Detailed inflow and outflow sections.
  - Automatic calculation of net cash flow.
  - Highlight periods of potential shortages or surpluses.
- **Example**: Plan for seasonal demand fluctuations.

4. Profit and Loss Statement

- **Purpose**: Track income, expenses, and profits over a specific period.
- **Key Features**:
  - Revenue and expense categories.
  - Automatic gross profit, net profit, and margin calculations.
  - Year-to-date comparisons for trend analysis.
- **Example**: Evaluate the profitability of business operations.

5. Break-Even Analysis

- **Purpose**: Determine the point at which revenue equals expenses.
- **Key Features**:
  - Inputs for fixed and variable costs.
  - Automated break-even point calculation.
  - Visual representation of break-even sales.
- **Example**: Assess the feasibility of a new product launch.

6. Resource Allocation Template

- **Purpose**: Plan and track how funds and resources are distributed.
- **Key Features**:
  - Categorize by project, department, or initiative.
  - Include start and end dates for allocations.
  - Track resource utilization and remaining budgets.
- **Example**: Ensure efficient use of resources across departments.

7. KPI Dashboard

- **Purpose**: Track financial metrics and key performance indicators.
- **Key Features**:
  - Automatically calculate metrics like ROI, gross profit margin, and CAC.
  - Interactive charts for visual performance tracking.
  - Customizable to highlight relevant KPIs.
- **Example**: Monitor overall financial health and strategic goals.

Tools for Creating and Customizing Spreadsheets

1. Microsoft Excel

- **Features**:
    - Pre-built templates for financial tracking.
    - Advanced formulas and pivot tables for customization.
    - Charting tools for data visualization.
- **Website**: Microsoft Excel

2. Google Sheets

- **Features**:
    - Free cloud-based spreadsheet solution.
    - Real-time collaboration and sharing.
    - Add-ons for advanced financial analysis.
- **Website**: Google Sheets

3. Tiller Money

- **Features**:
    - Automates data imports from bank accounts into Google Sheets or Excel.
    - Pre-built financial templates for budgeting and tracking.
    - Customizable dashboards for personal and business finances.
- **Website**: Tiller Money

4. Smartsheet

- **Features**:
    - Combines spreadsheet functionality with project management tools.
    - Ideal for team collaboration on financial planning.
    - Templates for cash flow, budgeting, and resource allocation.
- **Website**: Smartsheet

5. Airtable

- **Features**:
    - Combines spreadsheet functionality with database features.
    - Customizable templates for expense tracking and budgeting.
    - Integration with other business tools.
- **Website**: Airtable

Tips for Effective Use of Financial Spreadsheets

1. **Automate Calculations**
    - Use formulas to automatically calculate totals, averages, and variances.

2. **Keep It Organized**
   - Use clear headers, labels, and color coding for better readability.
3. **Update Regularly**
   - Maintain up-to-date data to ensure accurate financial insights.
4. **Use Visualizations**
   - Include charts and graphs to make data interpretation easier.
5. **Backup Data**
   - Save copies regularly to prevent data loss.

Benefits of Financial Planning Spreadsheets

1. **Cost Efficiency**: Often free or low-cost compared to advanced software.
2. **Flexibility**: Customizable to fit specific business needs.
3. **Transparency**: Provides a clear overview of financial health.
4. **Better Decision-Making**: Helps identify trends and allocate resources effectively.

By leveraging financial planning spreadsheets, businesses can gain greater control over their finances, streamline operations, and make informed strategic decisions to support growth and profitability.

Scenario Planning Framework

Scenario planning is a strategic method used to prepare for uncertain future events by developing best-case, moderate, and worst-case scenarios. This framework helps businesses anticipate potential challenges, assess risks, and identify opportunities to remain resilient and adaptable in dynamic environments.

Steps in Scenario Planning

1. Define the Objective

- **Purpose**: Clarify what you aim to achieve with scenario planning.
- **Examples**:
  - Assess the impact of a market downturn on revenue.
  - Prepare for supply chain disruptions.
  - Explore the potential success of a new product launch.

2. Identify Key Drivers of Change

- **Focus**: Determine the internal and external factors that could significantly impact your business.
- **Key Drivers**:
    - **Internal**: Operational efficiency, workforce availability, product innovation.
    - **External**: Market trends, economic shifts, regulatory changes, technological advancements.
- **Example**:
    - For a retail business, key drivers might include customer demand, supply chain reliability, and competitor activity.

3. Develop Assumptions

- Create plausible assumptions for each driver, ranging from optimistic to pessimistic.
- **Examples**:
    - Best-case: Sales increase by 20% due to strong market demand.
    - Moderate-case: Sales remain steady with no significant growth.
    - Worst case: Sales decline by 15% due to an economic downturn.

4. Build Scenarios

- Combine assumptions to develop distinct scenarios.
- **Types of Scenarios**:
    - **Best Case**: Everything goes better than expected, with maximum opportunities and minimal risks.
    - **Moderate-Case**: A realistic middle ground where current conditions remain stable or change gradually.
    - **Worst-case**: Adverse conditions prevail, such as economic recession, regulatory challenges, or operational disruptions.

Example:

Scenario	Sales Growth	Supply Chain	Customer Retention
Best-Case	20%	No disruptions	10%
Moderate-Case	0%	Minor delays	Stable
Worst-Case	-15%	Severe disruptions	-10%

5. Analyze the Impact

- Assess the financial, operational, and strategic implications of each scenario.
- **Key Metrics**:
  - Revenue and profit margins.
  - Operational costs and resources.
  - Customer satisfaction and retention.
- **Example**:
  - In the worst-case scenario, calculate how a 15% drop in sales would affect cash flow and identify necessary cost-cutting measures.

6. Develop Action Plans

- Create specific strategies to respond to each scenario.
- **Best-Case Actions**:
  - Scale up production, invest in marketing, and seize market opportunities.
- **Moderate-Case Actions**:
  - Maintain current operations, monitor key metrics, and prioritize efficiency.
- **Worst-Case Actions**:
  - Implement cost-saving measures, renegotiate supplier contracts, and focus on retaining loyal customers.

7. Monitor and Adapt

- Continuously track key drivers and indicators to identify shifts in conditions.
- Adjust strategies as needed to align with the evolving scenario.
- **Example**:
  - Use real-time sales data and market trends to determine if your current situation aligns with the moderate or worst-case scenario.

Scenario Planning Tools

1. **Excel or Google Sheets**
   - Build customizable scenario models with tables, graphs, and formulas.
   - Use "what-if" analysis tools for financial projections.
2. **Specialized Software**
   - **Crystal Ball**: Predictive modeling and risk analysis.
   - **PlanGuru**: Financial forecasting and scenario planning.
   - **Adaptive Insights**: Dynamic scenario analysis for budgeting and forecasting.
3. **SWOT Analysis**
   - Identify strengths, weaknesses, opportunities, and threats in each scenario.
4. **Simulation Tools**

- Use Monte Carlo simulations for more complex, probabilistic scenarios.

Benefits of Scenario Planning

1. **Improved Preparedness**: Anticipate risks and opportunities, enabling proactive decision-making.
2. **Strategic Agility**: Adapt quickly to changes in market conditions or operational challenges.
3. **Resource Optimization**: Allocate resources effectively across various scenarios.
4. **Risk Mitigation**: Develop contingency plans to minimize the impact of adverse events.
5. **Enhanced Decision-Making**: Gain clarity on potential outcomes to inform strategic priorities.

Scenario planning ensures businesses are prepared to navigate uncertainties while staying aligned with their strategic goals. By proactively addressing potential outcomes, businesses can reduce risks, seize opportunities, and maintain resilience in the face of change.

Contingency Planning Templates

Contingency planning templates help businesses prepare for unexpected events by providing a structured approach to creating backup plans. These templates ensure that businesses can respond effectively to risks and challenges, minimizing disruptions and safeguarding operations.

Key Components of a Contingency Plan

1. **Risk Identification**
   - List potential risks or events that could disrupt operations.
   - **Examples**: Supply chain disruptions, data breaches, equipment failure, market downturns.
2. **Risk Assessment**
   - Evaluate the likelihood and impact of each risk.
   - Prioritize risks based on their potential effect on business operations.
   - **Matrix**: Categorize risks as high, medium, or low based on likelihood and severity.
3. **Response Strategies**

- Develop specific actions to address each risk.
- **Examples**:
  - Supply chain disruption: Identify alternative suppliers.
  - Data breach: Implement a cybersecurity incident response plan.

4. **Resource Allocation**
   - Identify the resources needed to execute the contingency plan.
   - **Examples**: Budget, staff, technology, or external support.

5. **Roles and Responsibilities**
   - Assign tasks to team members or departments.
   - Ensure everyone understands their role in implementing the plan.

6. **Implementation Steps**
   - Create a step-by-step guide for executing the contingency plan.
   - Include timelines, checkpoints, and communication protocols.

7. **Monitoring and Review**
   - Define how the plan will be monitored and updated.
   - Establish triggers for activating the contingency plan.

Sample Contingency Planning Templates

1. General Contingency Plan Template

Section	Details
Risk	Describe the specific risk or challenge (e.g., cyberattack, natural disaster).
Likelihood	Rate the likelihood (high, medium, low).
Impact	Rate the impact on operations (high, medium, low).
Response Plan	Outline specific actions to mitigate the risk.
Resources Needed	List the required resources (e.g., budget, tools, personnel).
Assigned Team Members	Specify who is responsible for each action.
Activation Criteria	Define when the contingency plan should be activated.
Follow-Up Actions	List steps to return to normal operations.

2. IT System Failure Contingency Plan Template

Category	Details
Risk	IT system failure or server downtime.
Response Actions	- Notify IT team immediately.
	- Switch to backup servers.
	- Communicate downtime to affected customers or stakeholders.
Resources Needed	Backup servers, IT personnel, and communication tools.
Assigned Personnel	IT manager, customer support team, and operations manager.
Recovery Timeline	Resolve the issue within 24 hours; monitor systems for 72 hours post-repair.

3. Supply Chain Disruption Template

Category	Details
Risk	Supplier delays or shortages.
Response Actions	- Contact alternative suppliers.
	- Adjust production schedules to prioritize available resources.
	- Communicate potential delays to customers.
Resources Needed	Supplier directory, production plans, and customer communication channels.
Assigned Personnel	Procurement manager, production manager, and customer service team.
Recovery Timeline	Resolve supply chain issues within two weeks.

4. Data Breach Contingency Plan Template

Category	Details
Risk	Unauthorized access to sensitive data.
Response Actions	- Isolate affected systems.
	- Notify IT security team.
	- Report the breach to regulatory authorities and affected stakeholders.
Resources Needed	Cybersecurity tools, IT security team, and legal advisors.

Assigned Personnel	IT manager, legal counsel, and communication team.
Recovery Timeline	Secure systems within 48 hours; implement additional security measures.

5. Economic Downturn Template

Category	Details
Risk	Reduced revenue due to a recession.
Response Actions	- Reduce non-essential expenses.
	- Focus on core products or services with stable demand.
	- Offer discounts or flexible payment terms to retain customers.
Resources Needed	Financial forecasts, marketing team, and budget allocation.
Assigned Personnel	CFO, marketing manager, and sales team.
Recovery Timeline	Implement cost-cutting measures within one month.

Tools for Creating Contingency Plans

1. **Microsoft Word / Google Docs**
   - Use pre-formatted templates to document plans clearly and professionally.
   - **Best For**: Basic, text-based plans.

2. **Excel / Google Sheets**
   - Create structured tables for tracking risks, actions, and responsibilities.
   - **Best For**: Risk prioritization and resource allocation.

3. **Trello / Asana / Monday.com**
   - Organize contingency tasks as projects with clear assignments and timelines.
   - **Best For**: Collaborative planning and execution.

4. **Smartsheet**
   - Use templates for risk management and contingency planning.
   - **Best For**: Teams needing detailed tracking and reporting.

5. **Lucidchart / Visio**
    - Create visual flowcharts for contingency workflows.
    - **Best For**: Complex, process-driven plans.

Benefits of Contingency Planning Templates

1. **Proactive Risk Management**: Identify and prepare for risks before they occur.
2. **Improved Resilience**: Ensure business continuity during disruptions.
3. **Clarity and Accountability**: Clearly define actions, resources, and responsibilities.
4. **Time Savings**: Quickly implement responses with pre-planned strategies.
5. **Enhanced Communication**: Provide a clear roadmap for teams and stakeholders.

By using these contingency planning templates, businesses can prepare for potential risks, minimize disruptions, and ensure continuity during challenging times. Customizing these templates for your specific needs will further enhance their effectiveness.

Trend Monitoring Tools

Trend monitoring tools are essential for staying updated on market shifts, consumer behavior, competitor activities, and industry developments. These tools help businesses anticipate opportunities, adapt strategies, and maintain a competitive edge in dynamic markets.

Top Trend Monitoring Tools

1. Google Alerts

- **Purpose**: Monitor the web for new content about specific topics.
- **Key Features**:
    - Create alerts for keywords, brands, or competitors.
    - Receive notifications via email or RSS feed.
    - Track trends in real time.
- **Use Case**:
    - A retailer sets up alerts for "eco-friendly packaging" to stay informed about industry innovations.

- **Website**: Google Alerts

2. Feedly

- **Purpose**: Aggregate news, blogs, and industry publications into one feed.
- **Key Features**:
  - Subscribe to relevant RSS feeds and topics.
  - Organize content into custom boards.
  - Use AI-powered insights to highlight key trends.
- **Use Case**:
  - A tech startup uses Feedly to track developments in artificial intelligence and competitor announcements.
- **Website**: Feedly

3. BuzzSumo

- **Purpose**: Discover trending topics, content, and influencers in your industry.
- **Key Features**:
  - Identify popular content based on shares and engagement.
  - Monitor brand mentions and competitor activities.
  - Analyze trending keywords and hashtags.
- **Use Case**:
  - A digital marketing agency uses BuzzSumo to track trending topics for client campaigns.
- **Website**: BuzzSumo

4. TrendWatching

- **Purpose**: Provide insights into global consumer trends.
- **Key Features**:
  - Curated reports and trend briefings.
  - Focus on emerging trends and innovation.
  - Industry-specific and regional insights.
- **Use Case**:
  - A fashion brand uses TrendWatching to identify emerging sustainability trends in clothing.
- **Website**: TrendWatching

5. Statista

- **Purpose**: Access comprehensive statistics and trend data across industries.
- **Key Features**:
  - Industry-specific data and forecasts.
  - Consumer behavior and market analysis.

- Visualization tools for reports and presentations.
- **Use Case**:
  - A healthcare startup uses Statista to monitor global health tech trends.
- **Website**: Statista

6. Google Trends

- **Purpose**: Analyze search trends over time to identify popular topics and seasonal interests.
- **Key Features**:
  - Compare search interest across regions and time periods.
  - Identify related queries and rising topics.
- **Use Case**:
  - An e-commerce store uses Google Trends to predict peak demand for seasonal products like swimwear.
- **Website**: Google Trends

7. SEMrush

- **Purpose**: Monitor digital marketing trends and competitor performance.
- **Key Features**:
  - Keyword and traffic trend analysis.
  - Competitive analysis and content gap discovery.
  - Industry benchmarks and trend insights.
- **Use Case**:
  - A content creator uses SEMrush to track trending topics in their niche and optimize blog posts.
- **Website**: SEMrush

8. LinkedIn Pulse

- **Purpose**: Follow industry leaders, influencers, and trending topics on LinkedIn.
- **Key Features**:
  - Access curated articles and thought leadership content.
  - Follow hashtags and industry-specific updates.
  - Join groups for niche discussions.
- **Use Case**:
  - A B2B company follows "supply chain optimization" updates on LinkedIn Pulse to stay informed about logistics innovations.
- **Website**: LinkedIn

9. Industry-Specific Newsletters

- **Purpose**: Receive curated insights and updates directly in your inbox.

- **Examples**:
    - **Morning Brew**: General business and tech trends.
    - **TechCrunch**: Technology and startup news.
    - **Retail Dive**: Trends in retail and e-commerce.
- **Use Case**:
    - A retail business subscribes to Retail Dive for updates on consumer behavior and technology.
- **Websites**:
    - Morning Brew
    - TechCrunch
    - Retail Dive

10. Talkwalker Alerts

- **Purpose**: Monitor online mentions of keywords, brands, or competitors.
- **Key Features**:
    - Real-time alerts for mentions across social media, blogs, and news.
    - Track sentiment and analyze trends.
- **Use Case**:
    - A hospitality business uses Talkwalker Alerts to monitor customer feedback, and competitor mentions online.
- **Website**: Talkwalker Alerts

How to Use Trend Monitoring Tools Effectively

1. **Define Your Goals**
    - Focus on specific topics or industries relevant to your business.
    - Example: Monitor "sustainable packaging" trends for a packaging company.
2. **Set Up Alerts or Subscriptions**
    - Use tools like Google Alerts or Feedly to receive real-time updates.
3. **Analyze Trends**
    - Look for patterns or recurring themes in content and data.
    - Evaluate the impact of emerging trends on your business or market.
4. **Integrate Insights**
    - Use trends to inform product development, marketing strategies, and long-term planning.
5. **Review Regularly**
    - Update your monitoring preferences to stay aligned with current priorities.

Benefits of Trend Monitoring Tools

1. **Stay Ahead of the Curve**: Anticipate market shifts and prepare your business accordingly.
2. **Informed Decision-Making**: Use real-time data to guide strategies.
3. **Competitive Edge**: Gain insights into competitors' activities and emerging threats.
4. **Identify Opportunities**: Discover new markets, products, or services to explore.
5. **Improve Customer Engagement**: Align offerings with consumer preferences and behaviors.

By leveraging these trend-monitoring tools, businesses can remain proactive, adapt to changes, and capitalize on opportunities in an ever-evolving market landscape.

Digital Marketing Strategies

Digital marketing strategies encompass a variety of techniques to promote products, services, and brands online. By leveraging channels like online advertising, social media, email marketing, and more, businesses can connect with their audience, drive engagement, and achieve measurable results.

Key Digital Marketing Techniques

1. Online Advertising

Promote your business through paid ads on platforms like search engines, social media, and websites.

Techniques:

- **Search Engine Advertising (PPC)**:
  - Use platforms like Google Ads or Bing Ads to target specific keywords.
  - Example: A local bakery runs Google Ads targeting "best cupcakes near me."
- **Display Ads**:
  - Use banner ads on websites to increase brand visibility.
  - Example: A travel agency displays ads on popular travel blogs.
- **Retargeting Ads**:
  - Show ads to users who have previously visited your website or interacted with your content.

- Example: An e-commerce store retargets users who abandoned their shopping carts.

Best Practices:

- Use clear CTAs (Call-to-Actions) in your ads.
- Optimize ad copy for relevance and keywords.
- Monitor ROI and adjust bids regularly.

2. Social Media Marketing

Engage with your audience on platforms like Facebook, Instagram, LinkedIn, TikTok, and Twitter.

Techniques:

- **Organic Posts**:
  - Share engaging content like updates, images, videos, and polls.
  - Example: A fitness studio posts daily workout tips on Instagram.
- **Paid Social Ads**:
  - Use targeted ads to reach specific demographics.
  - Example: A clothing brand runs a Facebook ad targeting women aged 18-34.
- **Influencer Collaborations**:
  - Partner with influencers to promote your products to their followers.
  - Example: A skincare brand collaborates with a beauty influencer for product reviews.
- **Community Engagement**:
  - Respond to comments, participate in discussions, and engage with user-generated content.
  - Example: A tech startup answers customer queries on LinkedIn.

Best Practices:

- Tailor content to each platform's audience and format.
- Use analytics to track performance and refine strategies.
- Stay consistent with your posting schedule.

3. Email Marketing

Connect with your audience through personalized email campaigns.

Techniques:

- **Welcome Emails**:
  - Send automated emails to greet new subscribers.
  - Example: "Welcome to Our Brand! Here's a 10% Off Coupon."

- **Promotional Campaigns**:
    - Share special offers, sales, or product launches.
    - Example: A fashion brand sends an email announcing a Black Friday sale.
- **Segmentation**:
    - Divide your email list into groups based on behavior, location, or preferences.
    - Example: A travel agency sends tailored offers for beach vacations to one segment and mountain vacations to another.
- **Drip Campaigns**:
    - Send a series of automated emails based on user actions.
    - Example: An online course platform sends follow-ups to users who abandon the sign-up process.

Best Practices:

- Optimize subject lines to increase open rates.
- Keep emails concise and include strong CTAs.
- Regularly clean your email list to maintain high deliverability rates.

4. Content Marketing

Create valuable and relevant content to attract and retain your audience.

Techniques:

- **Blogging**:
    - Write articles that answer audience questions and provide solutions.
    - Example: A home improvement store publishes DIY guides for beginners.
- **Video Marketing**:
    - Use platforms like YouTube and TikTok for tutorials, testimonials, or behind-the-scenes content.
    - Example: A cooking brand shares recipe videos featuring its products.
- **Infographics**:
    - Use visually engaging graphics to present data or processes.
    - Example: A financial advisor creates an infographic explaining retirement savings tips.
- **E-books and Whitepapers**:
    - Provide in-depth content for lead generation.
    - Example: A SaaS company offers a free whitepaper on "Improving Team Productivity."

Best Practices:

- Align content with your audience's needs and interests.
- Use SEO techniques to improve visibility.
- Promote content across multiple channels.

5. Search Engine Optimization (SEO)

Improve your website's visibility on search engines to attract organic traffic.

Techniques:

- **Keyword Optimization**:
    - Use tools like SEMrush or Google Keyword Planner to find and target relevant keywords.
    - Example: A pet store optimizes its blog for keywords like "best dog food for puppies."
- **On-Page SEO**:
    - Optimize title tags, meta descriptions, and internal linking.
- **Technical SEO**:
    - Ensure your site is mobile-friendly, fast-loading, and free of errors.
- **Link Building**:
    - Gain backlinks from reputable sites to boost authority.

Best Practices:

- Publish high-quality, original content.
- Update and optimize older content for improved rankings.
- Monitor analytics for traffic and keyword performance.

6. Affiliate Marketing

Partner with affiliates who promote your products in exchange for a commission.

Techniques:

- Offer affiliates unique discount codes to share with their audience.
- Track referrals and conversions using affiliate links.
- Use platforms like Amazon Associates or ShareASale to manage affiliate relationships.

Best Practices:

- Choose affiliates whose audience aligns with your target market.
- Provide affiliates with clear guidelines and marketing materials.
- Regularly review affiliate performance.

7. Analytics and Data-Driven Marketing

Use data to refine campaigns and improve ROI.

Techniques:

- Use tools like Google Analytics to track website performance.
- Monitor KPIs such as click-through rates (CTR), conversion rates, and bounce rates.
- Conduct A/B testing to determine the most effective strategies.

Best Practices:

- Set clear goals for each campaign.
- Regularly review analytics to identify trends.
- Adjust strategies based on data insights.

Benefits of Digital Marketing Strategies

1. **Increased Reach**: Connect with a global audience.
2. **Cost-Effectiveness**: Target specific audiences with measurable results.
3. **Real-Time Insights**: Track campaign performance and ROI in real time.
4. **Enhanced Engagement**: Foster direct interaction with your audience.
5. **Scalability**: Adjust campaigns to fit your budget and goals.

By leveraging these digital marketing strategies, businesses can build brand awareness, attract customers, and drive growth in an increasingly digital-first world.

Customer Feedback Loops

A **customer feedback loop** is a system designed to collect, analyze, and act upon customer feedback to continuously improve products, services, and the overall customer experience. These systems close the gap between customer insights and actionable business strategies, fostering trust and long-term loyalty.

Key Components of a Customer Feedback Loop

1. **Collection**
   - Gather feedback from various touchpoints.
   - **Channels**:
     - Surveys (e.g., email, website pop-ups, in-app).
     - Customer reviews on platforms like Google, Yelp, or Trustpilot.
     - Social media mentions and direct messages.
     - Support interactions (tickets, chat logs, or call transcripts).
2. **Analysis**

- Extract actionable insights from feedback.
- **Methods**:
  - Categorize feedback by themes (e.g., product quality, pricing, customer service).
  - Use sentiment analysis to gauge customer emotions.
  - Identify recurring issues or trends.

3. **Action**

   - Develop strategies to address feedback and improve offerings.
   - **Examples**:
     - Resolve common complaints by updating a feature.
     - Enhance customer service training based on feedback about support quality.

4. **Communication**

   - Close the loop by informing customers about changes made based on their feedback.
   - **Examples**:
     - "We heard you! Based on your feedback, we've introduced [new feature]."
     - Share updates through emails, blogs, or social media.

5. **Iteration**

   - Regularly revisit feedback to ensure continuous improvement.
   - Update systems and strategies as needed to keep the loop effective.

Types of Feedback to Collect

1. **Product Feedback**

   - Identify customer needs and improve usability.
   - Example Question: "What features would you like to see added?"

2. **Service Feedback**

   - Assess satisfaction with support or interaction quality.
   - Example Question: "How would you rate your recent experience with our support team?"

3. **Experience Feedback**

- Understand the overall customer journey.
- Example Question: "How easy was it to navigate our website?"

4. **Brand Sentiment Feedback**

    - Gauge customers 'emotional connection with your brand.
    - Example Question: "How likely are you to recommend us to a friend?"

Customer Feedback Tools

1. Survey Tools

- **Examples**:
    - **SurveyMonkey**: Customizable surveys for detailed feedback collection.
    - **Typeform**: Interactive and engaging surveys for higher response rates.
    - **Google Forms**: Free, easy-to-use survey creation.
- **Use Case**:
    - A SaaS company uses surveys to collect post-purchase feedback about onboarding experiences.

2. Review Platforms

- **Examples**:
    - **Trustpilot**, **Yelp**, or **Google Reviews**: Collect public reviews for visibility and improvement.
    - **Capterra** or **G2**: Industry-specific platforms for SaaS businesses.
- **Use Case**:
    - A local restaurant monitors Yelp reviews to address common customer complaints about wait times.

3. In-App Feedback Tools

- **Examples**:
    - **Zendesk Feedback Tabs**: Collect feedback directly from customers during app usage.
    - **Usabilla**: In-app surveys and feedback buttons for website and mobile apps.
- **Use Case**:
    - A mobile app prompts users to rate their experience after completing a key action.

4. Social Listening Tools

- **Examples**:
    - **Hootsuite**, **Sprout Social**, or **Brandwatch**: Monitor mentions and sentiment on social media.
- **Use Case**:
    - An e-commerce business tracks Twitter mentions to identify pain points in delivery services.

5. Support Interaction Logs

- **Examples**:
    - Use ticketing systems like **Freshdesk** or **Zendesk** to analyze common customer queries and complaints.
- **Use Case**:
    - A software company reviews customer support tickets to identify recurring issues with a recent update.

How to Build an Effective Feedback Loop

1. **Set Clear Goals**
    - Define what you want to learn from customer feedback (e.g., product improvements, service enhancements).
2. **Choose Feedback Channels**
    - Use multiple channels to ensure comprehensive coverage of customer opinions.
3. **Create Feedback Collection Mechanisms**
    - Use surveys, feedback buttons, and review requests strategically.
4. **Analyze Regularly**
    - Schedule periodic reviews of feedback to identify trends.
5. **Take Action and Track Results**
    - Implement changes and monitor their effectiveness.
6. **Communicate Changes**
    - Let customers know their input is valued by sharing updates based on their feedback.

Example: Feedback Loop for an Online Retailer

1. **Collection**:

- Send post-purchase surveys via email.
- Monitor reviews on Google and social media mentions.

2. **Analysis**:
   - Identify trends, such as frequent complaints about shipping delays.

3. **Action**:
   - Partner with a new logistics provider to improve delivery times.

4. **Communication**:
   - Share updates with customers: "We've improved shipping speeds to ensure timely delivery."

5. **Iteration**:
   - Continue monitoring feedback to evaluate the new logistics provider's performance.

Benefits of Customer Feedback Loops

1. **Improved Offerings**: Gain insights into customer needs and refine products or services.
2. **Stronger Relationships**: Build trust by showing customers that their opinions matter.
3. **Proactive Problem-Solving**: Address recurring issues before they escalate.
4. **Data-Driven Decisions**: Use feedback as a foundation for strategic planning.
5. **Enhanced Customer Loyalty**: Foster long-term relationships through continuous improvement.

By implementing customer feedback loops, businesses can create a system of continuous improvement, leading to greater customer satisfaction and business success.

Sales Funnel Framework

A sales funnel framework is a structured approach to guide potential customers through each stage of the purchasing process, from awareness to conversion. By understanding the stages of the funnel and tailoring strategies for each, businesses can improve engagement, increase conversions, and foster loyalty.

Stages of a Sales Funnel

1. Awareness

Goal: Attract potential customers and make them aware of your brand or product.

Key Activities:

- **Content Marketing**: Blog posts, infographics, and videos that address customer pain points.
- **Social Media Marketing**: Posts, ads, and collaborations to boost visibility.
- **Search Engine Optimization (SEO)**: Optimize content to rank for relevant keywords.
- **Paid Advertising**: Google Ads, Facebook Ads, or other PPC campaigns.

Metrics:

- Website traffic.
- Social media impressions.
- Engagement rates (likes, shares, comments).

2. Interest

Goal: Engage potential customers by providing valuable and relevant information about your product or service.

Key Activities:

- **Lead Magnets**: Offer free resources (e.g., eBooks, templates, or webinars) in exchange for contact information.
- **Email Marketing**: Nurture leads with personalized emails that highlight benefits and solutions.
- **Retargeting Ads**: Show ads to users who visited your site but didn't take action.

Metrics:

- Email sign-ups.
- Download rates for lead magnets.
- Time spent on website pages.

3. Consideration

Goal: Build trust and provide detailed information to help prospects evaluate your offerings.

Key Activities:

- **Case Studies and Testimonials**: Highlight success stories and customer reviews.

- **Product Demonstrations**: Offer video demos, free trials, or samples.
- **Comparison Guides**: Provide detailed comparisons with competitors.

Metrics:

- Demo or trial sign-ups.
- Downloads of product information.
- Click-through rates on comparison pages.

4. Conversion

Goal: Persuade potential customers to make a purchase.

Key Activities:

- **Limited-Time Offers**: Create urgency with discounts or special promotions.
- **Clear CTAs**: Ensure purchase buttons and forms are easy to find and use.
- **Checkout Optimization**: Simplify the payment process to reduce cart abandonment.

Metrics:

- Conversion rate.
- Average order value (AOV).
- Cart abandonment rate.

5. Loyalty

Goal: Retain customers and encourage repeat purchases.

Key Activities:

- **Customer Support**: Provide excellent post-purchase support to ensure satisfaction.
- **Loyalty Programs**: Reward repeat purchases with discounts or points.
- **Exclusive Offers**: Share early access to sales or special promotions.

Metrics:

- Customer retention rate.
- Repeat purchase rate.
- Net promoter score (NPS).

6. Advocacy

Goal: Turn satisfied customers into brand advocates who promote your business.

Key Activities:

- **Referral Programs**: Offer incentives for customers who refer friends or family.

- **Social Proof**: Encourage customers to leave reviews or share testimonials.
- **Community Engagement**: Interact with customers on social media or through events.

Metrics:

- Referral rates.
- Customer reviews and ratings.
- Social media mentions and shares.

Sales Funnel Framework Template

Stage	Objective	Strategies	Metrics
Awareness	Attract potential customers	Content marketing, SEO, social media, PPC ads	Website traffic, impressions
Interest	Engage and educate	Lead magnets, email campaigns, retargeting ads	Email sign-ups, engagement rates
Consideration	Build trust and showcase benefits	Testimonials, demos, comparison guides	Demo sign-ups, page views
Conversion	Persuade to purchase	Limited-time offers, checkout optimization	Conversion rate, AOV
Loyalty	Retain and encourage repeat purchases	Loyalty programs, exclusive offers, support	Retention rate, repeat purchases
Advocacy	Turn customers into advocates	Referral programs, social proof, community engagement	Referral rate, customer reviews

Tools for Building and Managing Sales Funnels

1. **CRM Software**:
    - **HubSpot**: Manage leads and automate nurturing emails.
    - **Salesforce**: Track prospects and customer interactions.
2. **Email Marketing Platforms**:
    - **Mailchimp**: Design email campaigns and track engagement.
    - **ActiveCampaign**: Automate email sequences based on customer behavior.
3. **Landing Page Builders**:
    - **ClickFunnels**: Create optimized landing pages and sales funnels.
    - **Unbounce**: Design and test high-converting pages.
4. **Analytics Tools**:

- **Google Analytics**: Track website traffic and conversions.
- **Hotjar**: Visualize user behavior with heatmaps and session recordings.

5. **Social Media Platforms**:
   - **Hootsuite**: Schedule and manage posts across multiple platforms.
   - **Sprout Social**: Analyze social media performance and engagement.

Benefits of a Structured Sales Funnel

1. **Improved Customer Experience**:
   - Tailored strategies ensure prospects receive relevant information at each stage.
2. **Increased Conversions**:
   - Streamlined processes guide potential customers toward making a purchase.
3. **Better Resource Allocation**:
   - Focus efforts on high-impact activities at each stage.
4. **Enhanced Insights**:
   - Funnel analytics provide valuable data for refining strategies.
5. **Stronger Customer Relationships**:
   - Nurturing leads and rewarding loyalty build trust and advocacy.

By implementing this sales funnel framework, businesses can effectively attract, engage, convert, and retain customers while maximizing ROI and fostering long-term growth.

Stakeholder Alignment Tools

Stakeholder alignment tools and techniques help ensure that team members, investors, and partners share a unified vision and understanding of project goals, strategies, and progress. Proper alignment minimizes misunderstandings, streamlines decision-making, and increases the likelihood of project success.

Key Features of Stakeholder Alignment Tools

1. **Clear Communication**
   - Facilitate transparent and consistent communication among all stakeholders.
2. **Goal Setting and Tracking**
   - Define and monitor shared objectives to ensure focus and accountability.
3. **Collaboration and Feedback**
   - Enable real-time collaboration and incorporate feedback to refine strategies.
4. **Progress Visibility**
   - Provide dashboards or updates that show progress, milestones, and roadblocks.
5. **Decision Support**
   - Use tools that help stakeholders make informed decisions based on data.

Top Stakeholder Alignment Tools

1. Project Management Tools

Help stakeholders collaborate, track progress, and align on timelines and deliverables.

- **Examples**:
  - **Asana**: Create tasks, set deadlines, and assign responsibilities to ensure everyone is aligned.
  - **Monday.com**: Visualize project progress with customizable boards and timelines.
  - **Trello**: Use Kanban boards to organize tasks and provide status updates.
- **Use Case**: A product launch team uses Asana to align marketing, production, and sales teams on timelines and deliverables.

2. Collaboration Platforms

Facilitate seamless communication and document sharing among stakeholders.

- **Examples**:
  - **Slack**: Centralize team communication with channels for specific projects or topics.

- **Microsoft Teams**: Integrate chat, video calls, and file sharing for comprehensive collaboration.
- **Google Workspace**: Share documents, spreadsheets, and presentations for real-time collaboration.
- **Use Case**: A startup uses Slack to keep investors updated through a dedicated channel for key updates and discussions.

3. Goal Setting and OKR Tools

Align stakeholders on objectives and track progress toward measurable outcomes.

- **Examples**:
  - **Perdoo**: Align team and organizational goals using OKRs (Objectives and Key Results).
  - **WorkBoard**: Track OKRs and ensure everyone is working toward shared objectives.
  - **Betterworks**: Integrate OKR tracking with performance management.
- **Use Case**: A company uses Perdoo to align its leadership team and employees on quarterly revenue goals.

4. Visualization and Dashboard Tools

Provide stakeholders with a clear view of data, progress, and KPIs.

- **Examples**:
  - **Tableau**: Create data-driven dashboards to visualize performance metrics.
  - **Google Data Studio**: Integrate data from various sources into a single dashboard.
  - **Power BI**: Generate real-time reports and visualizations to share with stakeholders.
- **Use Case**: An e-commerce company uses Tableau to share sales performance metrics with investors during quarterly reviews.

5. Feedback and Survey Tools

Collect feedback from stakeholders to refine strategies and ensure alignment.

- **Examples**:

- **SurveyMonkey**: Create surveys to gauge stakeholder satisfaction and gather input.
- **Typeform**: Design interactive forms for qualitative and quantitative feedback.
- **Culture Amp**: Collect team feedback to identify alignment gaps within organizations.
- **Use Case**: A project manager uses SurveyMonkey to collect feedback from team members and partners after a major milestone.

6. Meeting and Decision-Making Tools

Ensure effective stakeholder meetings and decisions are well-documented.

- **Examples**:
  - **Miro**: Create visual brainstorming boards for collaborative planning.
  - **Lucidchart**: Develop flowcharts and diagrams to present ideas and plans.
  - **Doodle**: Schedule meetings and events with multiple stakeholders efficiently.
- **Use Case**: A consulting firm uses Miro during strategy sessions to align its team and clients on deliverables.

7. Strategic Planning Tools

Help teams define, document, and share strategic goals and roadmaps.

- **Examples**:
  - **Aha!**: Build product roadmaps and align on strategy with stakeholders.
  - **Roadmunk**: Create visual roadmaps to communicate plans across teams.
  - **Strategyzer**: Use business model canvases to align stakeholders on value propositions.
- **Use Case**: A SaaS company uses Roadmunk to align its product and marketing teams on a new feature launch roadmap.

Steps to Ensure Stakeholder Alignment

1. **Identify Stakeholders**
   - Map out all internal and external stakeholders, including team members, investors, and partners.
2. **Define Clear Goals**

    - Use tools like OKRs to set measurable, aligned objectives.
3. **Establish Communication Channels**
    - Use collaboration platforms (e.g., Slack, Teams) to centralize updates and discussions.
4. **Provide Regular Updates**
    - Share progress via dashboards, emails, or meetings to keep stakeholders informed.
5. **Gather Feedback**
    - Use surveys or direct interviews to understand stakeholder perspectives and adjust strategies.
6. **Foster Collaboration**
    - Encourage stakeholders to contribute ideas and solutions during planning sessions.
7. **Monitor and Adjust**
    - Continuously track progress and revisit alignment strategies to address evolving needs.

Benefits of Stakeholder Alignment

1. **Improved Decision-Making**: Shared understanding ensures better and faster decisions.
2. **Enhanced Collaboration**: Teams and partners work cohesively toward shared goals.
3. **Increased Efficiency**: Minimized misunderstandings lead to streamlined operations.
4. **Higher Stakeholder Satisfaction**: Transparency and involvement boost trust and engagement.
5. **Greater Success Rates**: Aligned teams are more likely to meet objectives and deliver successful outcomes.

By leveraging these stakeholder alignment tools and techniques, businesses can foster transparency, streamline collaboration, and ensure that all stakeholders remain engaged and aligned with shared goals.

Visual Presentation Tools

Visual presentation tools enable businesses to communicate complex data, concepts, and insights effectively using charts, graphs, infographics, and other visual aids. These tools make information easier to understand, enhance engagement, and support decision-making.

Top Visual Presentation Tools

1. Canva

- **Purpose**: Create professional-looking infographics, presentations, and charts.
- **Key Features**:
    - Drag-and-drop interface for easy design.
    - Pre-designed templates for infographics, presentations, and reports.
    - Integration with data sources for simple chart creation.
- **Use Case**:
    - A marketing team uses Canva to design visually appealing infographics for social media campaigns.
- **Website**: Canva

2. Microsoft PowerPoint

- **Purpose**: Create slides with charts, graphs, and visuals for presentations.
- **Key Features**:
    - Wide range of chart and graph options.
    - Customizable slide templates and animations.
    - Easy integration with Excel for real-time data updates.
- **Use Case**:
    - A sales team creates a presentation with dynamic graphs showcasing quarterly performance.
- **Website**: Microsoft PowerPoint

3. Google Slides

- **Purpose**: Create collaborative presentations with simple visuals.
- **Key Features**:
    - Cloud-based, allowing real-time collaboration.
    - Integrated with Google Sheets for seamless chart embedding.
    - Free templates for quick slide creation.
- **Use Case**:
    - A project manager uses Google Slides to present a project roadmap to stakeholders.
- **Website**: Google Slides

4. Infogram

- **Purpose**: Build interactive infographics, charts, and dashboards.
- **Key Features**:
    - Real-time data integration for interactive visuals.
    - Drag-and-drop interface with customizable templates.
    - Support for embedding visuals in websites or presentations.
- **Use Case**:
    - A financial analyst uses Infogram to create interactive dashboards for a quarterly report.
- **Website**: Infogram

5. Tableau

- **Purpose**: Visualize complex data sets using interactive charts and dashboards.
- **Key Features**:
    - Advanced data visualization options (heatmaps, treemaps, etc.).
    - Real-time integration with data sources like Excel, SQL, or APIs.
    - Interactive dashboards for presentations and reports.
- **Use Case**:
    - A business analyst uses Tableau to showcase key performance indicators (KPIs) during a team meeting.
- **Website**: Tableau

6. Venngage

- **Purpose**: Create infographics, reports, and data visualizations for storytelling.
- **Key Features**:
    - Easy-to-use editor with drag-and-drop functionality.
    - Hundreds of infographic templates for various industries.
    - Branding tools to maintain consistency in corporate visuals.
- **Use Case**:
    - An HR team uses Venngage to design a hiring trends report for internal stakeholders.
- **Website**: Venngage

7. Chart.js

- **Purpose**: Create customizable and interactive charts for websites.
- **Key Features**:
    - Open-source library supporting line, bar, radar, pie, and other chart types.
    - Integration with web applications for dynamic chart updates.
    - Highly customizable with JavaScript.
- **Use Case**:
    - A developer integrates Chart.js into a dashboard to display real-time analytics.

- **Website**: Chart.js

8. Piktochart

- **Purpose**: Design infographics, presentations, and visual reports.
- **Key Features**:
    - Intuitive editor with a focus on visual storytelling.
    - Built-in charts and maps for data visualization.
    - Templates tailored for marketing, HR, and education.
- **Use Case**:
    - A nonprofit organization uses Piktochart to create an annual impact report.
- **Website**: Piktochart

9. Adobe Illustrator

- **Purpose**: Create high-quality, detailed visuals for professional use.
- **Key Features**:
    - Advanced vector design tools for charts, diagrams, and infographics.
    - Integration with other Adobe Creative Cloud apps.
    - Precision editing for custom designs.
- **Use Case**:
    - A graphic designer uses Adobe Illustrator to create a detailed infographic for a client report.
- **Website**: Adobe Illustrator

10. Datawrapper

- **Purpose**: Create responsive charts, maps, and tables for online use.
- **Key Features**:
    - Simple interface for building charts without coding.
    - Automatic responsiveness for mobile and desktop displays.
    - Embedding options for websites or presentations.
- **Use Case**:
    - A news organization uses Datawrapper to display interactive election result maps.
- **Website**: Datawrapper

How to Choose the Right Tool

1. **Purpose**: Determine whether you need visuals for static presentations, interactive dashboards, or online sharing.
2. **Data Complexity**: For large or complex datasets, consider advanced tools like Tableau or Datawrapper.

3. **Ease of Use**: Choose tools like Canva or Infogram for user-friendly interfaces and templates.
4. **Collaboration Needs**: Tools like Google Slides or Venngage are ideal for team projects.
5. **Budget**: Many tools offer free versions with basic features, while premium tools provide more advanced options.

Tips for Effective Visual Presentations

1. **Simplify Complex Data**:
   - Focus on key insights and avoid overloading visuals with too much information.
2. **Use Consistent Design**:
   - Maintain a cohesive color scheme, font, and layout for professional results.
3. **Tailor Visuals to the Audience**:
   - Choose charts and infographics that resonate with your audience's needs and understanding.
4. **Incorporate Storytelling**:
   - Use visuals to tell a clear and compelling story about your data.
5. **Test for Clarity**:
   - Share drafts with colleagues to ensure visuals are easy to understand.

Benefits of Visual Presentation Tools

1. **Improved Communication**: Translate complex data into easily digestible visuals.
2. **Enhanced Engagement**: Capture and hold the audience's attention with visually appealing content.
3. **Better Decision-Making**: Provide clear insights to support strategic choices.
4. **Increased Productivity**: Save time with pre-designed templates and automation features.

By leveraging these visual presentation tools, businesses can effectively communicate insights, boost engagement, and make data-driven strategies accessible to diverse audiences.

Cloud Storage Solutions

Cloud storage solutions provide secure platforms for storing, sharing, and collaborating on files like business plans, updates, and other important documents. These platforms improve accessibility, streamline collaboration, and ensure data is backed up and protected.

Top Cloud Storage Platforms

1. Google Drive

- **Features**:
    - Free 15GB of storage per account (shared across Google services).
    - Integration with Google Workspace apps (Docs, Sheets, Slides).
    - Real-time collaboration and commenting on documents.
- **Best For**: Teams looking for seamless collaboration and integration with Google services.
- **Website**: Google Drive

2. Dropbox

- **Features**:
    - Simple file sharing and storage with robust syncing capabilities.
    - Advanced sharing controls (password-protected links, expiration dates).
    - Integration with popular tools like Slack, Zoom, and Adobe.
- **Best For**: Businesses prioritizing simple, reliable file storage and sharing.
- **Website**: Dropbox

3. Microsoft OneDrive

- **Features**:
    - 5GB of free storage and seamless integration with Microsoft Office apps.
    - Real-time collaboration on Word, Excel, and PowerPoint documents.
    - Built-in file versioning and recovery options.
- **Best For**: Teams using Microsoft Office or Windows-based systems.
- **Website**: Microsoft OneDrive

4. Box

- **Features**:
    - Enterprise-grade security and compliance features.
    - Integration with over 1,400 apps, including Salesforce and Microsoft 365.
    - Workflow automation for document approval and collaboration.

- **Best For**: Businesses with stringent security and compliance needs.
- **Website**: Box

5. iCloud Drive

- **Features**:
    - 5GB of free storage, optimized for Apple devices.
    - Automatic syncing across macOS, iOS, and iPadOS.
    - File sharing and collaborative editing for Apple users.
- **Best For**: Apple ecosystem users needing integrated cloud storage.
- **Website**: iCloud Drive

6. Amazon S3

- **Features**:
    - Scalable storage for large amounts of data.
    - Customizable access permissions and versioning.
    - Integration with AWS tools for advanced cloud management.
- **Best For**: Businesses requiring scalable and customizable cloud storage.
- **Website**: Amazon S3

7. pCloud

- **Features**:
    - Lifetime storage plans for one-time payment options.
    - Advanced encryption for secure file storage.
    - File versioning and extended file history features.
- **Best For**: Individuals and small businesses prioritizing privacy and cost efficiency.
- **Website**: pCloud

8. Sync.com

- **Features**:
    - Zero-knowledge encryption for enhanced security.
    - File sharing with password protection and expiration dates.
    - Easy collaboration with team accounts.
- **Best For**: Teams needing high-security storage options.
- **Website**: Sync.com

9. WeTransfer

- **Features**:
    - Simple, quick file sharing for large files (up to 2GB free).

- No account is required for basic sharing.
- Premium plans allow larger transfers and additional storage.
- **Best For**: Sharing large files with minimal setup.
- **Website**: WeTransfer

10. Mega

- **Features**:
    - 20GB of free storage with end-to-end encryption.
    - Secure file sharing with password protection.
    - Collaboration features like chat and real-time file editing.
- **Best For**: Teams focused on secure, privacy-centric storage.
- **Website**: Mega

Key Features to Consider

1. **Storage Capacity**:
    - Evaluate the amount of storage needed for your business needs.
    - Example: Small teams may require 50GB, while larger organizations might need terabytes.
2. **Collaboration Tools**:
    - Look for real-time editing, commenting, and version history.
3. **Security Features**:
    - Prioritize encryption, two-factor authentication (2FA), and compliance with data protection regulations.
4. **Integration**:
    - Ensure compatibility with tools your team already uses (e.g., Office 365, Slack).
5. **Accessibility**:
    - Opt for platforms accessible across devices (desktop, mobile, web).
6. **Pricing**:
    - Compare free tiers and paid plans for cost-effectiveness.

Benefits of Cloud Storage Solutions

1. **Remote Access**:
    - Access files from anywhere, improving flexibility and productivity.
2. **Enhanced Collaboration**:

- Real-time editing and sharing keep teams aligned and efficient.
3. **Data Security**:
    - Cloud platforms offer robust backup and encryption options to protect sensitive information.
4. **Cost Efficiency**:
    - Scalable pricing ensures businesses pay only for what they use.
5. **Disaster Recovery**:
    - Automatic backups and versioning help recover files in case of accidental deletion or cyberattacks.

By leveraging cloud storage solutions like Google Drive or Dropbox, businesses can securely store and share critical documents, streamline workflows, and enhance collaboration across teams. Choose the platform that best aligns with your needs for storage, collaboration, and budget.

Regular Progress Check-Ins

Regular progress check-ins are scheduled team meetings designed to review performance, adjust plans, and maintain accountability. They ensure alignment across teams, provide opportunities for feedback, and foster collaboration toward shared goals.

Key Objectives of Progress Check-Ins

1. **Performance Review**:
    - Evaluate team progress against goals and milestones.
    - Identify successes and areas for improvement.
2. **Plan Adjustments**:
    - Address roadblocks and revise strategies if needed.
    - Realign priorities based on new insights or circumstances.
3. **Accountability**:
    - Ensure team members are clear on responsibilities and deadlines.
    - Foster ownership and proactive problem-solving.
4. **Collaboration and Communication**:
    - Encourage open discussions and cross-functional teamwork.

- Share updates, feedback, and key learnings.

Steps to Conduct Effective Check-Ins

1. Set a Clear Agenda

- Outline the purpose of the meeting and the topics to be covered.
- Example Agenda:
    1. Review progress on current tasks and milestones.
    2. Discuss challenges and potential solutions.
    3. Adjust priorities or deadlines as needed.
    4. Confirm the next steps and assign responsibilities.

2. Use Performance Metrics

- Present data to objectively evaluate progress.
- Metrics to Include:
    - Key performance indicators (KPIs).
    - Milestone completion rates.
    - Budget or resource utilization.

3. Encourage Open Dialogue

- Create a supportive environment for team members to share updates and concerns.
- Use guiding questions:
    - "What progress have we made since the last check-in?"
    - "What challenges are slowing us down?"
    - "What resources or support do we need?"

4. Document Updates and Decisions

- Record key outcomes, adjustments, and new assignments.
- Share meeting notes with attendees for accountability.

5. End with Actionable Next Steps

- Summarize action items, responsible parties, and deadlines.
- Example: "Maria will finalize the report draft by Friday, and John will schedule the next client presentation for next Tuesday."

Formats for Progress Check-Ins

1. **Daily Stand-Ups (Scrum Meetings):**
    - Short, 15-minute meetings to review progress, blockers, and daily priorities.

- Best For: Agile teams with fast-moving projects.
2. **Weekly Check-Ins**:
    - Review ongoing tasks and align on short-term goals.
    - Best For: General team updates and task coordination.
3. **Monthly Progress Reviews**:
    - Assess performance against larger milestones and goals.
    - Best For: Strategic projects or long-term initiatives.
4. **Quarterly Business Reviews (QBRs)**:
    - Focus on overarching goals, outcomes, and lessons learned.
    - Best For: Evaluating long-term progress and planning.

Tools for Managing Check-Ins

1. Project Management Tools

- **Examples**:
    - **Asana**: Track tasks and deadlines during discussions.
    - **Monday.com**: Visualize progress with boards and timelines.
    - **Trello**: Use Kanban boards to update task statuses.

2. Video Conferencing Platforms

- **Examples**:
    - **Zoom**: Host virtual meetings with screen-sharing features.
    - **Microsoft Teams**: Integrate chat, video, and collaboration tools.
    - **Google Meet**: Simple video calls with screen-sharing capabilities.

3. Collaboration Tools

- **Examples**:
    - **Slack**: Use channels for daily updates and follow-ups.
    - **Notion**: Centralize meeting notes, task updates, and documentation.
    - **Google Docs**: Share and edit meeting agendas and minutes in real time.

4. Performance Tracking Dashboards

- **Examples**:
    - **Tableau**: Present data visualizations during check-ins.
    - **Power BI**: Share real-time progress metrics and analytics.
    - **Google Sheets**: Simple, collaborative progress tracking.

Best Practices for Progress Check-Ins

1. **Be Consistent**:

- Schedule meetings at regular intervals to establish a routine.
2. **Keep Meetings Focused**:
   - Stick to the agenda and avoid tangential discussions.
3. **Celebrate Wins**:
   - Acknowledge achievements to boost team morale.
4. **Address Roadblocks**:
   - Encourage problem-solving by identifying challenges early.
5. **Follow Up**:
   - Send meeting notes and action items promptly to ensure alignment.

Benefits of Regular Progress Check-Ins

1. **Increased Accountability**:
   - Team members stay focused and committed to their responsibilities.
2. **Improved Collaboration**:
   - Open communication fosters teamwork and mutual support.
3. **Enhanced Productivity**:
   - Regular reviews help prioritize tasks and resolve bottlenecks.
4. **Greater Flexibility**:
   - Teams can quickly adapt to changes in goals or circumstances.
5. **Data-Driven Insights**:
   - Performance metrics provide a clear picture of progress and areas for improvement.

By implementing regular progress check-ins, businesses can ensure teams remain aligned, adaptable, and motivated to achieve their objectives. These meetings provide the structure needed to track progress, address challenges, and celebrate successes.

Glossary of Terms

Here is an alphabetized glossary of terms relevant to the book:

Accountability
: The process of assigning responsibility for specific tasks, goals, or outcomes, ensuring individuals or teams take ownership and deliver results.

Break-Even Analysis
: A financial calculation used to determine the point at which total revenue equals total costs, indicating no profit or loss.

Business Plan
: A formal document outlining a business's goals, strategies, target market, financial projections, and operational plans.

Cash Flow
: The total amount of money being transferred into and out of a business, used to assess financial health.

Competitor Analysis
: The process of researching and evaluating competitors to understand their strengths, weaknesses, and market positioning.

Contingency Planning
Developing alternative strategies to address potential risks or unexpected challenges in business operations.

Customer Acquisition
: The process of gaining new customers for a business through marketing, sales, and outreach strategies.

Customer Demand
: The need or desire for products or services within a target market, driving sales and revenue.

Executive Summary
: A concise overview of a business plan, highlighting key elements such as purpose, market opportunity, and financial goals.

Financial Projections
Estimates of future income, expenses, and profitability are used to assess a business's financial viability.

Funding Requirements
: A detailed breakdown of the amount of money needed to start or grow a business, including its intended uses and anticipated return on investment.

Growth Potential
: The ability of a business to expand operations, increase revenue, and capture more market share over time.

Key Performance Indicators (KPIs)
are Measurable metrics used to evaluate the success of specific goals or activities within a business.

Market Analysis
: An assessment of industry trends, target audiences, and competitive landscapes to understand opportunities and challenges.

Milestone
: A specific, measurable checkpoint within a business plan used to track progress and measure success.

Minimum Viable Product (MVP)
: The simplest version of a product or service that meets the basic needs of customers, often used to gather feedback for improvements.

Operational Efficiency
: The ability of a business to deliver products or services effectively while minimizing waste and maximizing resources.

Profit Margin
A measure of profitability calculated as the difference between revenue and costs, expressed as a percentage of revenue.

Return on Investment (ROI)
: A performance metric used to evaluate the profitability of an investment, calculated as a ratio of net profit to investment cost.

Risk Mitigation
Strategies are designed to minimize potential challenges or losses in a business.

Scalability
: The capacity of a business to grow or expand operations without compromising efficiency or increasing costs disproportionately.

Self-Assessment Quiz
: A tool included in the book to help readers evaluate whether their venture operates as a business or hobby.

SWOT Analysis
: A framework for identifying a business's Strengths, Weaknesses, Opportunities, and Threats.

Target Market
: A specific group of customers that a business aims to serve with its products or services.

Timeline
: A schedule that outlines when specific milestones or goals should be achieved, helping track progress and maintain focus.

Value Proposition
: The unique benefits or advantages that a product or service offers to customers, differentiating it from competitors.

Bibliography

Books

- Abrams, Rhonda. *Successful Business Plan: Secrets & Strategies*. Palo Alto Press, 2020.
- Osterwalder, Alexander, and Yves Pigneur. *Business Model Generation: A Handbook for Visionaries, Game Changers, and Challengers*. Wiley, 2010.
- Kawasaki, Guy. *The Art of the Start 2.0: The Time-Tested, Battle-Hardened Guide for Anyone Starting Anything*. Portfolio, 2015.
- Collins, Jim. *Good to Great: Why Some Companies Make the Leap... and Others Don't*. HarperBusiness, 2001.

Articles and Reports

- Harvard Business Review. "Why Business Plans Are Still Relevant in Modern Entrepreneurship." *HBR*, March 2021.
- Small Business Administration (SBA). "Guide to Writing a Business Plan." *SBA Resources*, 2022.
- McKinsey & Company. "The Importance of Strategic Planning in Small Businesses." *McKinsey Insights*, 2021.

Online Resources

- Investopedia. "What Is a Business Plan?" https://www.investopedia.com
- SCORE. "How to Write a Business Plan." https://www.score.org
- Entrepreneur. "Top Tips for Starting and Scaling Your Small Business." https://www.entrepreneur.com

Case Studies

- "How Sarah's Gourmet Jam Transformed from a Hobby to a Thriving Business." *SCORE Case Study Series*, 2021.

- "Jane's Mobile Pet Grooming: Prioritizing Marketing for Growth." *Entrepreneur Success Stories*, 2022.

Statistical Reports

- Bureau of Labor Statistics. "Small Business Growth Trends." U.S. Department of Labor, 2022.
- Statista. "Consumer Preferences in Small Business Products and Services." Statista Report, 2021.